The Hemmings Book of

LINCOLNS

ISBN 1-591150-00-0
Library of Congress Card Number: 2002100087

One of a series of Hemmings Motor News Collector-Car Books. Other books in the series include:
The Hemmings Book of Postwar American Independents; The Hemmings Book of Buicks; The Hemmings Motor News Book of Cadillacs; The Hemmings Book of Postwar Chevrolets; The Hemmings Motor News Book of Corvettes; The Hemmings Motor News Book of Chrysler Performance Cars; The Hemmings Book of Prewar Fords; The Hemmings Motor News Book of Postwar Fords; The Hemmings Book of Mustangs; The Hemmings Motor News Book of Hudsons; The Hemmings Book of Mercurys; The Hemmings Book of Plymouths; The Hemmings Book of Oldsmobiles; The Hemmings Motor News Book of Packards; The Hemmings Motor News Book of Pontiacs; The Hemmings Motor News Book of Studebakers.

Hemmings Motor News
Collector Car Publications and Marketplaces
1-800-CAR-HERE (227-4373)
www.hemmings.com

The Hemmings Book of

LINCOLNS

Editor-In-Chief
Terry Ehrich

Editor
Richard A. Lentinello

Associate Editors
James Dietzler; Robert Gross

Designer
Nancy Bianco

Front cover: 1964 Lincoln Continental. Photo by David Gooley
Back cover: 1940 Lincoln Zephyr. Photo by Tim Howley

This book compiles driveReports which have appeared in *Hemmings Motor News*'s *Special Interest Autos* magazine (SIA) over the past 30 years. The editors at *Hemmings Motor News* express their gratitude to the following writers, photographers, and artists who made this book possible through their many fine contributions to *Special Interest Autos* magazine:

Arch Brown	Bob Hovorka	Michael Lamm
James Dietzler	Tim Howley	Roy Query
David Gooley	Bud Juneau	Russell von Sauers
Robert Gross		

We are also grateful to David Brownell, Michael Lamm, and Rich Taylor, the editors under whose guidance these driveReports were written and published. We thank Ford Motor Company and the Chrysler Historical Collection for graciously contributing photographs to *Special Interest Autos* magazine and this book.

CONTENTS

Special Interest Autos (SIA) magazine's back issues are referred to in this book by issue number. If in stock, copies may be purchased directly from Hemmings Motor News at 800-227-4373, ext. 550 or at www.hemmings.com/gifts.

drive report

1928 LINCOLN L
LOCKE DUAL-COWL PHAETON

NINETEEN twenty-eight was the very height of the Jazz Age. Lindbergh had crossed the Atlantic. The movies had learned to talk. Radio was coming into every home. Prosperity and optimism were everywhere. It seemed like the whole nation was on a roll. Meanwhile in Dearborn, Edsel Ford was creating some of the finest automobiles America had ever known, the fabulous Lincoln L's, veritable symbols of the Jazz Age.

The Lincoln Motor Company was founded in 1917, when Henry Leland, the grand old man of Detroit, left Cadillac to build Liberty Aircraft Engines under a corporate name that honored the Great Emancipator. Many may not know it, but the Lincoln name came from Leland's respect for Abraham Lincoln. It has been said that Leland cast his first vote for Honest Abe. It was only logical that after World War I Henry

By Tim Howley
Photos by David Gooley

Leland would turn his many talents to building a Lincoln automobile that would be an even finer car than his Cadillac. But the car had two drawbacks: ultra-conservative styling and limited financial resources. Moreover, it was introduced in late 1920 into a period of severe postwar recession. Then, in 1921, Henry Leland's Lincoln Motor Company faced its third demand from Internal Revenue to pay back taxes. Already financially troubled, the old master of precision engineering approached his long-time friend Henry Ford, and on February 4, 1922, Lincoln became a part of the Ford Motor Company. (See sidebar, page 10.) The Lelands' lawsuit

against Ford that followed dragged on for nearly a decade. This is a story in itself. What happened to Lincoln under Ford was a miracle of the age. Undisturbed by his dominating father, and unhampered by the financial constraints that makes like Peerless, Pierce-Arrow and Marmon suffered, Edsel Ford proceeded to turn the dowdy looking but mechanically faultless Lincoln L into one of the great Classic automobiles of the decade.

Underscoring Lincoln's highest standards of excellence was a factory at the corner of Warren and Livernois in Detroit which was kept as clean as a hospital. Not only were all of the tools and machinery kept spotless, but 40 painters were constantly at work on the building. As for the famous Johannsen gauge blocks imported to the United States by the Lelands, these were kept in a climate-controlled room, touched only by hands wearing surgeon's gloves.

Henry Leland's original Series L engine of 1920, a 60-degree, L-head, out of step" V-8, was so perfectly designed that it remained basically unchanged from 1920 to 1931. In 1925, this engine developed 80 horsepower @ 2,800 rpm, had a displacement of 357.8-c.i.d. and a compression ratio of 4.8 to 1. The engine was Lincoln's famous "fork and blade" design with long connecting rods and five main bearings. The rods were 12-1/2 inches from center to center, designed to reduce side thrust on the cylinder walls. This side-valve V-8 consisted of two separate blocks bolted at a 60-degree angle to a cast-aluminum crankcase. In 1928 the bore was increased from 3-3/8 inches to 3-1/2 inches, increasing the displacement to 384.8 c.i.d. Horsepower remained 90 at the same 2,800 rpm. There was a slight boost in compression ratio to 4.81 to 1 and larger 1-7/8-inch, rather than 1 3-3/4-inch intake valves, and a reshaped combustion chamber. Counterweights were now placed on the crankshaft to retain engine smoothness with the higher load resulting from the larger pistons. Also, there was now an engine oil filter and conical valve springs. Other unseen changes included new steering tube bearings and a lighter weight rear axle. Other than the engine change, Lincoln paid little attention to annual style change. Lincoln buyers were above such commercial trivia. In fact, the greatest change for 1926 may have been the addition of the greyhound radiator mascot made by Gorham to symbolize fleetness and grace. The 1927 Ford Model A was actually a miniature Lincoln, and in many ways reflected the quality ideals of the senior car.

Above: Lincoln's graceful greyhound points the way down the road. **Below left:** *Wire wheels require special wrench to mount and remove.* **Below right:** *Extra comfort with windwings on tonneau windshield.*

Visual and Visceral Beauty

Four-wheel brakes, which had been standard on the famous Lincoln Police Flyers since 1923, became the major change for all Lincolns for 1927. Actually, there were two more brakes for parking.

In addition to having a different engine, the 1928 model is differentiated from the 1927 by miniature cowl lamps (on some closed models) accompanying the bullet headlamps of 1927, chrome replacing nickel and the Lincoln-built wire wheels replacing the Buffalo wire wheels. Prior to this time, wire wheels were optional, although you will rarely see any Lincoln built after 1925 with wooden spoke wheels. Instrument panels were all new. Another new item was the ignition lock on the steering column, which later became a standard feature on all Ford-built cars.

Body styles were similar to those of 1927. But two new designs that year

were the Type 165 Locke club roadster with coach-molded driving compartment treatment and the Willoughby limousine with Landau leather rear quarters and arm-chair occasional seats. There were now 12 standard models and 11 semi-custom models; 105 chassis were shipped to the custom body builders for full custom bodies.

It was the Police Flyers (1923) that moved Lincoln into notoriety; these cars were chosen by lawmen and law breakers alike for their acceleration, high speed and excellent cornering for the period. Furthermore, Lincolns of the twenties had the strength to handle the extra weight of armor plate and bullet-proof glass. Nearly all of Chicago's most infamous gangsters chose Lincolns, as did the Chicago Police Department that pursued them.

Up until about 1925 the lawless usually chose open Lincolns, which allowed

them more room to swing around their tommy-guns. Later in the decade, they turned to Lincoln sedans, which offered them an extra degree of protection. Police departments continued to choose open Lincolns up until the early thirties. Lincolns were also the choice of Federal Dry Agents, the FBI and other minions of the law. It has been said that more "last rides" were taken in Lincolns than any other make. Certainly they were the most popular make to turn out at mobster funerals. One might think that this mobster image would tarnish Lincoln's reputation. On the contrary, the car's underworld reputation made it all the more appealing to the rich and famous. Lincoln L's were so well received that every US President of the era owned one. The list of notables who owned Lincoln L's in the mid to late twenties was awesome. Included were Washington Luis P. de Souza, president of Brazil;

1928 LINCOLN

Queen Marie of Romania; Crown Prince Olav of Norway: Gustaf Adolph of Sweden: the Presidents of Uruguay, Venezuela, Mexico, Cuba and Panama.

In the beginning, 1921-22, most of the Lincoln bodies were built by American Body, Murray, or Lincoln. From about 1925 forward, Edsel Ford adopted a greatly enlarged custom and semi-custom body-building program. This included bodies from Dietrich, Derham, LeBaron, Waterhouse, Fleetwood, Brunn, Murphy, Judkins, Willoughby, Holbrook, Lang, Locke and Murphy. Edsel would request that these builders submit designs. Those body styles selected and placed in production would be done in lots of 50 to 100 at a time, making the finest custom bodies available at far less than the cost of the "one-off" body. Much confusion exists between fully custom and semi-custom bodies. Actually, most of the bodies built by the custom body makers were available through the Lincoln dealers and were technically semi-custom bodies. The full custom bodies were usually ordered specially by the customer directly from the body builder, and would normally show up on sales records as the sale of a chassis only.

The tragedy of the Lincoln L was its aluminum body and aluminum crankcase. This made it a prime target for the World War II scrap drives. In those days, such cars were worth more as scrap metal than as transportation.

Above: Impressive phaeton has a lot of presence on the road. *Below left:* Dual-sidemount spares with accessory mirrors fill up the front fenders. *Right:* Three-lens taillamp was used on Lincoln for a number of years.

Driving Impressions

When *Motor Trend* tested a 1951 Lincoln, the car that won the Mobilgas Economy Run that year, writer Griff Borgeson brought along his 1928 Lincoln phaeton, a car very similar to our driveReport model. He wrote, "We talked about the long tradition of Lincoln quality, and about the most significant point of all today, Ford's almost three decades of experience with production of the V-8 engine. The Leland Lincoln became Ford's first V-8, and Ford has been the world's biggest producer of this type of engine, has had years of experience in acquiring and developing the know-how—a pleasant position to be in as the automotive world awakens to the superiority of the V layout.

"As far as I know, not even its manufacturer calls attention to the fact that Lincoln's engine is the biggest being fitted to a passenger car today, anywhere in the world—the reason being, I suppose, an understandable desire to avoid creating the impression of the gas-eating gargantua in the economy-conscious public mind."

Locke Bodies

Locke bodies were first introduced by Lincoln in 1925 in the form of a cabriolet. They were built in Rochester, New York. In 1926 a Locke semi-cabriolet and roadster were added. Locke bodies were extremely popular with Lincoln buyers and drew rave reviews from the motoring press. The 1926 Locke roadster, priced at $4,500, did not include wire wheels and sidemounts, although they were seldom sold without these and other sporty options. You could order your Locke roadster with either a trunk or rumble seat. Either way you got a golf compartment box in the bargain.

In 1927, Lincoln added a Locke sport touring, sport phaeton and dual cowl sport phaeton. In 1928, the touring and sport phaeton were priced at $4,600, and the dual-cowl sport phaeton was priced at $5,000. The sport phaeton, with or without the dual cowl, was the most popular of all Lincolns built. In the dual-cowl version, the tonneau cowl was counterbalanced to raise when either rear door was open. (We did not find this particular feature on our driveReport car.)

Even though Locke bodies were built by an independent firm in upstate New York, they were considered standard Lincoln bodies, and finally, in 1930, the three Locke sport phaetons offered were listed as "standard line" as opposed to the Locke roadster and a number of bodies by other custom builders as "custom line." Beginning with the 1932 Lincoln KB, Lincoln no longer listed Locke in its body offerings. The company may have gone out of business due to the Great Depression and lack of standing offers from Lincoln. All Locke bodies supplied to Lincoln were open. Beginning around 1932, the demand for open phaetons and tourings fell off sharply while the demand for convertibles and convertible sedans grew.

The 1951 Lincoln engine was the largest and last Ford flathead. It displaced 336.7 cubic inches, 48.1 less than the Lincoln-built engine of 1928. At 154 horsepower, the 1951 Lincoln engine developed nearly twice the horsepower of the 1928 model. In the Mobilgas Economy Run, it managed to average more than 25 mpg, or about two and a half times the average of the 1928 model. But Borgeson was right, its engine technology was deeply rooted in what Ford learned with the Lincoln L, as was the flathead Ford V-8 of the thirties.

Our driveReport car is one of 150 Locke-bodied dual-cowl sport phaetons that Lincoln produced for the 1928 model year, and one of 6,362 Lincolns produced for 1928. This compares to 5,512 Lincolns produced in 1922, Ford's first year of Lincoln operation, and 8,787 for 1926, the peak year of Classic Lincoln production.

The car is owned by Jim Crocker of Fullerton, California. The car was originally restored in the late fifties and won a CCCA grand national in 1960. Then it went into storage for over 30 years, until Crocker found out about it and purchased it in 1991. The cream yellow

Gorham Silver Co. made the Lincoln greyhound mascot from 1927 through 1933. Base material was brass, which was then plated with nickel or chrome.

paint job with brown trim was actually a 1928 Lincoln color. Cream yellow Locke phaetons were featured in 1928 Lincoln advertising. Unless custom ordered, 1928 Lincoln fenders were always black. This car is equipped with Winfield twin carburetors, mahogany running boards, chromed wire wheels and a trunk with trunk rack. This was in addition to the standard luggage rack on this body style. The radiator shutters were standard. In 1928, all Lincolns received a new nickel-plated instrument panel with ammeter, oil pressure gauge,

Edsel Ford And The Lincoln L

It has been written time and again that Edsel Ford was so dominated by his father that it drove him to an early death in 1943. Edsel's relationship with his father is one of the most complex stories in automotive history. In the area of design, Henry gave him a completely free hand. The styling of the Model A, the great Ford V-8s of the thirties, the Mercury and, certainly, the Lincoln-Zephyr and Lincoln Continental were purely products of Edsel's fine design sense and his talent for hiring top-notch stylists. All of the great Ford shows of the thirties were executed under Edsel. In all of these areas of artistic expression, his father left him alone. The engineering of these automobiles was another matter. Here, Henry Ford remained stubbornly old fashioned to the end.

But in the field of design, Edsel's unique talents were, in his father's eyes, both mysterious and highly respected, not to be interfered with. As Walter Dorwin Teague, designer of the Ford shows, noted in 1953, "Edsel was wise, generous, strong and simple, a combination of qualities that marks the greatest of men. In him an extreme sensitiveness was united with an unself-conscious modesty that left no need for the kind of compensations publicity has to offer. By choice, he moved quietly behind the scenes, where public eyes could not follow him. Thus, the fact that, among his many superb qualities, he was also a great designer was known to few except those who had the privilege of collaborating with him in his field."

That Ford even had a styling department in the thirties was a tribute to Edsel. That he selected and trained the best stylists in the business was the very basis of

Ford's great designs for the next 30 years. Daily, from 1935 on, he enmeshed himself in the work going on in the infant styling studio. Without resorting to fear tactics and dictatorship, as did Harley Earl over at General Motors, Edsel would collaborate with E.T. Gregorie and his associates, making suggestions, listening to ideas, and in a gentle, brotherly way, guiding Ford's designs into production. After hours, Edsel at home was doing modeling and painting and was a patron and finally president of the Detroit Institute of the Arts.

Edsel cut his teeth on automobile design with the Classic Lincoln L of the twenties. Whether his father bought the Lincoln Motor Company to get Edsel out of his hair or just because he saw a good bargain is academic. Remember, in 1919 Edsel became President of the Ford Motor Company. But as such he had no power to bring the Model T out of the dark ages. Yet, in turning the equally unattractive Leland Lincoln into a fine piece of automobile design, his father gave him no opposition whatsoever. Edsel entered the Lincoln arena with youthful zest and extreme talent for picking the best designs from the many custom coachbuilders of the day. By 1929 Edsel had turned Lincoln from a complete loser into a $2 million profit maker. But going back to 1926, Henry Ford fired top executive Ernest Kanzler for suggesting that the Model T be replaced. After this incident, Edsel raced back from Europe and convinced his father that a new Ford must be built and introduced in record time, and it should be styled after the current Lincoln L. From that point on, Edsel had the final

say in all Ford styling. The late twenties marks a special era in Edsel's design development. The Lincolns of this period represent the very finest executions of the custom body builder's wares. But they were still two-dimensional creations. The great custom designers of the day, such as Ray Dietrich, would draw their creations in chalk on a blackboard, and from here sketches would be made and blueprints would be drawn up. It was truly the golden age of the automobile, and working within the restrictions of this two-dimensional design, nothing surpassed the custom Lincolns.

But after 1931 a new age dawned. It was an age of purely automotive design, unhampered by the coachwork of kings, going back for centuries. It was the age of the streamlined automobile, designed in three dimensions by designers who could think and draw in three dimensions. With his design training rooted in the coachlike twenties' cars, one might think that Edsel would have stayed in that rut as many others did. But no; he moved with the times, adopting the Budd car designed by John Tjaarda and turning it into the Lincoln-Zephyr, suggesting the Lincoln-Continental to E.T. Gregorie, and collaborating to design the sleek Fords of the late thirties. When you stand back and look at our driveReport car, a 1928 Locke dual-cowl phaeton, you must think of Edsel Ford at the crossroads, In this car he had selected the best of Classic, squared-off twenties' design at its very crest. Perhaps sensing even then that this type of design had gone about as far as it could go, Edsel was about ready to carry Ford design in an exciting new direction.

specifications

illustrations by Russell von Sauers, The Graphic Automobile Studio
© copyright 1996, Special Interest Autos

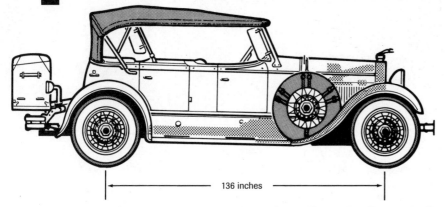

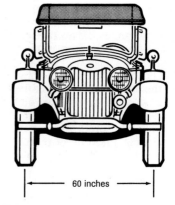

136 inches

60 inches

1928 Lincoln Locke Dual-Cowl Sport Phaeton

Base price	$5,000
Options	Electric clock, Winfield dual carburetor, chromed wire wheels, white sidewall tires, Police Flyer rear axle, mahogany running boards, trunk

ENGINE
Type	60-degree flathead V-8, cast-iron block with aluminum crankcase
Bore x stroke	3.5 inches x 5 inches
Displacement	384.8 cubic inches
Compression ratio	4.81:1
Horsepower @ rpm	90 @ 2,800
Torque @ rpm	N/A
Taxable horsepower	39.2
Valve lifters	Solid
Valve configuration	L-head
Main bearings	5
Induction system	Winfield 2-bbl carburetor
Ignition system	6-volt
Fuel system	Vacuum pump, camshaft driven
Exhaust system	Single

TRANSMISSION
Type	Sliding gear 3-speed manual, non-synchromesh
Ratios	N/A

CLUTCH
Type	Multiple dry plate
Actuation	Mechanical, foot pedal

DIFFERENTIAL
Type	Timken
Ratio	4.90:1 optional
Drive axles	Full-floating
Torque medium	Torque tube, radius rods with ball and socket

STEERING
Type	Worm and roller
Turns lock-to-lock	2.5
Ratio	N/A
Turning circle	50 feet

BRAKES
Type	4-wheel mechanical, internal expanding
Size	N/A
Effective area	N/A

CHASSIS & BODY
Frame	All steel, ladder type, 3 cross members
Body construction	Wood framing with aluminum skin
Body style	4-door, 6-passenger dual-cowl phaeton

SUSPENSION
Front	Half-elliptical springs
Rear	Half-elliptical springs
Tires	32 x 6.75 tube type
Wheels	Wire, one-piece construction

WEIGHTS AND MEASURES
Wheelbase	136 inches
Overall length	203 inches
Overall width	69.5 inches
Overall height	61 inches
Front track	60 inches
Rear track	58 inches
Weight	4,850 pounds

CAPACITIES
Crankcase	10 quarts
Cooling system	7.5 gallons
Fuel tank	20 gallons, plus 2.5 gallons, reserve
Transmission	3.5 pints
Differential	6.5 pints

Right: T-shaped door handles are another custom touch on driveReport car. Facing page, top: In its heyday, big Lincoln could cruise at 70 mph. Center left: Instrument panel features beautiful engine turning. Right: Tonneau has numerous compartments. Bottom: Locke body sweeps gracefully to rear from front cowl.

1928 LINCOLN

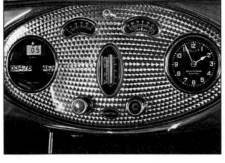

fuel supply thermometer, cigar lighter and 80-mph drum speedometer. An eight-day Waltham clock was standard equipment. This car had the optional Seth-Thomas electric clock, but no radio. In 1928, car radios were few and far between, even on luxury cars. This car does not have running lights or spot lights.

Driver's seat entry and exit is not easy. Moreover, the front seat is not adjustable. A fat man could not get behind the wheel of a 1928 Locke Lincoln even if he ordered the then-optional tilt-up steering wheel.

To start the car you unlock the igni-tion, depress the floor starter, and then release the huge hand brake to your right by first pulling back on it and releasing the button, then moving it forward.

While the engine is reliable to a fault, it is not the quietest of the Classic-era engines. In fact, it has been written that when Lincoln increased the bore in 1928, minor vibrations began to occur. In its day the Lincoln L had no peer. It was one of the fastest accelerating cars of the time and had a top speed of 90 mph. It would cruise effortlessly at 70 mph, meaning it can still stay with free-way traffic. The transmission has an aluminum casting housing, three forward speeds through straight-cut gears, and a multiple-disc clutch. The trans-missions are the most disappointing component in these automobiles. Since they are not synchromesh, shifting is very tricky. It takes a lot of practice to learn to shift one of these cars without grinding the gears. Downshifting from third to second is virtually impossible. You must be very aggressive when shifting a Lincoln L. Then, as soon as you are in first, you immediately shift into second. Actually, you can almost start off in second, and with the standard rear end you can almost start out in third. No form of freewheeling, overdrive or semi-automatic transmission was ever offered in the Lincoln L's.

Front compartment has the look and feel of an open-cockpit plane or a sleek vintage speed-boat.

1928 LINCOLN

In contrast, the four-wheel mechanical brakes stop extremely well, considering they have to deal with 5,000 pounds of pure automobile. Naturally, they are not up to hydraulics and are only marginal at highway speeds, but by the standards of their day they are quite good. They are unusually large, even for a car this big, and the cast-iron drums have deep cooling fins.

You have to judge the ride and handling by the period. The steering and suspension were quite good by the standards of the day, meaning that any Auburn or Pontiac built seven years later handled a lot better. The number of steering wheel turns lock-to-lock is a mere 2.5, meaning it takes the arms of Hercules to park one of these cars or to put it into a tight, low-speed turn. The turn circle is about 50 feet; hence it cannot be turned around on most any street or road without backing up a time or two. Precision control was not one of the fortes of twenties cars, nor was it

addressed by Henry Leland or Henry Ford in the twenties. The car is at its poorest on mountain roads. You really wouldn't want to drive a car like this in the Sierras or Rockies, and we wonder how anybody did. However, as a highway cruiser, it holds up extremely well, after nearly 70 years. Just ask any Lincoln Owner's Club member or CCCA club member who has driven his Lincoln L coast to coast, as a lot of them have.

This particular car has the optional Police Flyer rear end. The standard gear ratio on these Lincolns was 12 teeth on a pinion, 55 on the ring gear. On the Police Flyers it was 13 on the pinion and 49 teeth on the ring gear. This gives 59 mph at the previous 50 mph engine rpm. A change to a Lincoln Flyer rear end is authentic on any Lincoln L from 1923 on.

This author has his own jaded opinions on driving cars of this vintage. Number one: They are so valuable today that I shudder at the thought of driving them any distance. What would be even a minor collision today is a major expense in a car like this. The streets and highways of suburban Los Angeles, where we drove this car a considerable distance, are loaded with traffic that has no understanding of the limitations of twenties automobiles; i.e. lack of turn signals, limited rear visibility with the top up, and brakes that cannot respond effectively in modern emergency situations. When these cars were built, and for decades thereafter, the now-crowded Los Angeles basin was mostly peaceful country roads through citrus groves and oil fields. However, once away from the cities, the Lincoln L can be a pleasure to

How Leland Lost Lincoln to Ford

Henry Leland, like Henry Ford, was a man of destiny. He began his career as a machine tool engineer with Brown & Sharpe, and came to Detroit in 1890. There he established the Leland & Falconer Company, which built parts and engines for curved-dash Oldsmobiles. In 1902, a Detroit group which had twice backed young Henry Ford in unsuccessful ventures, called upon Henry Leland. What resulted was the formation of the Cadillac Automobile Company.

When the United States got into World War I in 1917, Henry Leland was still head of Cadillac, now a division of General Motors. W.C. Durant, then head of GM, would not hear of the Lelands' proposal to build war aircraft engines in the Cadillac plant, so they left to form the Lincoln Motor Company to build Liberty aircraft engines. Then, with the war ended in November 1918, the government refused to honor its wartime contracts with Lincoln. Already on the brink of financial disaster, Henry Leland and his son Wilfred decided to build a Lincoln automobile.

Now the Government demanded $5.7 in wartime income taxes, then backed down. This delayed the production of the new

Lincoln car and caused the beginnings of receivership. Then the feds dredged up the $5.7 million claim and withdrew it again. Next, followed the severe depression of 1921, and now a new tax claim from Uncle Sam for $4.5 million. Desperate, the Lelands turned to Henry Ford, who promised to take care of everything. Ford agreed to pay $5 million for the company and leave the Lelands to run it. But the judge refused to let the property go for less than $8 million, which Ford finally agreed to pay. Still it was a bargain. Allegedly, Ford made all kind of promises to the Lelands and their stockholders, all verbal, and on February 4, 1922, the ownership (via a court-ordered receivers' sale) was turned over to Ford.

What followed was no rose garden. Before the month was out, Ford executives appeared at the plant and took over. Walls were torn down, tools were strewn about, workers given their pink slips, and in June Henry Leland himself was carried out of his office and down the front steps of the building by Ford men, still sitting in his swivel chair. But Ford did make good on his word to pay off the suppliers, and eventually he paid over $12 million for

Lincoln. The Lelands then pursued Ford through the courts for years in an attempt to force him to pay off the stockholders, including themselves, who held the largest block of stock. Henry Ford could waltz through the courts as wonderfully as he danced old-time dances. The Lelands never got the best of him. Henry Leland died in 1932, broken and bitter.

In 1966, Wilfred Leland's wife published a book called *Master of Precision — Henry M. Leland*, which told the family's side of the story. There are really two sides of the story. Henry Ford bought the company at a receivers' sale. Had Ford not been there to bid, the Lelands would not have received a penny. Considering the financial state of the company, the Lelands probably got more than they deserved, and besides, nobody ever got the best of Henry Ford.

To Ford's credit, the Lelands' high standards of engineering continued, and the styling was enhanced through Ford's efforts. Had it not been for Henry and Edsel Ford, there would be no Lincoln car today, and Henry Leland and his contribution to the industry would probably be forgotten.

Above: *Vintage speedboat aura extends to wooden steering wheel.* **Right:** *Superb Lincoln V-8 is thoroughly understressed at 90 bhp.* **Below:** *Dual-throat Winfield feeds the cylinders.* **Below right:** *Tonneau windshield rises for access to rear compartment.*

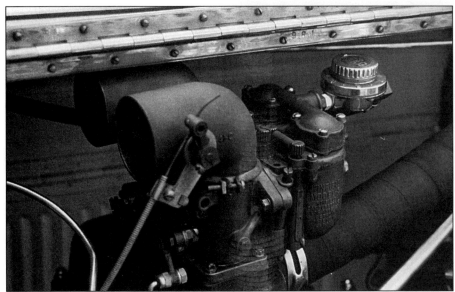

drive all day long on the Interstate cross country, getting off the Interstate when approaching major metropolitan areas. And out in the vast stretches of Texas, the old Lincoln L might be right at home and subject to a minimum of interference from the modern jellybean car traffic and the jellyhead mentality of the modern driver.

One especially interesting feature of the 1928 Lincoln is the two-and-a-half gallon auxiliary gas tank, in addition to the 20-gallon gas tank. Figuring a 1928 Lincoln averages 8 mpg, this gives you a mere 160-mile driving range. I noted that the indicator was low when we started our test. The owner assured us that there was plenty of gas. Well, we

ran out. Fortunately, the auxiliary switch and tank worked perfectly, aided by an electric fuel pump.

This was the first time he had ever tried out the auxiliary.

One final item: You never leave a 1928 Lincoln in reverse when you park it. These cars had backup lights, and the backup lights will stay on when the motor and ignition are off. No, this is not your modern Lincoln, where the lights come on and off automatically. ☜

Bibliography & Acknowledgments

"1951 Lincoln Motor Trial," Motor Trend, *July 1951;* "1925 and 1955 Lincoln Compared," Motor Life, *June 1955;* "Edsel Ford — Designer," Lincoln-Mercury Times, *May-June 1953;* The Old Car Book, *John Bentley, Fawcett Publications, 1953;* Famous Old Cars, *Hank Weiand Bowman, Fawcett Publications, 1954;* Lincoln, America's Car of State, *Maurice Hendry, Ballantine Books, 1971;* The Cars of Lincoln-Mercury, *George H Dammann & James C. Wagner, Crestline Publishing, 1987;* Master of Precision, Henry M. Leland, *by Mrs. Wilfred C. Leland and Minne Dubbs Millbrook, Wayne State University Press, 1966;* "The Lincoln Engine," Automotive Industries, *September 16, 1920;* The Jazz Age, *Henry Solomon and Richard Hanser, G.P. Putnam's Sons, 1959;* Standard Catalog of American Cars, 1805- 1942, *Krause Publications, 1985. Special thanks to Jim Crocker~Fullerton, California.*

That Wonderful Year, 1928

Ship to shore telephone service was established. Talking pictures swept the land. Network radio and radio programs boomed. Car radios were a new vogue. Amelia Earhart became the first woman to pilot a plane cross the Atlantic. A record flight was made from New York to Los Angeles in 19 hours, 10 minutes. Broadway musicals included *Rosalie,* George White's *Scandals,* Earl Carroll's *Vanities, Blackbirds of 1928, Rain or Shine,* and *Whoopee.* It was a year of hit songs including "Button Up Your Overcoat," "I Can't Give You Anything But Love," "I'll Get By," "Love Me or Leave Me," "Lover Come Back to Me," "Makin' Whoopee,"

"When You're Smiling" and "You're the Cream in my Coffee." This was the era of Irving Berlin and Rodgers and Hammerstein, who were not yet a team. George M. Cohan was still big box office, but the era of Cole Porter was yet to come.

In 1928, Auburns were the cat's pajamas, Ford sold Model A's like hotcakes, and Chevrolet hit an all-time production record of 1.2 million cars. Walt Disney made his first animated cartoon, *Steamboat Willie,* with Mickey Mouse; and Al Jolson made his second talkie, *The Singing Fool.* Al Smith lost the Presidential election to Herbert Hoover, and President Calvin Coolidge had nothing to say.

Battle of the Streamliners

Chrysler Airflow vs. Lincoln Zephyr

By Arch Brown
Photos by Bud Juneau

Originally published in Special Interest Autos #120, Nov.-Dec. 1990

I T was during the decade of the thirties that the world's automakers finally became aware of the importance of aerodynamics. Among the American cars that pioneered the concept of "streamlining," as it was popularly called, four come to mind. There was, first of all, the Pierce "Silver Arrow," a gorgeous machine built for display at the 1933 Chicago World's Fair. But only five examples were produced, and they sold for $10,000 a pop—at a time when a Ford V-8 sedan cost as little as $560.

Then there was the Aerodynamic Hupp (see *SIA #10*). But Hupmobile was already in its terminal slide by the time its streamliner was introduced in 1934, so it drew scant attention.

It was the other two that caught everyone's eye: the Chrysler Airflow and the Lincoln Zephyr. Much has been written about both of them, partly because, unlike the Pierce and the Hupp, they were built by two of the world's major automakers, and partly because each in its own way was unique—and a very advanced automobile for the time.

Let's begin with the Chrysler, whose 1934 introduction preceded its competitor's debut by two full years.

It was engineer Carl Breer who was responsible for Chrysler's initial interest in reducing wind resistance. According to company legend, one day in the fall of 1927 Breer was watching what appeared to be a flock of geese flying in formation. Presently he realized that he had been mistaken; what he saw was not geese, but rather military aircraft on maneuvers. And the thought came to him: If the airplane is designed to encounter minimum wind resistance, should not the same principle be applied to the automobile—especially now that speeds as high as a mile a minute were becoming commonplace?

A wind tunnel was constructed at Dayton, Ohio, and there the famous "Three Musketeers" of Walter Chrysler's engineering staff, Owen Skelton, Fred Zeder and Carl Breer, conducted the research that led to the development of the Airflow.

Parenthetically, the original idea was that the Airflow would be exclusively a De Soto. But Walter Chrysler, who took justifiable pride in his company s engineering leadership, wanted a streamliner with his name on it as well.

He ended up with four of them. That is, four series, all straight-eights, ranging in wheelbase from 123 to a whopping 146.5 inches and in engine displacement from 299 to 385 cubes. Prices started at $1,345 and extended all the way to $5,145, which was more than enough in those days to buy a 12-cylinder Cadillac.

The Airflow presented a startling appearance, far different from anything the public had seen before. As part of

Above and below: Both cars have a smooth rear aspect, although the Airflow's sheet metal is interrupted by outside spare. Bottom: Airflow taillamps look like afterthoughts; Lincoln's work much better with the car's total design.

the effort to reduce drag, it was given slab sides and a stubby, rounded nose. A vee-type, two-piece windshield was fitted to most models, though the largest, most expensive Custom Imperials used a one-piece curved glass windscreen—an industry "first." Rear fender skirts were standard.

The difference wasn't all on the surface by any means. Hidden beneath the body panels was a rigid, bridge-like steel skeleton that extended the full length of the car and even up into the roof, providing what has sometimes been called "semi-unitized" construction. Thus, the passengers rode within the frame, rather than on top of it. Typically, at least in recent years, "unit" construction has resulted in substantially reduced weight. This was not the case with the Airflows, however, for they were heavy brutes, outweighing their conventionally

styled 1933 counterparts by anywhere from 277 to 655 pounds.

The base series, known as the CU in 1934 and the Cl in '35, accounted for the bulk of Airflow sales. It was offered in four body types, with the sedan far outselling the other three combined. Other styles included the Town Sedan, featuring blind quarter panels; the two-door Brougham; and the five-passenger coupe. The latter, by all odds the best looking of the lot, was fitted with a pair of fold-down jump seats, and until 1936, was the only Airflow to feature an enclosed spare tire.

In the Chrysler tradition, the Airflows were sparkling performers, and with the overdrive, a popular option at about $35, they were relatively economical as well. An Imperial coupe was dispatched to the Utah salt flats, where it set no fewer than 72 new records including a

*Above: Airflow wins the engine accessibility contest hands down. **Below:** Chrysler's front windows are a clever combo; even the big ventpane can disappear for more "airflow." **Bottom:** Zephyr's vent is this attractive pivoting oval that's more windwing than window.*

SIA comparisonReport

speed of 95.7 miles an hour over the measured mile. Then to demonstrate the Airflow's safety as well as its durability, a brand new car was driven off a 110-foot cliff. It tumbled, teakettle over bandbox, landing at the bottom on its wheels—whereupon it was driven off under its own power!

These were comfortable cars, partly because the seats were moved as much

as 20 inches forward of their traditional location, spring rates having been adjusted accordingly. The result was that the pitching sensation, created when the rear seat was located directly over the axle, was virtually eliminated. This particular change was as simple as it was fundamental, and other manufacturers were quick to follow suit.

Seats were 50 inches wide, providing the sedans with ample space for six adults—an unusual feature at the time. Also contributing to passenger comfort was Chrysler's practice of elevating the

front seat a few inches off the floor, permitting fresh air from the cowl ventilators (and warm air from the optional heater) to circulate evenly throughout the car.

Chrysler's six-cylinder cars retained their conventional styling—which was evidently a good thing, at least from the stockholders' perspective. For although the Airflows received generally favorable reviews—Britain's *The Motor,* for instance, was "impressed by their graceful and attractive appearance—the radical styling was not well received by the public. Model year figures show that in 1933, the year before the Airflow's introduction, sixes accounted for 55 percent of the Chrysler Division's production. The following year, with the advent of the Airflow, 69 percent of all new Chryslers were the conventionally styled six-cylinder jobs. Meanwhile De Soto, whose 1934 production was confined to the six-cylinder Airflows, took a terrible bruising. At a time when most of the industry was scoring substantial sales gains—as much as 128 percent in the case of GM's Oldsmobile Division, for instance—De Soto's volume was off by nearly 39 percent.

In the meantime, over in Dearborn Edsel Ford was looking for a way to keep his Lincoln Motor Company viable. His father, the irascible Henry Ford, had appointed Edsel president of the Ford Motor Company in 1919, but the old man had never even pretended to relinquish even a modicum of control over the organization. At Lincoln, however, it was a different story. Henry Ford had once declared that he had "no use for any car that has more spark plugs than a cow has teats," and he permitted Edsel almost total freedom in running the Lincoln operation.

But the market for the big Lincoln, whose 1935 prices began at $4,200—about $1,800 higher than Cadillac's—had very nearly dried up. Production that year came to just 1,411 units, a thousand fewer than the previous season's already dismal total. Edsel was well aware that there were limits to his father's tolerance, and he realized that Lincoln's only hope of salvation would be the introduction of a more moderately priced automobile, one that would compete against Cadillac's La Salle.

Meanwhile, at the Briggs Body Company Dutch-born John Tjaarda, with the encouragement of his employers, had designed a streamlined, rear-engined automobile, powered by an aluminum V-8 and employing an automatic transmission. This car was shown at the 1934 Century of Progress Exposition in Chicago, where it drew rave reviews—with just one reservation. The rear engine was just too different, too controversial for the public's tastes.

Front-engined prototypes followed, and Edsel Ford expressed an interest in building the streamliner as a companion car for the big K-Series Lincoln. Ultimately it was decided that in order to clearly identify the new car as a Lincoln, a V-12 engine should be used; so a new powerplant was developed for the purpose. Diminutive as 12-cylinder engines went, at 267.3 cubic inches its displacement was nearly 17 percent less than that of the new Buick Century.

Based upon Ford rather than Lincoln technology, the new engine used a single block casting—most unusual for a V-12. Exhaust ports were routed through the block, in the Ford tradition, and connecting rods were actually interchangeable between the V-12 and the V-8. Cylinder banks were set at a 75-degree angle to one another.

The automatic transmission and certain other of the prototype's features were abandoned due to cost considerations (and perhaps in deference to traditional Ford practices), and a sharply pointed prow was adopted, with the result that apart from Tjaarda's graceful teardrop shape, the final product bore little outward resemblance to the car that had been displayed at Chicago. Tjaarda's lightweight, integral body-and-frame construction was retained, however. And by November 1935 the new car was ready to come to market as the 1936 Lincoln Zephyr.

It was, everyone agreed, a beauty. The New York Museum of Modern Art called it the "first successful streamlined car in America." There were two body styles initially: two- and four-door sedans, each with ample room for six-passengers. Prices were $1,275 and $1,320. No other manufacturer was producing a 12-cylinder car at anywhere near that figure in 1936, though in 1932 the Auburn Twelve had sold for as little as $975.

Lincoln built 14,994 Zephyrs that year—most of them in the four-door style. The factory even turned out 908 right-hand-drive sedans for the export market. Production nearly doubled during the 1937 model run, by which time a three-passenger coupe and a town limousine had been added to the line. Prices were cut, the coupe selling for a time at just $1,090 — though that figure was later raised to $1,165.

Perhaps more than most automobiles, the Lincoln Zephyr had great strengths, offset by enormous weaknesses. On the plus side, in addition to its good looks, the Zephyr boasted an engine that was one of the smoothest to be found anywhere. The car would cruise easily at 75 miles an hour, and had a top speed of at least 90. Its ride was comfortable, despite its conventional I-beam axle and archaic transverse springs. And under normal driving conditions the owner could expect between 15 and 18 miles to the gallon in highway travel.

But on the downside, crankcase ventilation was inadequate and sludge tended

Hood ornaments are appropriate to the designs of both cars. Zephyr's looks almost like a jet plane.

to build up in the V-12 engine, particularly if there was a lot of stop-start driving. Passing the exhaust ports through the engine block helped in warming up the engine on a cold morning, but—like the Ford V-8—the Zephyr sometimes tended to overheat and develop vapor lock. Mechanical brakes were used, per Henry Ford's dictum, and oddly enough the Zephyr's binders provided less lining area than those of the Ford—even though the Ford was the lighter of the

two cars by some 600 pounds.

The recession of 1938 hurt sales throughout the auto industry, though the Lincoln Zephyr was affected less than most makes. Hydraulic brakes were finally adopted in 1939, and a major restyling was undertaken for 1940. The bore was enlarged that year, then expanded again for 1942. Meanwhile, in 1940 the Zephyr-based Lincoln Continental had appeared, drawing rave reviews as one of the handsomest auto-

1935 Chrysler Table of Prices, Weights and Production

	Price	Weight	Production
Airstream Six, Series C6 (118" w/b, 241.5 c.i.d.)			
Business coupe	$745	2,863	1,975
Coupe with r/s	$810	2,953	861
Sedan, 2-door	$820	2,990	400
Touring Brougham	$820	2,99	1,9018
Sedan, 4-door	$830	3,013	6,055
Touring Sedan	$860	3,048	12,790
Chassis	N/a	N/a	476
Airstream Eight, Series CZ (121" w/b, 273.8 c.i.d.)			
Business coupe	$910/$930	3,103/3,138	100
Coupe with r/s	$935/$955	3,138/3,233	550
Touring Brougham	$960/$980	3,203/3,293	500
Sedan, 4-door	$975/$985	3,213/3,333	2,958
Touring Sedan	$995/$1,015	3,263/3,338	4,394
Convertible coupe	----/$1,015	----/3,298	101
Chassis	N/a	N/a	237
Note: Prices and weights above slash refer to standard models; figures below the slash refer to Airstream Deluxe cars			
Airstream Eight, Series CZ (133" w/b, 273.8 c.i.d.)			
Traveler Sedan	----/$1,235	----/3,513	245
Sedan, 7 passenger	----/$1,235	----/3,538	212
Airflow Eight, Series C1 (123" w/b, 323.5 c.i.d.)			
Business coupe	$1,245	3,823	72
Coupe, 6-passenger	$1,245	3,883	307
Sedan, 4-door	$1,245	3,828	4,617
Imperial Airflow, Series C2 (128" w/b, 323.5 c.i.d.)			
Coupe, 6-passenger	$1,475	4,003	200
Sedan, 4-door	$1,475	3,998	2,398
Imperial Custom Airflow, Series C3 (130" w/b, 323.5 c.i.d.)			
Sedan, 4-door	$2,245	4,208	69
Town Sedan, 4-door	$2,245	4,308	1
Sedan Limousine	$2,345	4,387	53
Town Sedan Limousine	$2,345	4,478	2
Imperial Custom Airflow, Series CW (146.5" w/b, 384.8 c.i.d.)			
Sedan, 8-passenger	$5,000	5,785	15
Town Sedan, 8-passenger	$5,000	5,885	0
Sedan Limousine	$5,145	5,990	15
Town Sedan Limousine	$5,145	6,090	2

Specifications

	1935 Chrysler Airflow	1937 Lincoln Zephyr
Price, f.o.b. factory	$1,245	$1,090 (Nov. '36), $1,165 (Jul. '37)
Standard equipment	Dual trumpet horns, safety glass windshield, 2 w/s wipers, dome light, 2 stop/taillamps, 2 inside sun visors	2 stop/taillamps, 2 sun visors, clock, lighter, safety glass throughout, 2 w/s wipers
Options on feature car	Overdrive, white sidewall tires	Columbia axle, white sidewall tires, radio
Engine	Straight-eight	75-degree V-12
Bore x stroke	2.75 inches x 3.25 inches	3.25 inches x 4.875 inches
Stroke/bore ratio	1.500:1	1.364:1
Displacement (cu.in.)	323.5	267.3
Compression ratio	6.20:1	6.70:1
Horsepower @ rpm	115 @ 3,400	110 @ 3,900
Torque/rpm	240 @ 1,200	186 @ 2,000
Taxable horsepower	33.8	36.3
Valve lifters	Solid	Solid
Main bearings	5	4
Lubrication	Pressure to main, con rod, cam-shaft bearings, timing drive	Pressure to main, con rod, cam-shaft bearings, timing drive
Fuel system	Stromberg 1.5" plain tube single downdraft carb, camshaft pump	Stromberg 1" dual downdraft carb, camshaft pump
Cooling system	Centrifugal pump	Centrifugal pump
Exhaust system	Single	Single
Electrical system	6-volt	6-volt
Clutch	Single dry plate	Single dry plate
Diameter	11"	10"
Actuation	Mechanical, foot pedal	Mechanical, foot pedal
Transmission	3-speed selective	3-speed selective
Location of lever	Floor	Floor
Ratios, 1st/2nd/Reverse	2.53/1.52/3.16	2.82/1.60/3.63
Overdrive (opt.)	Borg-Warner	Columbia
Differential	Spiral bevel	Spiral bevel
Ratio	4.10:1	4.33:1
Drive axles	Semi-floating	3/4-floating
Steering	Worm & roller	Worm & roller
Ratio	20.25:1	18.0:1
Turns, lock-to-lock	4.5	4.9
Turning diameter	37 feet	44.0 feet
Brakes	Lockheed hydraulic	Mechanical, servo-type, cable conduit control
Drum diameter	13 inches	12 inches
Effective area	198.8 sq. in.	168.0 sq. in.
Construction	Semi-unitized all-steel; bridge-truss frame	Unit type with bridge-type structure
Body style	4-door, 6-pass. sedan	3-pass. coupe
Front suspension	Tubular axle, 44" x 2" longitudinal leaf springs	I-beam axle, 40.5" x 2" transverse leaf spring
Rear suspension	Live axle, 56.125" x 2" longitudinal leaf springs	Live axle, 46.5" x 2.25" transverse leaf spring
Shock absorbers	Double-acting hydraulic	Double-acting hydraulic
Wheels	Pressed steel	Pressed steel
Tires	7.00/16	7.00/16
Crankcase capacity	6 quarts	6 quarts
Cooling system capacity	19 quarts	27 quarts
Fuel tank	21 gallons	19 gallons
Wheelbase	123 inches	122 inches
Overall length	206.4375 inches	202.5 inches
Overall width	70.25 inches	70.5 inches
Overall height	67 inches	69 inches
Front track	57 inches	55.46875 inches
Rear track	57 inches	58.25 inches
Min. road clearance	8.375 inches	8.5 inches
Shipping weight	3,828 pounds	3,214 pounds
Horsepower/c.i.d.	.3555	.4115
Lb./horsepower	33.29	29.22
Lb./c.i.d.	11.83	12.02
Lb./sq. in. (brakes)	19.26	19.13
Top speed	"Over 90 mph"	93 mph (est)
Acceleration 0-30		5.8 seconds
0-40		8.7 seconds
0-50	13.6 seconds	10.8 seconds
0-60	20.4 seconds	16.0 seconds
0-70		23.6 seconds
0-80		31.7 seconds
Stopping distances		
From 30 mph	33'6"	N/a
From 50 mph	104'	N/a
	(From Motor, 1/1/35)	(From Rod and Custom 1/70, quoting The Autocar, 3/27/37)

mobiles ever to come out of Detroit. And in the postwar world the Lincoln Zephyr re-emerged, virtually unchanged, as the unhyphenated Lincoln.

In the meantime, Chrysler, having been disappointed in the Airflow's 1934 model year sales of 11,239 cars, undertook a facelift, which provided the 1935 models with a more conventional frontal appearance. But the Airflow still failed to catch on; production sank to 7,751 units, which amounted to just 19 percent of the Chrysler Division's total output for the season.

Modifications for 1936 included a built-in trunk, permitting easier access to the luggage area. But nothing helped; not even the partial economic recovery being experienced at the time. Only 6,275 Airflows were built that year, followed by 4,600 during the 1937 model run—the latter figure representing just 4.3 percent of the Chrysler Division's total production for the year. There was no point in continuing the battle. The Airflow was every bit as advanced an automobile as its makers claimed, but the public simply didn't accept it.

Driving Impressions

When Editor Dave Brownell asked for a comparisonReport pitting a Chrysler Airflow against a Lincoln Zephyr, we expected to have no difficulty In finding a suitable Zephyr. The Airflow, we thought, might present a problem, for it had been some time since we had seen a well-restored example.

Exactly the opposite proved to be the case. With the help of the WPC Club, we learned almost immediately that Lon Normandin, the Chrysler-Plymouth dealer in San Jose, had a fine 1935 Airflow Series Cl on his showroom floor. But the Zephyr eluded us. Our neighbor, John Cavagnaro, used to have a fine '36 sedan, but that one is back on the East Coast now. Lincoln Zephyr authority Dave Cole has a similar car, but Dave lives 300 miles south of here. There were two or three blind leads, and we were commencing to become discouraged, but finally, at the 1990 Palo Alto Concours d'Elegance we found Rico Ghilardi with this lovely 1937 Zephyr coupe.

The question may arise: How come we paired a 1935 model with a '37? Ideally, we should have pitted a '36 Airflow against a Zephyr of the same vintage. But of course we had to take what we could find. In setting up these comparisons, it's obviously necessary to use two cars that are located within a reasonable distance of one another, and that's not always easy to do. But the truth of the matter is, the 1935 Chrysler Airflow Eight is virtually the same car, apart from the grille and a few other minor details, as its 1936 counterpart. Similarly, the 1937 Lincoln Zephyr was carried over from 1936 with only very minor differences. So the comparison is a fair one.

We met at the Normandin dealership, a place with a fascinating history that will be worth telling some day. Lon's great grandfather founded the business in 1875. At that time he was selling buggies of his own manufacture, and one of great grandpa's vehicles is on display in a gallery above the showroom.

Then the automobile came upon the scene, and—with Lon's grandfather in charge this time—Normandin's became a Franklin agency. (In fact, when the Chrysler Airflow was moved out of the showroom for our photo session, its place was taken by a 1915 Franklin that had been sold to its original owners by Normandin's. Incredibly, the old Franklin remained in the same family until 1988, when Lon was able to buy it back at an estate sale!) Fleet manager Paul Normandin, who hosted our visit, represents the fifth generation of the Normandin family to be active in the business.

The early history of Normandin's Airflow is clouded in obscurity. When Lon bought it in 1985 it was in boxes, having been disassembled many years earlier by an owner who expected to restore it. But somehow the restoration had never even been started, a not-unfamiliar story in this hobby.

Lon hauled the pieces back to the Normandin shop, not even knowing whether all the components were present. He was fortunate. Apart from a few minor pieces, such as the knobs that are supposed to open the two-piece windshield (items that Lon is still searching for, by the way), it was all there. A complete mechanical and cosmetic restoration followed, so the old Chrysler drives like a new car, and it looks almost as good as it runs.

Rico Ghilardi is a veteran Ford salesman. He's supposedly retired now, but he still spends some time at San Bruno Ford, taking care of his old customers. His Lincoln Zephyr was restored a number of years ago, but it's still a remarkably sharp looking automobile.

We were fortunate to be able to contact Bill Schmidt, of Saratoga, California, a long-time Lincoln aficionado who had owned Rico's car many years ago and was responsible for its restoration. It was back in 1962 when a friend told him of seeing the Zephyr, rotting away on a lot in Vallejo. Bill checked it out, finding the coupe to be literally no more than a hulk. It had neither engine nor transmission, and Bill theorizes that it must have been a desert car, for all the rubber parts had been fried in the sun

Above: Although both cars are big and relatively heavy, they handle hard cornering with aplomb. ***Below:*** Zephyr's spare consumes a huge amount of available trunk space. ***Bottom:*** Airflow's spare takes no trunk space at all. ***Bottom right:*** Zephyr owner was instructed on how to close trunk lid.

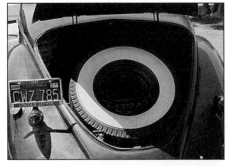

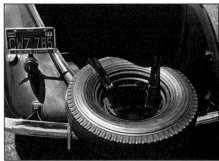

Both the Lincoln and Chrysler engines nestle deep in their respective bays. Service access is a breeze compared to modern cars.

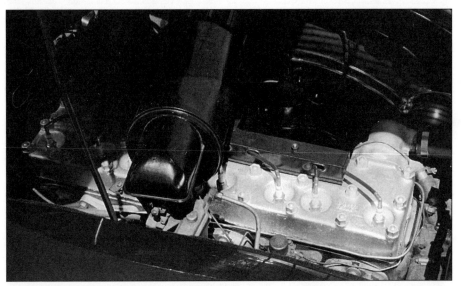

1935 Chrysler Table of Prices, Weights and Production

	Price	Weight	Production
Lincoln Zephyr V-12			
122" w/b, 267.3 c.i.d.			
Coupe-Sedan, 6-passenger	$1,245	3,329	1,500
Coupe, 3-passenger	$1,165	3,214	5,199
Sedan, 4-door, 6-passenger	$1,265	3,369	23,159
Town Limousine, 6-passenger	$1,425	3,398	139
Lincoln Model K V-12			
136" w/b, 414.8 c.i.d.			
Sedan, 5-passenger, 2-window	$4,450	5,492	48
Sedan, 5-passenger, 3-window	$4,450	5,522	136
Coupe, 5-pass. (Willoughby)	$5,550	N/a	6
Convertible victoria (Brunn)	$5,550	5,346	13
Conv. roadster (LeBaron)	$4,950	N/a	15
Coupe, 2-pass. (LeBaron)	$4,950	5,172	24
Lincoln Model K V-12			
145" w/b, 414.8 c.i.d.			
Sedan, 7-passenger	$4,750	5,697	212
Limousine, 7-passenger	$4,850	5,647	248
Non-coil. Cabriolet (Brunn)	$6,550	N/a	10
Semi-coil Cabriolet (Brunn)	$6,750	5,646	7
Brougham, 7-passenger (Brunn)	$6,750	6,781	28
Touring Cabriolet (Brunn)	$6,950	N/a	10
Conv. Sedan (part.) (LeBaron)	$5,650	N/a	12
Convertible Sedan (LeBaron)	$5,450	5,547	37
Sedan Limo, 7-pass. (Judkins)	$5,950	5,732	27
Berline, 2-window (Judkins)	$5,650	5,622	47
Berline, 3-window (Judkins)	$5,750	5,682	19
Touring, 7-pass. (Willoughby)	$5,550	N/a	7
Limousine (Willoughby)	$5,850	5,801	60
Sport Sedan (Willoughby)	$6,850	N/a	6
Panel Brougham (Willoughby)	$7,050	N/a	4

until they were brittle. But of course dry desert air causes no rust, so the Zephyr — with a straight, solid body — was an ideal subject for restoration.

Schmidt recalls that his worst problem in restoring the Lincoln Zephyr had to do with the engine. At first he was unable to find the correct V-12, so a Ford V-8 was substituted temporarily. A few years later a '37 Lincoln Zephyr engine was located, so Bill rebuilt it using new-old-stock parts throughout, and installed it in the car.

Schmidt owned the Zephyr until the mid-1970s. A succession of owners followed, until Rico Ghilardi purchased it in December 1988. Bill Schmidt's cosmetic restoration, completed something like 25 years ago, still looks remarkably good, and the V-12 engine runs as smoothly as it ever did.

Visually, there's some similarity between our two feature cars — at least to the extent that both were aerodynamically advanced for their time. But under way it's quite another matter. In advertising the Airflow, Chrysler took justifiable credit for its comfortable ride — the result, in large measure, of the forward location of the engine. Inevitably, the arrangement had its downside, for it placed the heavy straight-eight engine directly over the front wheels, contributing to the Airflow's relatively heavy steering.

As a matter of fact, our comparisonReport Chrysler outweighs our Lincoln Zephyr by 614 pounds. Admittedly, coupes are typically lighter than sedans, but even if we had used a four-door Lincoln Zephyr for this comparison, the difference would have come to 459 pounds. Small wonder that the Zephyr is significantly easier to steer than the Airflow.

Just one more observation regarding the Airflow's steering: It has a surprisingly short turning diameter, 37 feet, a full seven feet shorter than the Lincoln Zephyr.

Both cars seem to "track" well; both handle hard cornering without heeling over excessively, and both offer a comfortable ride — though the Chrysler appears to hold the edge in that respect. The Airflow is evidently better insulated, for its doors close with a deep "thunk," and on the road it is substantially quieter than its competitor.

Another, equally noticeable difference has to do with low-end torque. The Zephyr's V-12 needs to rev over at a fairly brisk pace in order to flex its muscles adequately, while the Airflow's straight-eight is a stump-puller, displaying tremendous power at very low engine revs.

Both cars have smooth clutches that require only moderate pedal pressure. Both are easy to shift, though we'd have to give the edge in that respect to the Lincoln. There's a lot of play in the Chrysler's linkage, and the synchronizers are not quite as effective as those of its competitor. To some extent this may reflect the respective conditions of the two cars, but based upon past experience we'd say that Lincoln did a better job with its synchronizers than Chrysler. In any case, we quickly got the hang of the Airflow's transmission and were able to shift it without difficulty.

Since the Lincoln has mechanical brakes while the Chrysler uses hydraulics, we expected to find a big difference in stopping power — particularly since the Zephyr's lining area is a bit skimpy (smaller, in fact, than the '37 Ford V-8 85). In a longer, harder test, no doubt the Chrysler would have had the advantage, particularly in terms of fade resistance. Certainly over time the mechanicals would need more adjustment. But in our brief drive we'd have to say that the binders in both cars did their job well. Years ago we owned a Ford with cable-controlled brakes similar to those of the Zephyr. They worked well enough, but they made a groaning sound that we found annoying. No such problem here; the Lincoln's brakes were as quiet as those of the Chrysler.

As the years creep up on us, seating comfort becomes increasingly important. Both of these cars deserve high marks in that respect, though the edge clearly goes to the Chrysler, which seems to offer better support to the lower back. Wide, three-abreast seats were a major selling point for both the Chrysler Airflow and the Lincoln Zephyr. back in the 1930s. And deservedly so.

That's all to the good, but the luggage compartments in both cars must have been designed by a chiropractor bent on expanding his practice. In the case of the Chrysler, the storage space can be reached only from inside the car. (The same is true, by the way, of the 1936 Zephyrs.) It almost takes a contortionist to hold the rear backrest aloft while the suitcases and other gear are stowed away. The Zephyr coupe is different, but no better. One has to lean far forward, grab the 50-pound spare wheel and tire, pull it upright and then ease it down toward the bumper. It's a task that would be physically impossible for many people.

On the other hand, once access has been gained, the Zephyr coupe's luggage space is nothing short of cavernous. That of the Airflow is much more limited, and the same would be true of the Lincoln Zephyr sedans.

We don't indulge in high-speed driving with these older cars, so we had no opportunity to compare the two different overdrives. The Zephyr uses the

Above: Both cars use elegant chrome framing on their seats. **Below:** Even though they were the last word in modern design at the time, both cars retained small split rear windows, which severely limited visibility.

Above: Airflow's instrument panel, left, is easier to read than Zephyr's centrally located gauges. Below left: Airflow's trunk access is difficult. Below right: But when down, Airflow rear seat is ultra-comfortable.

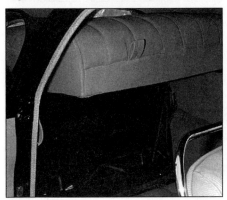 

SIA comparisonReport

Columbia two-speed axle, while the Airflow employs a first-generation Borg-Warner unit. These early B-W jobs don't have the "kick-down" of the later models, which enable the driver to shift back to conventional high simply by flooring the accelerator. So it's advisable for the driver to look alive, lest he find himself sailing down a steep mountain grade without the ability to engage his engine to help with the braking.

Personally, we enjoy using an overdrive. We like the quiet that results from reduced engine rpms, and of course we appreciate the extra gas mileage. Our favorite setup is the later Borg-Warner with the "kick-down" switch. But between the earlier B-W used in our comparisonReport Chrysler and the Columbia unit, we'd feel a little more secure with the Columbia.

And so, we come to the bottom line. Let's say it's the mid-thirties again, and we're about to purchase one of the streamliners of that era, Which to choose?

There's no clear, hard-and-fast answer. The lady at our house would pick the Zephyr, hands down, first because of its graceful lines (admittedly,

a matter of individual taste, but one that was widely shared), and second because of its easier steering. But the driver who values lots of torque, either for mountain travel or simply to minimize downshifting, or the individual who places a premium upon maximum comfort and minimum noise would doubtless be happier with the Airflow.

Both were highly advanced designs for their time. And both, in our view, represented stellar values in the medium-price range. ᦲ

Acknowledgments and Bibliography
Automobile Trade Journal, *March 1935, July 1937*; Automotive Industries, *February 23, 1935; November 21, 1936; February 27, 1937*; Chrysler Division factory literature; Cole, Richard. *"The Chrysler Airflow and the Lincoln Zephyr,"* The Way of the Zephyr, *Vol. 6, No, 3*; Dammann, George H., Seventy Years of Chrysler; Kimes, Beverly Rae, *"Chrysler: From the Airflow,"* Automobile Quarterly, *Vol. VII No. 2*; Kimes, Beverly Rae and Henry Austin Clark, Jr., Standard Catalog of American Cars, 1805-1942; Lamm, Michael *"Drivetest of the 1937 V-12 Lincoln Zephyr,* Rod and Custom, *January 1970*; Lincoln Motor Company factory literature; Langworth, Richard M., *"In the Track of the Zephyr,"* Automobile Quarterly, *Vol. XVI, No. 2*; Langworth, Richard M. and Jan P. Norbye, Chrysler: The Complete History; Motor, *January 1935*; The Motor, *March 27, 1934, and January 1, 1935*; Woudenberg, Paul R., Lincoln and Continental: The Postwar Years.

Our thanks to Joe Caruso, San Jose, California; John Cavagnaro, Stockton, California; Leilo Giorgi, San Mateo, California; Bill Gordon, Las Vegas, Nevada; Holy Family Catholic Church, San Jose, California; Bill Schmidt, Saratoga, California. Special thanks to Rico and June Ghilardi, Milbrae, California; Lon and Paul Normandin, San Jose, California.

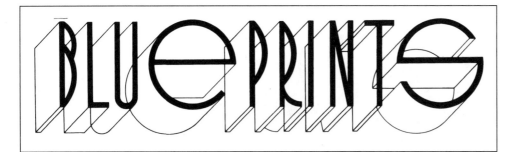

BLUEPRINTS

1928 Lincoln
By Bob Hovorka

THE speedometer stopped at 80, but the cars could easily hit 90. A favorite of lawman and criminal alike, the twenties Lincolns were a paradox in wood and steel.

Designed by the master of precision, built by the mastermind of mass production, they offered unheard-of quality for the price. Although the purchase of Henry Leland's company by Henry Ford made many people wonder what would happen to Leland's precise manufacturing methods, most fears were unfounded. While brochures addressed their concerns on paper, the real proof lies behind the wheel.

Here, 357-cubic-inch V-8s still idled with marshmallow-soft smoothness. Beautifully finished bodies were still plain to a point just short of homely, and custom coach builders still plied their trade on chassis built by Lincoln. Internally, aluminum pistons replaced the iron Leland versions. Externally, Lincoln emblems began sporting "Ford – Detroit" in place

of the original "Leland Built."

For 1927, four-wheel brakes were added to the line. Brochures called them a "Six-brake System." "This comprises mechanical four-wheel brakes of Bendix design, with special Lincoln refinements providing braking efficiency far in excess of all ordinary requirements." In addition, "The hand or emergency brake operates independently on the rear wheel drums, giving to Lincoln a "Six-brake System."

The following year the 60-degree V-8 was bored an eighth inch, increasing displacement to 384 cubic inches. Some say it resulted in a rougher idle. Ford engineers felt the improved torque curve was worth it, adding balance weights to filter out any vibrations. However, instead of mechanical improvements, brochures stressed safety and quality.

"Nowhere is the safety advantage of quality more apparent than in body construction...." Extolling the virtues of a steel-reinforced framework of specially selected hardwoods, it stated, "Where

wood is joined to wood it is mortised, glued and screwed together with expert care. Every one of the 700 screws is hand set — not power set — to prevent overstrain and breakage."

Even glass was "especially selected" Triplex shatter-proof glass. It was used in all Lincoln windshields, as well as all closed car windows.

But if safety was important, quality was an obsession. Not only body parts, but axles, steering gear, wheels, hubs, shackles — even bolts and nuts — were individually tested. "And individual testing does not mean that just a few samples out of a group must pass inspection — it means that each and every part must be separately tested to prove its fitness for Lincoln use."

Yet, for all the talk of quality and safety, those early Lincolns are probably best remembered from the old gangster flicks; swerving down rain-stained city streets — dodging machine gun bullets — both being chased and doing the chasing. ✍

Originally published in Special Interest Autos #150, Nov.-Dec. 1995

by Michael Lamm, *Editor*

THE AUTOCAR (British) road-tested a Zephyr V-12 when the car first appeared for 1936, and then they tested another one in 1939. Why they ran two such similar tests back to back we don't know, but reading both reports today, they sound very much like rave reviews, and with good reason.

Both AUTOCAR tests concluded that Zephyrs were fast, handsome, well put together, and a bargain at the price. This was equally true in the second test as the first. Britishers liked the idea of a not-too-expensive V-12, and Zephyr engines appeared not only in exported Zephyrs but in prewar Allards, Atalantas, plus one-offs by Brough and Jensen.

The convertible coupe you see here is owned by Jerry Emery of San Jose, California. Jerry is the car's fourth owner; it's an Ohio car, and Jerry bought it while on vacation in 1970. At the time of our driveReport, the odometer showed 94,542 careful miles. Everything but the paint and the top was original, even the leather upholstery.

Best way to summarize the Zephyr's overall personality is to liken it to a big, pumped-up Ford. In every way, it handles, sounds, drives, rides, and even smells like a bigger, heavier Ford of the same era. The smell is the barely perceptible odor of blow-by coming from the oil filler just ahead of the slightly porous firewall.

The Zephyr takes off with that delightful Ford crispness. You hear the carb suck air, the fan starts to moan as speed picks up, there's the subdued but rising burble of the exhaust. Shifting takes a little getting used to, since the Zephyr's long lever pokes out from the left side of a floor-to-dash console and is therefore slightly indirect, although no more so than a column-mounted lever.

The convertible has pretty bad visibility to the rear with the top up, and the driver can't see either right fender, so it's hard to tell how wide the car is. Other than that, the car is easy and a great pleasure to drive. Steering's a bit heavy, but the brakes aren't, nor is the clutch. In cornering, the Zephyr sticks flatter and more predictably than most cars of that era, and it's amazing what Ford could do with transverse springs. It's a very sophisticated suspension system—highly refined. The convertible rides with admirable gentleness, and it seems to us a good long-distance car.

Among the Zephyr's subtler features, we appreciated the trunk light

Originally published in Special Interest Autos #6, Jul.-Aug. 1971

1939 Lincoln Zephyr

Zephyr's 267-c.i.d. V-12 was Ford's flathead V-8 with an extra four cylinders added. Lower grille opening for 1939 necessitated fan attached to crankshaft. The inner fender panels are generously louvered to let out engine heat.

Big dial dominates Zephyr dash. Battery-condition gauge replaces ammeter. Key locks steering; gearshift pokes out of console; all knobs are recessed.

Tools stow in special compartment under rear seat. Running board is concealed when doors shut. This convertible sports original leather.

Spare bolts to A-frame that tilts back for access to trunk. Springs help cantilever the tire, but it's still awkward—you have to reach over it.

To make convertible, Briggs merely modified club coupe, finished doors with chrome plates.

Zephyr's cornering remains amazingly flat, especially considering single body attachment to each transverse spring. 1939 marked the first year for Zephyr's hydraulic brakes, and car does not stop well.

Twin glove compartments and double ashtrays lend symmetry plus a bonus of extra stowage.

Hills don't faze the Zephyr—it's a good cross-country tourer. Columbia 2-speed rear axle improves gas mileage approximately four mpg at 60 mph, so it was well worth the extra $75 it cost.

There's plenty of leg room front and rear. Only 640 Lincoln Zephyr convertible coupes were made for 1939. 136-inch springbase gives a smooth, comfortable ride despite archaic suspension.

Windwings that came with Jerry Emery's Lincoln are prototypes that never were produced.

Chrysler Historical Collection

Rear-engined Tjaarda-Briggs proto was shown at 1934 Chicago World's Fair—one of many built. Porsche saw this car, so it may have influenced VW.

that comes on when you pivot the spare tire out of the trunk; also the oil-level sight gauge atop the block, the hydraulic valve lifters, the aluminum heads, and the optional Columbia 2-speed rear axle. In proving grounds tests, the Columbia raised the Zephyr's fuel mileage from 12.6 to 16.4 mpg at a steady 60mph.

Now that Jaguar has brought out a new one, V-12s might come back into vogue. Porsche already makes an Opposed 12 racing engine, Ferrari has favored V-12s for nearly a quarter century, and Cadillac keeps tinkering with a modern V-12 or so it's been rumored these last few years.

Best-selling V-12 of all time, though, was the Zephyr's. Lincoln began offering V-12s in 1932, and from 1933 through 1948, you couldn't buy a Lincoln without one.

The Zephyr, introduced in November 1935, was Ford Motor Co.'s very clever and beautifully timed way of cashing in on V-12 prestige. Packard had long championed V-12s and, in the early 1930s, if you had the cash, you could choose between V-12s from not only Packard and Lincoln but also Cadillac, Pierce, Auburn, and Franklin. Those, plus the Marmon and Cad V-16s, marked the height of Depression-era luxury, the rule of thumb being the more cylinders the better.

The Zephyr might never have been born if hard feelings hadn't broken out between the Ford Motor Co. and the Briggs Body Co. Briggs had lost much of its FoMoCo earnings in 1931-32. Strained relations developed between Ford and Briggs because Ford's production boss, Charles Sorensen, felt Briggs was paying too much attention to its Chrysler business and not enough to Ford's. Then, too, Lincolns weren't selling well, and Briggs had previously counted on finishing and trimming many more Lincoln bodies.

So to get back into Ford's good graces, Briggs hired two men: Howard Bonbright and John Tjaarda. Bonbright was a personal friend of Edsel Ford's, and the idea was to let Bonbright woo Edsel with the concept of an all-new, medium-priced Lincoln. Tjaarda was hired to design that car, and Briggs, of course, would build bodies for it.

Tjaarda had been with Locke & Co., had worked with Harry Miller on Duesenberg race-car designs, had put time in at GM's Art & Colour Section and, in 1929, was hired by Briggs' LeBaron studios. In an article published in *Motor Trend* in 1954, Tjaarda wrote. "I was to work on designs for Briggs customers, and for Ford in particular.... The new assignment was just what the doctor had prescribed for both Briggs and myself."

Tjaarda had long been doodling with a far-out, streamlined, unit-bodied, rear-engined layout that he now updated. As soon as Tjaarda got

sketches and models presentable, Bonbright arranged a meeting with Edsel Ford. (Briggs was purposefully skirting Old Henry and Sorensen, wooing Edsel instead, knowing he'd be more receptive.) Edsel saw the models and needed no further convincing a new mid-priced Lincoln was just what the company needed, and Tjaarda's radical ideas appealed to him, particularly his thoughts on bridge-truss body framing. Tjaarda later wrote, "It was a happy time for me to see some of my long-nourished dreams coming true, and it was truly a pleasure to be associated with an individual of such good taste and discernment as Edsel Ford."

Since Briggs was working with Chrysler on the Airflow at the same time, the Zephyr project had to be kept strictly secret, even from most Briggs execs. Tjaarda worked almost alone on the locked fifth floor of the Briggs plant, and Edsel used to stop by several mornings a week on his way to the office. Tjaarda's first proposals included one rear-engined version and one front-engined design. Initially, the idea was to use a hopped-up Ford V-8 in the rear, but that engine didn't work out, and the placement seemed too unconventional, so Frank Johnson, Lincoln's chief engineer, came up with a small V-12 based on the Ford V-8 block. After all, it was common industry practice to create a Straight 8 by tacking two cylinders onto an existing 6, so why not make a V-12 by adding four to an existing V-8?

Around mid-1932, the Zephyr project reached the point where Edsel had to tell his dad and Sorensen about it. Luckily, Edsel seems to have had no trouble selling the idea. Ford and Sorensen went along from the start but insisted that suspension and running gear continue in the Ford mode. Tjaarda's slope-nosed prototypes were shown in 1934 at the Chicago World's Fair, and reaction was wildly favorable. Public opinion reinforced the choice of front engine placement, so E. T. Gregorie, Ford's styling chief, designed the distinctive 1936 Zephyr prow-cum-alligator-hood and refined Tjaarda's general lines and interior. Thus the Zephyr made its debut in November 1935. It sold well, but more important than that, its styling was copied by nearly every other automaker in later years. Tjaarda's early drawings included a convertible, and Edsel Ford kept those. The Zephyr eventually led to the Continental of 1940, and after the war, though the name Zephyr disappeared, the car and the V-12 remained basically unchanged until 1949. ෨

The editors wish to thank Jerry Emery, San Jose, California; the Lincoln Zephyr Owners Club, Inc., Box 185, Middletown, PA 17057; the Lincoln Continental Owners Club, Box 549, Nogales, AZ 85621; Lincoln-Mercury Div. of Ford Motor Co., Dearborn; Bill Schmidt; John MacAdams; Jack Passey; E. T. Gregorie; and the Ford Archives, Henry Ford Museum, Dearborn.

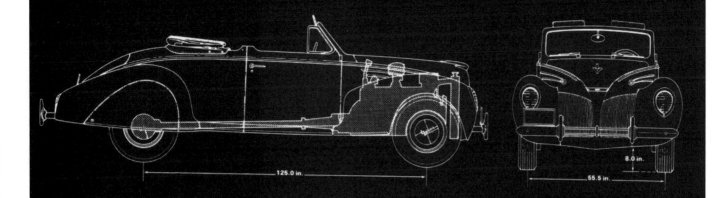

125.0 in.   8.0 in.   55.5 in.

SPECIFICATIONS
1939 Lincoln Zephyr Model 96-H Convertible Coupe

Price when new................$7,148 f.o.b. Dearborn (1939)

Current valuation* ....Xlnt., $4,190; good, $2,710

Options................................Windwings, heater, whitewall tires, bumper guards

ENGINE
Type..L-head V-12, water-cooled, cast-iron block,
aluminum heads, 4 mains, full pressure lubrication
Bore x stroke ....2.75 inches x 3.75 inches
Displacement ....267.3 cubic inches
Max. bhp @ rpm....................110 @ 3,900
Max. torque @ rpm ....186 @ 2,000
Compression ratio 6.7:1

CHASSIS & BODY
Frame..Channel-section steel with bridge-truss body framing
Body construction ....Steel
Body style ....2-door convertible coupe, manual top

SUSPENSION
Front ....I-beam axle, transverse leaf spring, hydraulic
lever shocks
Rear ....Solid axle, transverse leaf spring, hydraulic
lever shocks
Tires ....7.00 x 16 inch 4-ply, whitewalls
Wheels ....Pressed steel, drop-center rims, lug-bolted
brake drums

WEIGHTS
AND MEASURES
Wheelbase..................................125 inches
Overall length...........................210 inches
Overall height...........................63.25 inches
Overall width ....74 inches
Front track..................................55.5 inches
Rear track ....58.25 inches
Ground clearance..................8.0 inches
Curb weight...............................3,790 pounds

CAPACITIES
Crankcase....................................5 quarts
Cooling system ....30 quarts
Fuel tank....................................19 gallons

FUEL CONSUMPTION
Best..18.2 mpg
Average ....14.1 mpg

PERFORMANCE (from Autocar road test of 1939 Zephyr sedan 6/23/39)
0-30 mph......................................4.4 sec.
0-50 mph......................................10.8 sec.
0-60 mph......................................15.5 seconds
0-70 mph......................................21.4 sec.
Top speed ....90-91 mph

*Courtesy Antique Automobile Appraisal

1941 LINCOLN CONTINENTAL

by Arch Brown
photos by Bud Juneau

IF there is one automobile that ranks above all the others as a monument to Edsel Ford's good taste, It is the original Lincoln Continental of 1940-41.

During the summer of 1938 Edsel had been traveling on the Continent. Upon his return he commissioned stylist E.T. "Bob" Gregorie to design a one-off convertible for his own use. The car was to be based upon the Lincoln Zephyr, using the Zephyr's mechanical components and as much Zephyr sheet metal as possible. Yet its styling was to have a continental flair, and its rear-mounted spare tire was to be left exposed. Delivery was to be made in time for Edsel and Eleanor Ford's Florida vacation, scheduled for the following March. Which, of course, gave Gregorie an almost impossibly short time in which to develop the car.

A clay model was ready in November, however, after which the first Lincoln Continental was meticulously hand built. The body was based on the Lincoln Zephyr convertible of 1938-39, sectioned at the belt line and lowered by three inches. The hood was stretched an extra seven inches, front fenders were lengthened accordingly, and the passenger compartment was shifted rearward on the chassis. A squared-off, top-loading trunk completed the Continental's long-hood, short-deck appearance, a radical innovation at that time. Thus the Zephyr's proportions were substantially changed, and the result was sheer elegance. For, as the late Gordon Buehrig has reminded us, good design is largely a matter of proportion.

Not only was Edsel Ford enormously pleased with the result, but architect Frank Lloyd Wright referred to the Continental as "the most beautiful car of all time." And the reaction among Edsel's friends was so enthusiastic that some 200 orders were reportedly received, in case the decision was made to produce the car in significant numbers. It surely was not Edsel's intent to create such a stir; that simply was not his style. But his love of beauty permeated

EDSEL FORD'S LEGACY

Driving Impressions

It was during 1954 that Heinz Schu — then 13 years old and living in his native Germany—first became enchanted by the Lincoln Continental. The car was owned by an American serviceman who lived in an apartment complex not far from the Schu home. Young Heinz made up his mind that some day he would own a car like that.

A year later, Heinz came with his family to the United States. His dream of owning a Continental was very much alive in December 1957, when he found a 1948 model on a used car lot. The youngster couldn't afford it, so to get rid of the anxious salesman he said he was looking for a '41 Continental.

A month later Heinz's mother received a telephone call from the salesman. He had a car for Heinz: a 1941 Lincoln Continental cabriolet, priced at $650!

Of course, Schu bought the car. It was in decent running condition, and Heinz used it as his daily driver. Within a year the Continental began using oil, so Heinz—unable to afford the $700 it would take to go through the V-12 engine — installed a flathead Mercury V-8. And then, piece by piece, he began to acquire the parts he would need for a full restoration.

In 1961 Heinz quit driving the Continental and tore it down, installing the Mercury engine in a 1947 Hudson. Every nut and bolt on the car was dismantled. The engine was totally rebuilt, using all new parts except for the block and the crankshaft. Bearings and seals were replaced throughout, with Heinz doing all the mechanical work himself.

The meticulous cosmetic work was also young Schu's work, though the new upholstery was sewn by a specialist. Altogether it took nine years before the car was fully restored to showroom condition. And for 20 years now, Heinz has proudly driven his Continental on club tours as well as family outings. He has driven it to Lincoln and Continental Owners Club meets in Boise, Portland and San Diego, and he expects to participate in the Classic Car Club's Canadian tour in 1991.

We asked Heinz, "What was the most difficult part to find?" "The steering wheel," he replied. After years of searching, he was able to buy a new-old-stock item from an old Ford dealership in Carson City, Nevada. Almost as difficult to locate were the aluminum cylinder heads, which turned up in a San Carlos, California, wrecking yard. At a swap meet he found a pair of new-old-stock 1941 California license plates, still in the original envelope.

We expected the Continental's acceleration to be rather slow, but while it won't send anyone to the chiropractor with whiplash, it's actually fairly brisk. The clutch chatters lightly, in a fashion familiar to anyone who has driven flathead Ford V-8s. Shifts are easy, and the snychromesh is very effective. Steering is both slow — five turns, lock-to-lock — and heavy, which is hardly surprising, considering the big ragtop's considerable weight. The car leans rather heavily in the turns. Brake pressure is also heavy. The binders seem to do their job well, but given the somewhat skimpy lining area we would expect them to fade under very hard use.

Front leg room is adequate, though one could hardly call it generous, especially for the tall driver. It's a bit cramped in the rear, as one might expect of this body style. The trunk is very spacious, however it wouldn't be easy to load, especially if the luggage was heavy. Our only major criticism is the inevitable one: that long stretch of canvas top constitutes a terrible blind spot for the driver.

We asked Heinz about the Continental's fuel mileage, knowing that in its day this engine took its share of honors in economy runs. He replied that at 70 miles an hour with the overdrive engaged, it regularly returns 17 miles to the gallon in highway travel. And, he adds, it will cruise without complaint at 90.

Given the stunning good looks of the 1941 Lincoln Continental, one could hardly complain if the car didn't run at all! But according to its owner, this one is a fine traveling companion as well as a head-turning beauty.

tions being the polished aluminum cylinder heads and the side-mounted air cleaner, the latter made necessary by the Continental's low hood line. The engine was the Lincoln Zephyr's 75-degree. 292-cubic-inch V-12, by that time the only 12-cylinder engine being produced by an American manufacturer. The transmission was a conventional three-speed manual gearbox, controlled—for the first time in a Ford product—by a column-mounted shift lever. The Columbia two-speed axle was available at extra cost for buyers who wanted an overdrive.

Suspension was by means of transverse leaf springs, with rigid axles front and rear—an archaic arrangement, retained at the insistence of Henry Ford.

Above: The word "timeless" has been used to describe the Continental's design, and we can't disagree with it at all. Right: Push-button door handles contribute to smooth flanks on the car. Far right: Engine i.d. is found in a tiny badge at front of the hood. Below: Parking lamps are the same as on regular Zephyrs.

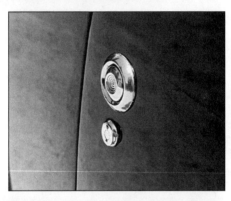

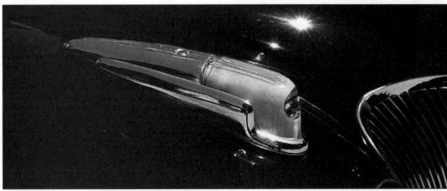

1941 LINCOLN

his entire life, and his keen eye for line and design had always been a major influence upon Lincoln styling (see sidebar, page 31).

And so in April 1939, just a month after the first Lincoln Continental had been delivered to him, Edsel ordered the car into production, to be based this time upon the 1940 Lincoln Zephyr convertible. The first production cabriolet rolled off the line in September 1939, spoken for by the youthful screen star Jackie Cooper. The formal introduction took place on October 2 at the Ford Rotunda in Dearborn, followed two weeks later by presentations at the New York and Los Angeles automobile shows. But production was extremely

limited; by the end of the 1939 calendar year, just 25 of these gorgeous automobiles had been built.

The Lincoln Zephyr Continental was, as Tom Bonsall has observed, an "instant classic," and demand quickly began to build, despite the car's premium price. Series production got under way, though the numbers were still small. This was, after all, a semi-custom job, and at $2,840 it cost $1,045 more than the Cadillac 62 convertible—a difference of 58 percent. (Even so, it is believed that Lincoln lost money on every Continental it produced.)

A coupe—a true "hardtop," derived from the convertible body—was introduced in April, and by the end of the 1940 model year 404 Lincoln Continentals had been built: 54 coupes and 350 ragtops.

Mechanically, the Continental was pure Lincoln Zephyr, the only modifica-

Brakes were hydraulics; old Henry had resisted their use, but had finally bowed in 1939 to public opinion and the demands of his dealers. However, their lining area was only seven square inches greater than that of the Ford V-8—a difference of four percent—though the Continental outweighed its corporate sibling by more than 900 pounds.

Styling remained virtually the same for 1941, though there were a few superficial changes such as the adoption of pushbutton door latches. Prices were shaved just slightly, to $2,778 for the cabriolet, $2,737 for the coupe. And the word "Zephyr" was dropped from the title. Thenceforth, Edsel's handsome new car would be known simply as the Lincoln Continental.

More important were a number of mechanical changes. common to both the Lincoln Zephyr and the Continental for 1941. Springs were longer and wider, with rubber interleaf inserts. Shock absorbers were given greater capacity, and the rear tread was widened by two and a half inches. Wheel rims were also wider, though the tire size remained unchanged.

The Borg-Warner overdrive joined the option list, though the Columbia axle was still available for those who preferred it. An electrically powered top replaced the earlier vacuum-powered unit in the cabriolet. Electric windshield wipers were a new option, and hydraulically powered windows and front seat were also available.

Far left: Taillamps blend smoothly into body shape. *Left:* License plate has its own illumination.

Edsel

"Edsel, you shut up"

This was Henry Ford, speaking to his only son. (Or at least, his only acknowledged son.) The occasion was an executive luncheon at Ford headquarters. Edsel, who rarely disagreed publicly with his father, had had the temerity to suggest that the time had come for the Ford Motor Company to adopt hydraulic brakes. Henry, furious at what he regarded as Edsel's disloyalty, glared across the table at his son, then turned and abruptly left the meeting.

The incident is illustrative of the way Edsel Ford was treated by his father throughout his adult lifetime. Time after time the elder Ford humiliated his son. There can be no question but that Henry Ford loved Edsel dearly, in his own perverse way. He was simply, as he explained to Harry Bennett, trying to build character in his son—presumably by goading him into fighting back. But conflict was not in Edsel's nature.

On one occasion, Edsel—a man of impeccable taste—had hired an interior decorator to refurbish his office. Especially pleased with the new marble fireplace, Edsel ordered a duplicate to be installed in his father's office—a lovely, thoughtful gift. Henry promptly had it torn out and replaced with brick.

At another time, informed by the production people that new coke ovens were needed, Edsel, the titular head of the company, had them built. Henry, without a word to his son, ordered them destroyed.

On yet another occasion Edsel had contracted for the construction of a new office building, since both accounting and the sales department had long since outgrown their quarters.

It is probably no coincidence that Henry Ford had been out of town when plans for the new building were drawn and the contract let. Upon his return the elder Ford took note of the excavation that was under way and demanded to know what was going on. Edsel, doubtless with a mixture of pride and dread, described the new building, which would supply the company with badly needed office space.

"Space for who?" the old man demanded.

In retrospect, that should have been Edsel's cue to make a pitch for the needs of the sales department; Henry could have understood that. Instead, his son mentioned first the accountants. Without waiting to hear any more, Henry Ford turned on his heel and left.

Next morning, when the accountants reported for work they found their offices stripped. No desks, no chairs, no files, no telephones. Even the carpeting was gone, and their jobs had been eliminated. Henry Ford had abolished the accounting department, with which he had never had any patience anyway; and overnight he had seen to the removal of its furniture and equipment.

Betaking himself to his son's office, Henry blithely informed the hapless Edsel that there was plenty of room available now for the sales staff.

Only rarely did Edsel Ford reveal his emotions to anyone, save perhaps to Eleanor, his wife, and to Ernest Kanzler, his wife's brother-in-law. But toward the end of his life, after his father had sided for at least the hundredth time with his security chief, the infamous Harry Bennett, Edsel burst out in angry frustration, "The hurtful thing is that Father takes Harry's word and he won't believe mine."

In his youth Edsel Ford attended the Detroit University School, an excellent preparatory institution. But although he made a fine record there, he was not permitted to go on to college, where his keen mind and artistic inclinations would have profited enormously from a liberal arts education. Henry Ford, whose own education had begun and ended in a one-room country school, believed that the factory would supply Edsel with all the education he would ever need.

The one area in which Henry Ford appears to have recognized his son's talents was that of styling. Walter Dorwin Teague recalled, "Here his unique ability was, in his father's eyes, both mysterious and highly respected, not to be interfered with. This was a matter of immense importance to the success of the Ford Motor Company during a difficult interval, and it also provided for Edsel an indispensable outlet, an escape into his profoundest and most satisfying interests, the creative arts."

Edsel's artistic interests led him, despite widespread criticism, to finance Diego Rivera's murals at the Detroit Institute of Arts, and he became that museum's principal benefactor. It was Edsel who saw to it that when the Model T was finally superseded by the Model A, at the close of 1927, the new Ford had an elegant appearance that had clearly been inspired by the Lincoln. From that time until his death, Edsel played an important role in the styling of all Ford cars; and as Tom Bonsall has noted, "Whatever else their shortcomings, they were, thanks to Edsel, nearly always handsome."

But it was at the Lincoln Motor Company where he made his greatest impact. "His method," Bonsall has explained, "was to solicit designs from the leading coachbuilders of the day...and then order selected designs in lots of 50 or 100 or more. In this fashion Edsel was able to offer the highest quality designs at prices far below what would have been charged for one-offs." And with the Lincoln Zephyr, in whose design Edsel collaborated every step of the way, Lincoln was able to offer much of the elegance of the larger Lincolns at a price within the reach of middle America.

As World War II approached, Edsel was widely perceived, both within the company and elsewhere, as the stabilizing force at the Ford Motor Company. His father, who had suffered a stroke in 1938, was becoming increasingly unpredictable, and it was Edsel, a far better administrator than Henry, who held the badly disorganized company together.

Pressure, combined with frustration and suppressed rage, makes a poor recipe for good health and a long life. Not surprisingly, Edsel Ford fell victim to ulcers, and then to something far worse. Early in 1942 he underwent abdominal surgery. Ten months later he was hospitalized again, this time with undulant fever. As part of his bland diet, Edsel had been drinking milk from his father's dairy farm; and, of course, stubborn old Henry would not permit even the testing of his herd, much less the pasteurization of the milk.

But the doctors found something far worse than undulant fever, bad as that was. Edsel's ulcers had become cancerous, and his condition was deemed inoperable. He was sent home to die.

Henry Ford stubbornly refused to admit the truth about his son's condition. It was all due to Edsel's high-flying lifestyle, he declared. If Edsel would only eat a proper diet; if he would just stop smoking; it was the fault of the doctors—what Edsel needed was a chiropractor. But early on the morning of May 26, 1943, with his hand held by his beloved Eleanor, Edsel Ford escaped forever from his father's tyranny. He was only 49.

What a tragedy, and what a waste!

specifications

illustrations by Russell von Sauers, The Graphic Automobile Studio

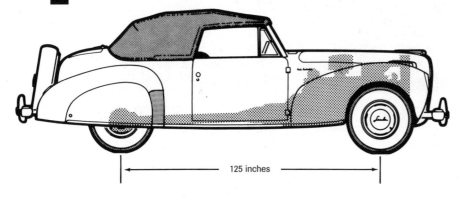

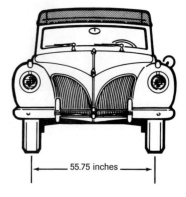

125 inches

55.75 inches

1941 Lincoln Continental

Original price	With standard equipment, $2,778 f.o.b. factory, federal taxes included
Standard equipment	Dual windshield wipers, electric clock, glove compartment with lock, rear wheel shields, twin synchronized horns, turn signals, outside rear-view mirror
Optional equipment	Overdrive, radio, heater, white sidewall tires

ENGINE

Type	75-degree V-12, cast en bloc
Bore x stroke	2.875 inches x 3.75 inches
Displacement	292.0 cubic inches
Compression ratio	7.00:1
Horsepower @ rpm	120 @ 3,500
Torque @ rpm	220@ 2,000
Taxable horsepower	39.6
Valve configuration	L-head
Valve lifters	Hydraulic
Main bearings	4
Fuel system	Dual downdraft carburetor, camshaft pump
Cooling system	Centrifugal pump
Lubrication system	Pressure to main, connecting rod and camshaft bearings
Exhaust system	Single with cross-over
Electrical system	6-volt

CLUTCH

Type	Long single dry plate
Diameter	10 inches
Actuation	Mechanical, foot pedal

TRANSMISSION

Type	3-speed selective, column-mounted lever; synchronized 2nd and 3rd gears; Borg-Warner overdrive
Ratios: 1st	2.33:1
2nd	1.57:1
3rd	1.00:1
Reverse	3.00:1
Overdrive	0.70:1

DIFFERENTIAL

Type	Hypoid
Ratio	4.44
Drive axles	3/4-floating
Torque medium	Torque tube

STEERING

Type	Gemmer worm-and-roller
Ratio	18.4:1
Turns lock-to-lock	5
Turning diameter	44' 6"

BRAKES

Type	4-wheel hydraulic, drum type
Drum diameter	12 inches
Braking area	168 square inches

CHASSIS & BODY

Construction	All-steel construction with integral body and frame
Body style	6-passenger convertible cabriolet

SUSPENSION

Front	I-beam axle, 44.5" x 2" transverse 16-leaf spring; torsional stabilizer
Rear	Live axle, 49" x 2.25" transverse 16-leaf spring

Shock absorbers	Double-acting hydraulic, tubular type
Tires	7.00 x 16, 4-ply
Wheels	Pressed steel, drop-center rims

WEIGHTS AND MEASURES

Wheelbase	125 inches
Overall length	209.82 inches
Overall width	75 inches
Overall height	62 inches (unloaded)
Front track	55.75 inches
Rear track	60 inches
Road clearance	9 inches (minimum)
Shipping weight	3,860 pounds

INTERIOR MEASUREMENTS

Hip room	50" front, 49" rear
Shoulder room	52" front, 50" rear
Head room	38" front, 35" rear
Leg room	39.5" front (rear n/a)
Luggage area	18.25 cu. ft.

CAPACITIES

Crankcase	5 quarts
Cooling system	27 quarts
Fuel tank	19.5 gallons
Transmission	2.75 pt.
Differential	4 pt.

CALCULATED DATA

Stroke/bore ratio	1.304:1
Hp per c.i.d.	.411
Weight per hp	32.2 lb.
Weight per c.i.d.	13.2 lb.
Lb. per sq. in. (brakes)	23.0 lb.

Right: Chromed hex bolt holds fender skirts in place. *Far right:* The famous "Continental spare." At a time when spare tires were moving into autos' trunks, this may have seemed like a regressive step, but in reality it worked elegantly.

1941 LINCOLN

Standard interiors for the Lincoln Continental came in a choice of full leather or leather and whipcord, while interior hardware carried a soft gold finish. And for the coupes, custom interiors were available in a choice of tan, blue, maroon or green "shadow stripe" broadcloth.

In response to demand, Continental production was increased for 1941. If the car wasn't a money-maker for Lincoln, at least it did good things for the marque's prestige. But the supply was still far short of demand: Only 400 cabriolets and 850 coupes were built for the 1941 model year.

For 1942, both the Zephyr and the Continental were fitted with a new two-part grille with horizontal bars, accenting the car's more massive form. Weight was increased, by 170 pounds in the case of the Continental coupe. In order to compensate for the additional heft, the engine was bored a sixteenth of an inch, increasing the displacement to 306 cubic inches and raising the horsepower to 130. Even that figure was less than fully competitive, since the contemporary Cadillac was rated at 150 horsepower and the senior Packards at 160.

But that wasn't the half of it. As revised for the abbreviated 1942 model run, the V-12's cylinder walls were perilously thin, and the factory experienced considerable waste in the casting operations. Then, as time went on, owners found that the engine was difficult, if not impossible, to rebore. Early in the postwar era, Lincoln would revert to the earlier, 2-7/8-inch bore.

Adding to the woes of 1942 Lincoln Continental and Zephyr owners was the vacuum-operated Liquimatic transmission, a $189 option. This unit proved to be so unsatisfactory that virtually every car that had been so equipped was recalled and retrofitted with the standard gearbox and Borg-Warner overdrive.

Then there were other problems with the Zephyr-cum-Continental engine. The oiling system, for instance, was never its strong point. "The original oil pump was none too large," Paul Woudenberg has written, "and if clearances opened up anywhere, pressure fell. There were simply more places for the oil to go in a 12-cylinder engine." Crankcase ventilation was inadequate, and cars used primarily for stop-and-go urban driving tended to develop a great deal of sludge. Some owners complained of excessive oil consumption, while others experienced problems with vapor lock.

The V-12 was at its best in long-distance highway travel, where it could

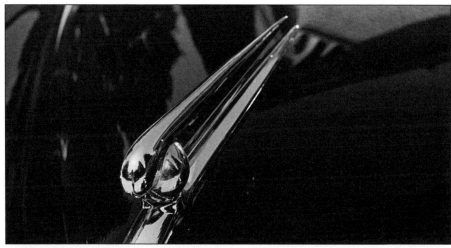

Above: Sleek-looking hood ornament was also used on Lincoln Custom models. *Below:* It's a high lift over the spare for luggage. *Bottom:* Delicate grille and bumper treatment give Continental a light and graceful appearance despite its large size.

Comparison Table: 1941 Luxury Convertibles

	Lincoln Continental	Lincoln Zephyr	Cadillac 62	Packard Deluxe 160
Price	$2,778	$1,801	$1,645	$2,067
Wheelbase	125"	125"	126"	127"
Overall length	209.8"	209.8"	216.0"	206.2"
Weight (lb.)	3,890	3,840	4,055	3,985
Engine	V-12	V-12	V-8	Straight 8
Displacement (cu.in.)	292.0	292.0	346.4	356.0
Compression ratio	7.00:1	7.00:1	7.25:1	6.45:1
Horsepower @ rpm	120 @ 3,500	120 @ 3,500	150 @ 3,400	160 @ 3,600
Valves	L-head	L-head	L-head	L-head
Final drive ratio	4.44:1	4.44:1	3.77:1	3.92:1
Steering	Worm/roller	Worm/roller	Worm/nut	Worm/roller
Ratio	18.4:1	18.4:1	23.6:1	20.2:1
Braking area (sq. in.)	168.0	168.0	208.0	196.0
Drum diameter	12"	12"	12"	12"
Tires	7.00/16	7.00/16	7.00/15	7.00/16
Indep. front suspension?	No	No	Yes	Yes
Automatic transmission?	No	No	Optional	No
Overdrive?	Optional	Optional	No	Optional
Stroke/bore ratio	1.30:1	1.30:1	1.29:1	1.32:1
Horsepower/c.i.d.	.411	.411	.433	.449
Lb./horsepower	32.4	32.0	27.0	24.9

stretch its long legs, and where crankcase dilution was minimal. To give the engine its due, given proper care and plenty of exercise, it could be a tough. dependable unit, and a remarkably economical one as well. And in its time it was arguably the smoothest powerplant on the American market.

Styling of the 1946-48 Continentals was largely carried over from the 1942 models, a heavy die-cast grille being the principal distinction. Prices were up, to $4,474 for the cabriolet, $4,392 for the coupe during 1946; and by 1948 those figures had risen to $4,662 and $4,746, respectively. Production dipped to 466 units for 1946, then rose to 1,569 and 1,289, respectively, during the 1947 and 1948 model runs.

Production of the Lincoln Continental was halted during March 1948. Sketches of a proposed 1949 model were prepared, but no such car was ever produced, even in prototype form. But the accolades continued to come, as they come to this day. In 1951 the Continental was one of eight automobiles chosen by the Museum of Modern Art, "for their excellence as works of art." Eight years later, *Time* magazine ranked it among the top ten in its list of the 100 best-designed commercial products. And among today's collectors the Lincoln

Right: Push buttons are also used for inside door actuation. Below: Zephyr V-12 was the Achilles' heel of the Continental. Many owners eventually yanked the troublesome unit out and replaced it with a more modern ohv V-8.

Continental is a prized possession.

Perhaps Walter Dorwin Teague said it best: "Edsel Ford had produced a masterpiece, not yet approached, and certain to maintain its historical position throughout the future of motor car design." 👓

Acknowledgments and Bibliography
Automotive Industries, *March 1, 1940, and October 15, 1940; Bonsall, Thomas E.,* The Lincoln Motorcar: Sixty Years of Excellence; *Kimes, Beverly Rae and Henry Austin Clark, Jr. (editors),* Standard Catalog of US Cars, 1805-1942; *Lincoln Motor Company factory literature; May, George S., "Edsel Bryant Ford,"* Encyclopedia of American Business History and Biography; Motor Age, *January 1941; Woudenberg, Paul R.,* Lincoln and Continental, the Postwar Years.

Our thanks to Ray Borges and Linda Huntsman, William F. Harrah Foundation's National Automobile Museum, Reno, Nevada; Ralph Dunwoodie, Sun Valley, California; Harry Wynn, Antioch, California. Special thanks to Heinz Schu, Los Gatos, California.

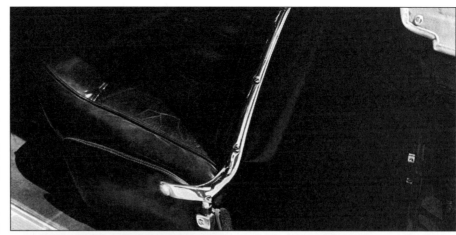

Above: *Chromed seat trim is typical of Continental's luxurious attention to details.*
Left: *All the vital info is right in front of the driver in two round instrument clusters.*
Below: *There's not an awkward line on the car, thanks to Edsel's taste and Bob Gregorie's deft touch at the drawing board.*

Cream of the Postwar Crop

1947 Cadillac 62 vs.
1948 Lincoln Continental

Originally published in Special Interest Autos #137, Sept.-Oct. 1993

by Arch Brown
photos by Bud Juneau

We saw them side by side at the Hillsborough Concours d'Elegance: the two American luxury convertibles of the immediate postwar era. The Cadillac Sixty-Two was a 1947 model, while the Lincoln Continental was a year newer. No matter; the 1947 and '48 Lincolns were virtually identical, so the match-up was valid. And as we stood there, eyeballing these two beautiful automobiles, comparisons began to take shape in our mind. Comparisons and contrasts, for it would be difficult to imagine two more diverse concepts of luxury motoring than these two cars represented.

Both, of course, featured warmed-over prewar designs. The Continental's styling dated from 1940, updated for the postwar market by means of a bold new grille. But a total of only 886 Lincoln Continental cabriolets and 1,104 coupes had been produced during the three prewar model years, 1940-42; so even without the new grille, one could hardly think of these lovely cars as having suffered from over-exposure.

Cadillac, meanwhile, had been completely restyled for the abbreviated 1942 season. The company built only 308 ragtops that year; so although the 1946-47 cars were little changed, to all intents and purposes their design was fresh and new.

Mechanical components were also carried over from prewar times. The Cadillac engine, for example, was simply a refined version of the monobloc V-8, first introduced in 1936 (see *SIA* #69). A stout, 346.4-cubic-inch L-head with a comparatively low 1.286:1 stroke/bore ratio, it had acquitted itself admirably — one could almost say heroically — during the war, when it was used to power the United States Army's M-5 and M-24 tanks (see sidebar, page 42). Horsepower was rated at 150, which was creditable enough, but the torque, at 274 foot-pounds, was even more impressive.

The Cadillac's standard transmission was a three-speed manual with a column-mounted shift control. It was an excellent gearbox, but the HydraMatic, first employed by Cadillac during 1941 and offered for 1947 as a $186 option, proved to be so popular that it was fitted to 95 percent of that year's production. Like the V-8 engine, the HydraMatic had proven itself in combat, and had undergone a number of improvements as a result of that experience.

Powering our featured Lincoln Continental — and all the 1946-48 Lincolns,

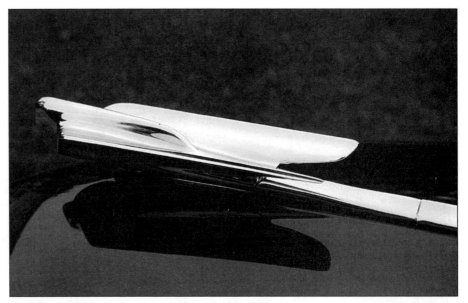

Cadillac's graceful flying lady hood ornament looks a bit old fashioned compared to Lincoln's futuristic ball.

for that matter — was the only V-12 engine still being offered by an American manufacturer. During the 1930s there had been Twelves from Cadillac, Pierce-Arrow, Auburn, Franklin and — perhaps most notably — Packard. But all of these were gone now, leaving only Lincoln's comparatively small (292.1-c.i.d., 125-horsepower) V-12, an engine dating from the 1936 Lincoln-Zephyr.

At a concours some years ago, we heard the announcer — who should have known better — describe this powerplant as having been inherited from the great K-Series Lincolns of the 1930s. Far from it! The Zephyr-cum-Lincoln was basically a 12-cylinder version of the flathead Ford V-8. And it was not, to put it delicately, a distinguished piece of machinery. It shared the V-8's tendency to vapor lock under certain conditions, and, as Lincoln authority Paul Woudenberg has noted, the oiling system was never its strong point. An improved oil pump, fitted to the postwar models, was a step in the right direction, but to some extent the difficulties persisted.

Furthermore, its power was no better

than marginal, especially when the postwar models proved to be nearly 300 pounds heavier than the 1940 original. Commencing on January 6, 1942, the V-12 had been bored an extra sixteenth of an inch, increasing its displacement to 305 cubic inches and raising its horsepower from 120 to 130. Unfortunately, as owners were quick to discover, this left the cylinder walls perilously thin. In the interest of dependability, therefore, early in 1946 the engine was returned to its original dimensions. The compression ratio was increased from 7.00:1 to 7.20:1, which brought the horsepower to 125 for the postwar engine.

Unlike Cadillac, Lincoln did not offer an automatic transmission. Not until the arrival of the 1949 models would that convenience become available to Lincoln buyers, and even then — doubtless to the embarrassment of the company's engineering staff — it was the familiar HydraMatic, purchased from General Motors. What Lincoln *did* offer, while Cadillac did not, was the Borg-Warner overdrive. Coupled to the standard three-speed gearbox, it permitted a

Cadillac's "sombrero" wheel covers carry traditional coat of arms while Lincoln is identified with elegant script.

SIA comparisonReport

30 percent reduction in engine revolutions, which of course led to quieter operation, increased fuel economy and longer engine life.

Suspension was another point of contrast between Cadillac and Lincoln. While the Cad employed longitudinal semi-elliptic springs at the rear and independent A-arms with coil springs at the front, Lincoln clung to its rigid axles and transverse leaf springs all around — essentially the same suspension system that Henry Ford had employed for his legendary Model T back in 1908.

Even the styling reflected two distinct themes. The Continental, which had originated as a one-off intended for the personal use of Edsel Ford, featured crisp, clean lines and a minimum of brightwork. Edsel himself had come up with the concept, instructing stylist Eugene T. "Bob" Gregorie to give the car a "continental" flavor — right down to the exposed spare tire. In so doing, as Dammann and Wagner have noted, he "unknowingly built his own memorial."

Taking the Lincoln Zephyr as his base, Gregorie shaved three inches off its overall height, added three inches to the length of the hood and brought up the rear with a squared-off trunk. The result was absolutely stunning. Gordon Buehrig once commented to this writer that "good design is largely a matter of proportion," and in the case of the Lincoln Continental, the proportions were exquisite. The result, in the words of automotive journalist Dick Langworth, was "one of the most stunning automotive designs of the decade, and perhaps of all time." Even the renowned architect, Frank Lloyd Wright, who owned one, called the original Lincoln Zephyr Continental (as it was called at first) "the most beautiful car ever designed."

There have been complaints that the heavy grille fitted to the postwar Continentals spoiled the purity of the original design. While there may be some validity to that view, the later models were still among the most beautiful, and certainly the most distinctive cars on the road. And they rank among the very last cars to be recognized by the Classic Car Club of America.

Cadillac, on the other hand, was caught up in the "bigger is better" craze. Three inches longer in wheelbase than its predecessor and 360 pounds heavier, the 1942 Series 62 was a big automobile by just about anyone's definition. Lines were softly rounded; fenders were elliptical in shape, extending halfway across the front doors. And for the first time, the convertible came equipped with quarter-windows, a welcome convenience as well as an important safety measure.

Only minimal changes were made in the appearance of the postwar Cadillacs. For 1947 a stamped grille replaced the previous die-cast type. "Sombrero" wheel covers, taking their name from a popular broad-brimmed Mexican hat, were a popular option at $25.08 a set. And bright metal stone shields replaced the earlier black rubber type.

Four series were offered, down from six in 1941-42. As before, the price leader was the Series Sixty-One, which came as either a four-door sedan or a two-door sedanet, both fastbacks with body shells held over from 1941. Built on a 126-inch wheelbase, these were the bargain-basement Cadillacs, with prices starting at $2,200 — a premium of less than $100 over the cost of a Buick Roadmaster.

Next up was the Series Sixty-Two, riding on a 129-inch wheelbase and featuring the styling that had been new (and highly acclaimed) for 1942. In addition to the two- and four-door sedans, the Sixty-Two Series included Cadillac's only convertible. With prices just an easy step above those of the Sixty-One, this series was, by a wide margin, Cadillac's best seller.

Then there was the Fleetwood Sixty Special. Gone were the classic lines of Bill Mitchell's 1938-41 models. Basically, this car, which was built only as a four-door sedan, was a stretched and sumptuously trimmed version of the Sixty-Two. Built on an exclusive 133-inch wheelbase, it was surprisingly popular, despite a price tag that was nearly $700 higher than the Sixty-Two.

And finally, at the top of the line was

the Fleetwood Seventy-Five, which came in five sedan configurations, all on a wheelbase of 136 inches and ranging in price from $4,368 to $4,887.

Lincoln's inventory was much more limited. The basic line was essentially a continuation of the prewar Lincoln-Zephyr line, though the Zephyr name had been dropped by war's end. Available in sedan, club coupe, or cabriolet form, it was priced to compete, in most body styles, with the Cadillac Sixty-Two. The cabriolet, however, was $240 higher than the Cadillac ragtop, which put the Lincoln, nee Zephyr, in pretty heady company.

But the Lincoln that turned a lot of heads and generated a great deal of publicity was the Continental. It came in two forms, club coupe and cabriolet, both sharing the 125-inch wheelbase of the "regular" Lincolns. A great deal of hand work went into the manufacture of these lovely cars, and as a result, they were very expensive. During 1947 and '48 the coupe sold for $4,662, the cabriolet for $4,746. To put those numbers in perspective, look at it this way: For the price he paid for our featured Lincoln Continental cabriolet, its original owner could have purchased a standard Lincoln ragtop, plus a Chevrolet Fleetmaster sport coupe, with a couple of hundred dollars left over.

Despite the efforts of the Office of Price Administration (OPA), inflation ran rampant during the war years and for some time thereafter. Our featured 1947 Cadillac convertible, for instance, cost 76.4 percent more than its 1941 counterpart. By 1948, the price would be more than double the prewar figure. The tab for our Lincoln Continental, meanwhile, was hiked by 70.8 percent between 1941 and 1947-48.

After nearly four years during which no new cars had been built for the civilian market, demand was at an all-time high. So despite the fact that most people considered the OPA "ceiling" prices to be outrageous, there was a flourishing "gray" market for new automobiles. Most in demand were the luxury models, since the well-to-do were obviously in a better position than most people when it came to paying a premium price for a new set of wheels. Paul Woudenberg has noted, for example, that in 1947 a Cadillac convertible could command nearly twice its government-established ceiling price of $2,902. Not until 1949 would the automobile market return to anything resembling a "normal" condition.

Driving Impressions

Our featured Cadillac has been a California car from the beginning, having been sold originally (in June 1947) by the Don Lee dealership in San Francisco. The first owner was a woman of

Above and below: *Restrained use of chrome trim characterizes Cadillac rear styling. Continental spare gives Lincoln instant identity.* **Bottom:** *Cadillac's gas cap is cleverly hidden. Lincoln opts for fender flap.*

some means, who kept the car garaged and gave it meticulous care. Upon the lady's death, the Cadillac passed to her son, and it was from him that it was purchased, in 1967, by Ed Gunther, of San Jose. By that time the convertible had logged some 80,000 miles.

Gunther confesses to a special affinity for 1946 and '47 Cadillacs, which he had admired so much as a youth. Over the years, he has owned something like 20 of them. This may suggest that Ed Gunther is something of a horse trader, but he regards this particular Cadillac as a "keeper." (Incidentally, his inventory of Cadillacs presently includes a 1941 Series 62 coupe, a 1949 convertible and a 1937 LaSalle ragtop — all of them sold

originally by the Don Lee agency.)

Gunther purchased a military surplus Cadillac engine for his convertible. But then, in order to preserve the numbers, he retained the original block, fitting it with the internal parts of the new engine. Fortunately, maximum taper was no more than three thousandths of an inch, so a rebore was not required. He also put new bands in the HydraMatic transmission, rebuilt the brakes and installed new tie-rod ends. Otherwise, the chassis was in excellent shape.

Gunther did his own mechanical work, but the cosmetics were farmed out to specialists. New paint was applied in the original Beldon Blue color. Brightwork was rechromed, and the interior

Cadillac heels over in a controllable fashion in cornering; Lincoln's primitive transverse leaf suspension does a very creditable job of roadholding.

1947 Cadillac Prices, Weights and Production

	Price	Weight	Production
Series 61 (126-inch wheelbase)			
#6107 Club Coupe	$2,200	4,080	3,395
#6109 Sedan, 4-door	$2,364	4,165	5,160
Total production, Series 61			8,555
Series 62 (129-inch wheelbase)			
#6207 Club Coupe	$2,446	4,145	7,245
#6267 Convertible Coupe	$2,902	4,455	6,755
#6269 Sedan, 4-door	$2,523	4,235	25,834
#62 Chassis	N/A	N/A	1
Total Production, Series 62			39,835
Series 60-Special (133-inch wheelbase)			
#6069 Sedan, 4-door	$3,195	4,370	8,500
Series 75 (136-inch wheelbase)			
#7519 Sedan, 5-passenger	$4,471	4,875	300
#2523 Sedan, 7-passenger	$4,686	4,895	890
#7523L Business Sedan, 9-pass.	$4,368	4,790	135
#7533 Imperial Sedan, 7-pass.	$4,887	4,930	1,005
#7533L Business Imperial, 7-pass.	$4,560	4,800	80
#75 Chassis	N/A	N/A	3
Series 75 (163-inch wheelbase)			
#75 Commercial Chassis	N/A	N/A	2,423
#75 Business Chassis	N/A	N/A	200
Total Production, Series 75 (both chassis lengths)			5,036
Total Cadillac Production, 1947 model year:			61,926
Total Cadillac Production, 1947 calendar year:			59,436

SIA comparisonReport

was completely reupholstered. We were surprised, initially, to find that although the seats are done in leather, door panels are upholstered in whipcord. But upon reflection, the combination makes a lot of sense. For one thing, it's attractive. But more important, fine leather was in short supply in 1947. The fabric-covered door panels were born of necessity.

We've been unable to trace very much of the history of our featured Lincoln Continental. Evidently it had been a Southern California car, though it was in San Jose when it was purchased by Al Weiry, of Niles, California.

Weiry, who owned several cars, never got around to restoring the Continental, which was in pieces when he acquired it. Eventually, some 15 years ago, he sold it to its present owner, J.W. Silveira, of Oakland. Fortunately, it was essentially complete, but it came with a 283-c.i.d. Chevrolet V-8 in lieu of the Lincoln V-12. A sacrilege to the purist, of course, but for driving purposes the Chevy engine would actually have been a good deal more competent than the original mill. A comparison of the specifications tells the story:

	C.I.D.	HP	Torque
Lincoln V-12	292.1	124/3,600	214/1,600
Chev. 283 V-8	283.0	170/4,200	275/2,200

Still, to use the Chevrolet V-8 in a restored Continental was out of the question. Eventually, Silveira found a proper V-12 engine, and turned the car over to Rod Marconi, of R & M Classics, for a high-point restoration, including a superb new finish in a shade of blue

Specifications: '47 Cadillac 62 vs. '48 Lincoln Continental

	1947 Cadillac 62	1948 Lincoln Continental
Base price	$2,902	$4,746
Standard equipment	Hydro-lectric windows, power top, clock	Power top, power windows
Options on feature cars	HydraMatic transmission, radio/power antenna, heater, "sombrero" wheel covers, w.s.w. tires	Overdrive, radio, heater, w.s.w. tires
Engine	90-degree V-8	75-degree V-12
Bore x stroke	3.5 x 4.5 inches	2.875 x 3.75 inches
Displacement	346.4 cubic inches	292.1 cubic inches
Compression ratio	7.25:1	7.20:1
Horsepower @ rpm	150 @ 3,600	125 @ 3,600
Torque @ rpm	274 @ 1,600	214 @ 1,600
Taxable horsepower	39.2	39.6
Main bearings	3	5
Valve configuration	L-head	L-head
Valve lifters	Hydraulic	Hydraulic
Lubrication system	Pressure	Pressure
Carburetor	1.25-inch dual downdraft	1-inch dual downdraft
Fuel feed	Camshaft pump	Camshaft pump
Cooling system	Centrifugal pump	Centrifugal pump
Electrical system	6-volt battery/coil	6-volt battery/coil
Exhaust system	Single	Single
Clutch	None	Single dry plate
Diameter		10 inches
Actuation		Mechanical, foot pedal
Transmission	HydraMatic 4-speed automatic planetary	3-speed selective, synchronized 2nd and 3rd; overdrive
Ratios: 1st/2nd/3rd/4th/Reverse	3.82/2.63/1.45/1.00/4.31	2.12/1.43/1.00/0.70 (OD)/2.72
Differential	Hypoid	Spiral bevel
Ratio	3.77:1	4.44:1 (3.11 w/overdrive)
Drive axles	Semi-floating	Semi-floating
Torque medium	Springs	Torque tube
Steering	Recirculating ball	Worm and roller
Ratio	23.5:1	18.4:1
Turning diameter	40.2 feet	45 feet
Turns, lock-to-lock	3.94	4.75
Brakes	Drum type	Drum type
Drum diameter	12 inches	12 inches
Effective area	208 square inches	184 square inches
Chassis and body	Body-on-frame	Integral body/frame
Frame	Rigid X-type	N/A
Body construction	All steel	All steel
Body type	Convertible coupe	Convertible cabriolet
Front suspension	Independent, coil springs, torsional stabilizer	Rigid axle, transverse leaf spring, torsional stabilizer
Rear suspension	Rigid axle, semi-elliptic springs, cross-link stabilizer	Rigid axle, transverse leaf spring
Shock absorbers	Delco double-acting	Monroe direct-acting
Wheels	Pressed steel, drop-center rims	Pressed steel, drop-center rims
Tires	7.00/15 4-ply	7.00/15 4-ply
Wheelbase	129 inches	125 inches
Overall length	219.19 inches	218.1 inches
Overall width	80.75 inches	77.8 inches
Overall height	63.0625 inches	62 inches
Front track	59 inches	59 inches
Rear track	63 inches	60.69 inches
Minimum road clearance	7.66 inches	7.5 inches
Shipping weight	4,455 pounds	4,135 pounds
Crankcase capacity	7 quarts	5 quarts
Cooling system capacity	25 quarts	19.5 quarts
Fuel tank	20 gallons	27 gallons
Transmission	13.5 quarts (dry)	3.75 pounds (inc. o/d)
Differential	5 lb.	4 lb.
Horsepower/c.i.d.	.433	.428
Lb./horsepower	29.7	33.1
Lb./c.i.d.	12.9	14.2
Lb./sq. in. brake area	21.4	22.5
Stroke/bore ratio	1.286:1	1.304:1

Caddy uses old style twist and pull door handles. Lincoln offers ultra modern push-button access.

that, by coincidence, almost exactly matches that of Ed Gunther's Cadillac. The engine was done by Bill Schmidt, top and interior by Cook's Upholstery of Redwood City, and by the end of 1990 the job was complete.

The Silveiras — J.W. and his charming wife Barbara — have put very little mileage on the Continental. They've shown it a number of times, however, and have collected a few trophies including First Place at Silverado 1991, and another "First" at a Classic Car Club meet in San Francisco.

Unlike the Silveiras, Ed Gunther uses his Cadillac as a driver. The odometer now shows 44,900 miles, the second time around, with about 45,000 of that figure having been run up during the

*Dashboards are similar in layout with Cadillac, **top**, using round gauges throughout while Lincoln uses combo of round and rectangular.*

The Luxury Car Goes To War

For the builders of American luxury cars to have played an important role in the manufacture of military hardware during World War II was nothing new. The Lincoln Motor Car Company, in fact, had been founded in 1917 by former Cadillac general manager Henry M. Leland, for the express purpose of building Liberty aircraft engines for the United States government.

Cadillac eventually followed suit, with production of the Liberty engine getting under way by May 1918. But as early as 1915 Cadillac had built America's first fully armored car. And when the United States became a full participant in the conflict, Cadillac touring cars were designated as the official staff vehicles, with literally thousands of them shipped to France for that purpose. General John J. "Black Jack" Pershing, Commander of the American Expeditionary Force, was driven in a Cadillac limousine. Colonel Edward J. Hall, co-designer of the Liberty engine, would later comment, "I believe these cars from my observation gave better service than any other make of car in France.... I never saw a Cadillac tied up for trouble of any kind." Upon his return to the United States following the Armistice, Colonel Hall backed up his words by purchasing a Cadillac for his own use.

By the time war broke out again, in 1939, Lincoln had long since become a part of Henry Ford's industrial empire, and the Cadillac Division of General Motors had become an infinitely stronger organization than it had been a generation earlier. Both companies turned their energies to the war effort.

Fifty-five days after the last 1942 Cadillac rolled off the assembly line, production commenced on the M-5 light tank, powered by two Cadillac V-8 engines, each linked to a HydraMatic transmission. According to John F. "Jack" Gordon, Cadillac's chief engineer from 1943 to 1946 and later president of the division, the twin engine/HydraMatic arrangement was eventually extended to 11 distinct types of military vehicles, manufactured in Canada, Britain and Australia, as well as the United States. Applications included three types of Howitzer motor carriages, M19 gun motor carriages, Australian cruiser tanks, amphibians and — most notably — the M-24 light tank, a larger, faster, more sophisticated battle tank that replaced the M-5 during 1944.

Lincoln, too, played an important role in the war effort, building, among other items, bodies for all the amphibious jeeps and some 145,000 standardized jeeps. But the division's really unique contribution — one that seems to have been accorded little recognition — was the manufacture of engines for the big Sherman tanks and M-10 tank destroyers. These were huge, 1,100-c.i.d. V-8s, fitted with four valves per cylinder and rated at 500 horsepower.

SIA comparisonReport

past three and a half years. Trips, mostly in company with Classic Car Club Caravans, have taken Ed and his car to places as far distant as Nova Scotia, Banff, British Columbia, Florida, and twice to New York. Performance, Gunther reports, has been flawless.

We've done a number of these comparisonReports for *Special Interest Autos*, but we don't recall another in which the cars contrasted quite so sharply in terms of performance and handling.

We drove the Cadillac first. Seating is very comfortable. Seats are wide, and they offer good support to the back. There's even adequate knee room in the rear, though we'd have to say that trunk space, thanks to an intrusive spare tire, is limited.

Acceleration is brisk, and the ride is marvelously smooth, as one might expect of a Cadillac. The HydraMatic transmission shifts crisply, changing gears with less of a surging sensation than we've experienced in some HydraMatic-equipped cars.

The Cad heels over somewhat in hard cornering, but it's not excessive, and control is easy enough to maintain. We were surprised, however, to note how heavy the steering feels. Not that we didn't expect to exert some muscle; after all, this automobile has a road weight of about two and a half tons, and there is no power assist. But we road-tested a similar car several years ago for a driveReport (see *SIA* #91), and at that time, according to our notes, we found the steering lighter than we had expected. (Disturbing question: Does Ed Gunther's car really steer heavier than that other one, or is it that we're seven years older now?)

In all honesty, we must admit that we put this car through a particularly demanding trial, turning it around on a narrow lane in the cemetery that served as Bud Juneau's photo location. But yes, in this sort of maneuver the steering was very heavy indeed.

Not surprisingly, the Cadillac is at its best on the open road. It cruises quietly and smoothly at 70 miles an hour, with enough reserve for passing should the need arise. It's no econobox, of course, but 15 miles to the gallon isn't too bad. And the brakes are excellent. There's no power assist, yet we didn't find the pedal pressure to be excessive.

On, then, to the Lincoln Continental. Once again the front seat is roomy and comfortable, but this time the trunk is deep and roomy while rear seat knee room is seriously cramped. We'd hate to have to ride back there on a trip of more

1948 Lincoln Prices and Production

	Price	Weight	Production
Lincoln Series			
Sedan, 4-door	$2,554	4,015	See note
Club Coupe	$4,533	3,915	See note
Cabriolet	$3,142	4,245	See note
Continental Series			
Club Coupe	$4,662	4,125	847
Cabriolet	$4,746	4,135	452
Total, Continental Series			1,299

Note: Model year production for the Lincoln series was 6,470. No breakdown by body style is available.

Top left: Both instrument clusters require driver to glance down and take his eyes off the road ahead. **Above and below:** Caddy's strong, quiet V-8 was nearing the end of production in 1947. For Lincoln, '48 marked the final year for the Zephyr V-12.

than a few minutes' duration.

Given the Lincoln's comparatively primitive suspension system, we were agreeably surprised at how well it rides. There's a slight degree of choppiness, to be sure; this car is clearly no match for the Cadillac in that respect. But it's smoother than we expected.

The Continental carries 11.5 percent more weight per horsepower than the Cadillac, and of course the difference shows up in its acceleration, which seemed to us to be no better than adequate. An even more striking difference is found in the torque output of the two engines, with the Cadillac enjoying a 28 percent advantage. We were unable to take the two cars through the Oakland hills, but it is safe to assume that the Cadillac would hold an enormous advantage there.

Similarly, the nod goes to the Cadillac for braking power. The Lincoln's binders take more pressure than those of the Cad, and although we make no pretense of having made a precise test of their effectiveness, it seemed to us that they displayed significantly less stopping power.

On the other hand, the Lincoln Continental's steering is somewhat lighter than that of the Cadillac. We duplicated as carefully as we could, the test to which the Cad had been put, and in this particular respect the Lincoln was the clear winner.

The Continental's three-speed transmission shifts easily, although the action of the column shift couldn't be called precise. And in contrast to many Ford Motor Company products of its era, we found virtually no chatter in this car's clutch.

Like the Cadillac, the Continental is at its best on the open road, where it can stretch its long legs. With the overdrive engaged, its overall gear ratio is 3.11:1, enabling the engine almost literally to loaf at highway speeds.

So, how to choose between the Cadillac Sixty-Two and the Lincoln Continental? How does one choose between chocolate cake and apple pie? The two are radically different from one another, and we like them both.

Almost anyone would agree, we think, that the Continental's greatest strength lies in its styling. This automobile is so beautiful that it almost wouldn't matter if it didn't run at all. Beyond that, we like the overdrive, and we're impressed by the Lincoln's comparatively light steering. Admittedly, there's a penalty here: A U-turn takes nearly five feet more than the Cadillac requires, and more wheel-winding is required, as well.

A further advantage to the Continental

*Above left and right: Lincoln also uses push-buttons inside; Cadillac offers traditional door handles. **Below and bottom:** Cadillac's spare chews up lots of trunk space compared to Lincoln's cubic feet out back.*

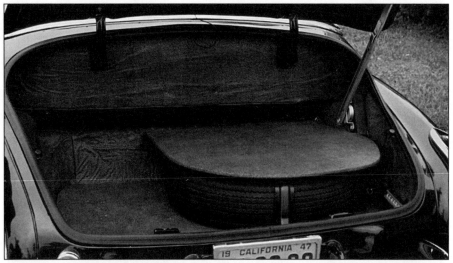

has to do with fuel mileage. With the help of the overdrive, it was not unusual for the flathead V-12 to deliver 18 or even 20 miles on a gallon of gasoline.

But in terms of performance, it's Cadillac's game, nearly all the way. The Cad is faster, more powerful, and — as experience has proven — more durable than the Lincoln of this vintage. It is more comfortable to ride in; it has better seating, at least in the rear, and its brakes are definitely superior. And with an $1,844 price advantage, it was, in its own time, obviously the better buy of the two.

In our view, it's not a choice that any person could legitimately make on behalf of someone else, for we all have our own priorities. The buyer to whom beauty was the first concern would have no difficulty justifying the premium price of the Lincoln Continental. But the driver whose priorities had to do chiefly with comfort and performance was well advised to select the Cadillac convertible — as 6,755 of them did, during the 1947 model year.

❑

Acknowledgments and Bibliography
Automotive Industries, *March 15, 1947, and March 15, 1948; Bonsall, Thomas E.*, The Lincoln Motorcar; *Clymer, Floyd,* The Lincoln Continental; *Dammann, George H. and James K. Wagner,* The Cars of Lincoln-Mercury; *Hendry, Maurice D.,* Cadillac: The Complete History; *Juneau, Bud (ed.),* The Cadillac-LaSalle Self-Starter, *Vol. XVIII; Langworth, Richard M.,* Encyclopedia of American Cars, 1940-1970; *McCall, Walter M.P.,* 80 Years of Cadillac-LaSalle; *Schneider, Roy A.,* Cadillacs of the Forties; *Woudenberg, Paul R.,* Lincoln & Continental, The Postwar Years.
Our thanks to Mountain View Cemetery, Oakland, California; Bob Rushing, Niles, California; Al Weiry, Niles, California. Special thanks to Ed Gunther, San Jose, California; J.W. and Barbara Silveira, Oakland, California.

Lincoln Continental, 1940-48
Prices and Production

	Cabriolet		Club Coupe		
	Price	Production	Price	Production	Total
1940	$2,840	350	N/A	54	404
1941	$2,778	400	$2,727	850	1,250
1942	$3,174	136	$3,174	200	336
1946	$4,474	201	$4,392	265	466
1947	$4,746	738	$4,662	831	1,569
1948	$4,746	452	$4,662	847	1,299
TOTAL PRODUCTION, 1940-48					5,324

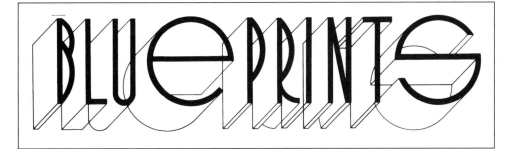

1937 Lincoln Zephyr
By Bob Hovorka

Although it was built in the shadow of Henry Ford, it was touched by Edsel's unmistakable hand. Based on the aircraft construction techniques espoused by John Tjaarda, the Lincoln Zephyr offered "a new, rigid, steel one-piece body and frame...with the advanced features that set new standards of comfort, safety, roadability." And while its gracefully streamlined prow pointed towards an aerodynamic future, its transverse springs and mechanically operated brakes clung to a horse and buggy past.

Even its much touted 12-cylinder engine owed more to Mr. Ford's flathead V-8 than any previous Lincoln casting. Maybe this is what prompted Lincoln to advertise: "Remember that the Lincoln-Zephyr has been designed by Lincoln, is built by Lincoln."

However, the engine needed more than words to overcome its quickly tarnished reputation. Youngsters often quipped that a lingering puff of smoke at a stoplight meant a Zephyr had just left. Yet, for all the bad-mouthing, the undeniably smooth 12-cylinder served

Lincoln for over a decade. Treated respectfully, it could cruise with the best of them while furnishing a smoothness many would envy today.

But it wasn't the engine that set Zephyr apart from the crowd, it was the styling. Originally offered only as torpedo-shaped two- or four-door sedans, a slinky three-passenger coupe was added for 1937. "The beauty of the Lincoln Zephyr is the beauty of swift-flowing streamlines." And *stream lines* they were!

Individual front fenders arched inward towards a narrow V-lined grille; teardrop-shaped headlamps swelled from their uppermost sections. Vestigial running boards not only mimicked the flowing body contours, they curved upwards to meet the lower door edges. Out back, drive wheels were half hidden by covers that echoed the elongated sweep of the tapering rear fenders. From the front of its sharply pointed grille to the tip of its projectile taillamps, it was stunning!

Of course, interiors were styled to match. Seats were edged with simple tubular chrome frames, while a centrally located tower held speedometer and other gauges. Tapering down from the edge of the dashboard, the tower visually split the front compartment between driver and passenger. A leather flying helmet and scarf would have completed the unmistakable aircraft cockpit feeling. Sales for 1937 nearly doubled. It was Zephyr's best year.

Long looked upon as a second class cousin to the original Continental, the Zephyr deserved better. In fact, if it had done nothing more than sire the Continental, it would have reached heights many manufacturers merely dream of. With Lincoln sales falling, it was probably Zephyr alone that kept Lincoln from joining the ranks of Auburn and Cord. Without Edsel, it may never have happened. Maybe his name should be more closely linked with his success in saving Lincoln than with the misfortunes of his shortlived namesake. ✍

1950 LINCOLN

MORE THAN A MERCURY?

By Tim Howley
Photos by the author

FROM 1949 through 1951 Lincoln offered two distinct lines of cars, the Lincoln on a 121-inch wheelbase and the Lincoln Cosmopolitan on a 125-inch wheelbase. Both shared a new 336.7-c.i.d., 90-degree L-head V-8, the largest Ford-built flathead V-8 since the Lincoln 385 was retired in 1932. The Lincoln Cosmopolitan had a completely separate body. The Lincoln carried the Mercury body with the Cosmopolitan front end modified slightly.

These two lines of Lincolns came about in a rather oblique way, as discussed in *SIA* #12. Up until early 1947 there were to be four distinct lines of Ford postwar cars: a compact Ford, a full-sized Ford, a Mercury on two different wheelbases, and a Lincoln on three different wheelbases. In mid-1946, when the Ford Division decided to build an entirely new 1949 Ford, it dropped plans to build a compact, and there was considerable reshuffling. The 188-inch-wheelbase Ford became the 1949 Mercury. The two Mercurys on 120-inch

and 123-inch wheelbases became one Lincoln on a 121-inch wheelbase. The Lincoln on a 125-inch wheelbase became the Lincoln Cosmopolitan, and plans for larger Lincolns and a Lincoln Continental were dropped. The two distinct lines of Lincolns were dropped in 1952 when the marque went to a single car on a 123-inch wheelbase. This was simply a bad marketing decision, as Ford very much needed a car mid-way between the Mercury and Lincoln Cosmopolitan in order to compete with GM at the high end. The need for such a car was recognized in 1952 with the recommendation of a new make to be called Monterey and the re-introduction of the Lincoln Continental. Unfortunately, Ford's upper management was mired down in a complex set of political circumstances at the time, which eventually led to the Edsel, priced between the

Ford and the Mercury. Had Ford continued to build two Lincolns in the fifties rather than experiment with new names and sub-names, the Lincoln-Mercury Division might have been a formidable competitor. As things turned out, the Mercury-bodied Lincoln was discontinued after 1951, and the car is now nearly forgotten.

In this driveReport we will discuss only the Lincoln, not the Lincoln Cosmopolitan. (See *SIA* #16.) Lincolns for 1949 were offered in three body styles: a coupe, a sport sedan and a convertible coupe. The cars are instantly recognized from the front end by their deeply sunken headlamps. It was designer Bob Gregorie's original intent to have hideaway headlamps, á la 1942 De Soto, but cost and time constraints put the eyelids on the shelf after the tooling was already made, and deep chromed bezels were substituted. The sides of the front fenders carried a clean sweep of stainless steel as opposed to the Cosmopolitan's bulbous stainless

Originally published in Special Interest Autos #130, Jul.-Aug. 1992

Driving Impressions

Our driveReport car is a 1950 Lincoln sport sedan owned by collector Don Williams of San Diego. This is an all-original, 70,000 mile car which was owned for 33 years since new by a woman in Red Bluff, California. It was garaged all of its life and sold only when she went into a nursing home in 1983. Since it was delivered September 23, 1950, it had the more desirable late 1950-51 engine. It might well be the best remaining *original* example of a 1950 Lincoln extant. It has HydraMatic rather than standard transmission and overdrive like the Mobilgas Economy Run winner. Since 1983 it has passed through the hands of several collectors who have all maintained the original integrity of the car. The present owner has done a motor vehicles search on the car and finds that only 26 1950 Lincoln sport sedans are currently registered in United States. The current Lincoln and Continental Owner's Club Directory lists seventeen 1949 Lincolns, four 1950 Lincolns and fourteen 1951 Lincolns. These figures do not include Lincoln Cosmopolitans, which appear to have a somewhat higher survival rate.

Needless to say, 1949-51 Lincolns have an extremely low survival rate, perhaps the lowest of any mass-produced car of the era. The only explanation we can offer is that there has always been a very low awareness of these cars, even compared to the Lincoln Cosmopolitans.

Our driveReport car was photographed and tested on San Diego's Fiesta Island, where it drew a lot of attention. Everybody who came over to look at the car thought it was a Mercury and was surprised to learn that Lincoln ever built such a car. Our own impression of the car was that it seemed like a Mercury with a Lincoln engine; the same concept as the Olds 88, only flathead instead of overhead. The car beautifully combines all of the best features of both Lincoln and Mercury and actually tests out better than either of them. It is more powerful than a 1950 Mercury, handles much better than a 1950 Lincoln Cosmopoli-

tan, and in our opinion has the best overall styling of any Ford product that year.

In *SIA* #124, July-August 1991, we compared a 1950 Mercury club coupe and a 1950 Olds 88 two-door sedan. According to *Motor Trend* tests of 1950, performance figures for the 1950 Mercury and Lincoln, both with standard transmission and overdrive, are nearly identical, although the Lincoln has a top speed of 97.08 mph compared to the Mercury's 83.75. This is with a 152-horsepower flathead V-8 pulling 3,470 pounds of automobile, compared to a 255.4-c.i.d., 110-horsepower, flathead V-8 pulling 3,470 pounds. The HydraMatic does not pull down the Lincoln's performance figures significantly, especially at the high end.

When we tested the Mercury we were impressed with the handling in the turns. This is one area where the Lincoln falls down, but not a lot. "The road wants to turn, the Lincoln wants to go straight," notes owner Don Williams. However, the car's tendency to plow into the turns is not particularly annoying and is probably somewhat less than that of GM makes of the era. The steering is remarkably light, even when parking, which amazed us, for a car lacking power steering. The steering is also quite slow, 5.5 turns lock-to-lock, even slower than the Mercury. The faster you drive the Lincoln, the better it handles, and its handling at highway speeds is extremely pleasing. There is very little wind or road noise transmitted to the interior. The car just moves along steadily and confidently, and you can hardly hear the engine. The ventilation system is a breath of fresh air, as pointed out enthusiastically by Williams. It's the best ventilation system we have ever experienced on a car of this era. We tried the car out in San Diego in January, hardly the place to test the heater, but we strongly suspect that it keeps all the occupants toasty warm, even in upper Michigan and Minnesota.

We liked this HydraMatic a lot better than the one on the Olds 88 we tested in

1991. It was smoother at all speeds. While there are only two speeds indicated on the column, Lo and Drive, there are four forward driving ranges, and at any speed over 20 there is a kickdown that instantly puts the transmission in second. But in order to put the transmission in reverse, you have to go through Lo, which is a time-consuming annoyance.

The Lincoln is an ideal size, big enough to carry five passengers in comfort yet small enough to retain agility. What we liked best about the car was the total pleasure of driving it, thanks to its combination of size/weight, fine construction, suspension design and power train. What we liked least was the difficulty in entering the rear seat and limited rear seat leg and knee room. The rather small "suicide" rear doors only swing out about two-thirds of the way, and any six-footer sitting in the back seat will find his knees in his lap. Parking was difficult, not because of the lack of power steering, but because you cannot see the trunk or rear fenders. The rear window is much too small and high. It was made slightly larger in 1951, but not until 1952 was it easy to see out the rear.

We've driven a lot of cars of this era, in their day and in recent years. Like most everybody else, we've completely overlooked 1949-51 Lincolns. They are just filled with quality features and pleasurable driving design that should give them a lot of appeal. Plus they are truly unique cars guaranteed to turn a lot of heads at shows. Unless you must have neck-snapping performance, this is just about the nicest 1950 collector car you are going to find to own and drive. It offers a world of improvement over the old Lincoln V-12 and compares very favorably with Oldsmobiles, Buicks and Cadillacs of the same year, despite their more advanced engines. Truly, this car is the ultimate flathead Ford V-8, which won over millions of motorists during the thirties, forties and early fifties, and still has extremely wide collector appeal. Despite all this, prices remain a bargain.

1950 LINCOLN

Above: '50 Lincoln's grille design, left, is squarer and less fussy than 1949's offering. **Below:** *Door handles were shared with Mercury.* **Bottom:** *With no real hardtop designs to offer in 1950, Lincoln countered with gussied-up Capri and Lido sport coupes.*

airfoil. From the rear the car looks very much like a Mercury with a three-piece rear window, but with Lincoln's own gunsight tail-lamp treatment. Inside, the '49 Lincoln carried a bizarre instrument panel with "church organ" controls. The upholstery was a cut above the Mercury's, a cut below the Lincoln Cosmopolitan's.

The 336.7-c.i.d., 900-pound flathead V-8 developing 152 horsepower @ 3,600 rpm was a vast improvement over the old V-12. It had a 3.5-inch bore, 4.35-inch stroke, 7:1 compression ratio and maximum torque of 265 ft/lb. @ 2,000 rpm. But in contrast to the new Cadillac ohv V-8, soon to appear, weighing some 200 pounds less, it was antediluvian. Originally this engine was developed for Ford trucks, and was introduced in January 1948 in the Ford F-7 and F-8 lines. As late as 1946 the 1949 Lincoln was slated to carry an improved V-12. However, total reorganization of the company and the '49 Ford project preempted further development of the V-12 and management opted to modify the truck V-8 slightly for the new Lincoln.

Instead of a cast crankshaft like the Ford and Mercury V-8s, it had a drop forged crankshaft and zero lash hydraulic valve lifters. The former single downdraft carburetor was exchanged for a large dual-concentric downdraft carburetor with an air-cooled fuel chamber. There was now a separate exhaust system for each bank of cylinders located outside of the engine V to permit better exhaust cooling, and a more orthodox arrangement of accessories on top of the engine compared to the V-12, especially the distributor and fuel pump. Further cooling improvement was afforded through a completely redesigned cooling system and a new low-profile radiator. About the only thing that wasn't improved was vibration damping. On early 1949 models engineers employed a viscous-type fluid in the damper. This did not work out at all.

The transmission was a conventional three-speed gearbox with or without Borg-Warner overdrive, coupled to Hotchkiss drive and hypoid gears. Lincoln-Mercury engineers had been working overtime on an automatic transmission, but it never proved very reliable so it was not offered. Finally, from mid-1949 on Lincoln offered an optional GM HydraMatic gearbox.

The frame was Ford's new K type with front coil springs in wishbone pressed steel arms and parallel leaf springs in the rear. There was nothing new about

Continued on page 57

Color Gallery

Photograph by David Gooley

Photograph by Vince Wright

1928 L-Locke Dual-Cowl Phaeton
Wearing a similar body to the previous year's Lincoln, with only minor bolt-on revisions, the Lincoln for 1928 was undoubtedly one of the most lavish automobiles of its time. Replacing the smaller V-8 was a larger, 384.8-cu.in. V-8 that made 90hp. Coachbuilt bodies were the way to go on Lincolns in the pre-Depression era, as seen by this stunning example fitted with a Dual-Cowl Phaeton body fabricated by Locke.

1933 KB
Long, flowing, elegant bodies and a 150hp, 381.7-cu.in. V-12 engine. Sure, there might have been economic turmoil throughout the country in 1933, but Lincoln would have nothing of it. This beautiful Brunn Convertible body is one of only 15 built for this year. Chrome-plated wire wheels, dual sidemounts and Pilot Ray driving lamps were among its noteworthy options.

Photograph by Tim Howley

1936 Model K

With production limited to just a single example, it doesn't get any rarer than this Brunn Touring Cabriolet, which was built atop a 147.5-inch wheelbase 1936 Lincoln chassis. While it has a fixed roof, the rear portion folds down for semi-convertible pleasure. Power comes from one of two V-12s this year. This example used the larger, 414-cu.in. version that makes 150hp.

Photograph from Hemmings Motor News archives

1937 Zephyr

With response so favorable to the introductory Zephyr, Lincoln changed it very little for its sophomore year in 1937. A masterpiece of streamlined design, it incorporated sharply raked windshield and smooth, curved headlight housings integrated into the front fenders. Under the long, slippery hood was a 267.3-cu.in. V-12 that developed 110hp. As Lincoln's best seller in 1937, more than 23,000 four-door sedans were produced.

Photograph by Tim Howley

1940 Zephyr
A major styling change for the Zephyr took place in 1940. Its wheel-base was stretched to 125 inches, sealed-beam headlights were now being used, gear selector was to be found on the column, and its V-12 engine displacement was increased to 292 cubic inches, for 120hp. Although it was the second most popular Lincoln built this year, the Club Coupe as seen here only accounted for about 3,500 sales.

Photograph by Bud Juneau

1941 Continental
The Lincoln Continental originated as a factory-customized 1939 Lincoln Zephyr convertible coupe. Edsel Ford insisted on a sporty version of the Lincoln Zephyr and brought Continental to life for 1940. Little changed for 1941, save for minor cosmetic refinements. Under the long hood was a 292-cu.in. V-12 that managed 120hp, and with overdrive engaged was good for 70 mph.

1948 Continental

While Lincoln was frantically laboring over its new postwar model, its offering for 1948 was much like the prewar 1942 version. Low, sleek automobiles that oozed elegance, these Lincolns were still stately and loaded with class. Engine availability for all Lincolns this year was the 130hp, 305-cu.in. V-12 that was first used in 1946. This is one of only 846 Club Coupes built in 1948.

1950 Cosmopolitan

Still wearing the restyled body first seen in 1949, the Lincoln line for 1950 saw only minor revisions in the grille and trim areas. Under the hood was still a 152hp, 336.7-cu.in. V-8, and a three-speed manual gearbox came standard. Though just over 10,000 of the high-end Cosmopolitans were ordered, the suicide-door sedan as seen here was the most popular and accounted for more than 8,000 units.

1955 Capri

Shadowed by the revered Pan Americana race cars and the anticipation of the newly styled 1956 line, the 1955 Lincolns seemed to rank among the forgotten favorites from FoMoCo. With many one-year-only add-ons, Lincoln could sell only 27,222 of its 1955 models. Even a new V-8 engine of 341-cubic-inches was not enough to help bring in more business. Today these striking Capris rank very high among the rarest and most elusive postwar Lincolns.

1956 Premiere

Attractive and stylish, the 1956 Lincolns took on the typical styling cues of cars from the mid-1950s. Hooded headlamps and extended rear quarter panels were among its rather obvious redesigned features in the Capri and Premiere line. Engine size was increased again to 368-cubic-inches. While the lavish Continental Mark II had a 300hp version of this V-8 engine, the Premiere and Capri settled for 285hp.

Photograph by Don Spiro

Photograph from Hemmings Motor News archives

1957 Mark II

For the second and final year, Lincoln offered the sophisticated Mark II as its top-shelf model. Under its long, low hood sat the same 300hp, 368-cu.in. V-8 and Turbo Drive automatic that was also found in the Capri and Premiere that year. With a cost of $10,000, this exclusivity came at a high price. It is no wonder that only 444 Mark II coupes and just two convertibles were built this year.

1958 Mark III

Sitting at the top of the Lincoln lineup in 1958 was the Continental Mark III. All Lincolns this year were given new bodies that included quad headlamps and squared-up styling. Although the Marks shared the same body as the lower-priced Capri and Premiere, they did have a few unique features, one of which was a sliding rear window. A 375hp, 430-cu.in. V-8 and other equipment was shared with the rest of the Lincoln models.

Photograph from Hemmings Motor News archives

1960 Lincoln

Diagonally fixed dual headlamp pods, and small, ever-present rear fender spears that were first seen on 1958 models were retained through 1960. The example here is a 1960 coupe, one of only 1,670 produced this year. Its massive 430-cu.in. V-8 was rated at 315hp, and a Turbo Drive automatic came standard. Air conditioning and power features were optional.

Photograph by David Newhardt

1961 Continental convertible

In 1961, no other car emulated luxury more than the Lincoln Continental. Where most cars in this era started out stark and basic, Lincoln came fully stocked with accessories such as power steering and power brakes—thus justifying its rather high price tag. Although air conditioning was optional, 65 percent of all Lincolns built this year were ordered with it. Under its large hood was a 300hp, 430-cu.in. V-8, mated to a Turbo Drive automatic.

1967 4-door convertible

After getting a facelift in 1966 that included a 4-inch-longer body, revised grille area and a wraparound front bumper, there were only subtle revisions for the 1967 model. Four-door convertibles, as seen above, came with a glass rear backlight, leather trim and a remote trunk release switch. Air conditioning was its most popular option — more than 95 percent were ordered with it. Power came from a 368-cu.in. V-8 that developed 340hp.

1970 Continental

Hidden headlamps, horizontally styled front grille and conventional rear-door entry on four-door models were some of the styling features of the 1970 Lincoln Continental. Standard power was still a 365hp, 460-cu.in. V-8 with the Select Shift automatic transmission. While more than 28,600 sedans were built, a mere 3,000 coupes like the one shown here were ordered.

1950 LINCOLN
Continued from page 48

this type of suspension except among Ford products, which had been bouncing along on transverse buggy springs since 1903. The rear axle was also new, a semi-floating type replacing the old 3/4-floating rear axle. All of these suspension changes were shared with the Cosmopolitans. The Lincoln weighed about 400 pounds less than the Cosmopolitan, which went a long way to improve handling.

In writing for *Mechanix Illustrated*, dean of auto testers Tom McCahill cited the '49 Lincoln as the first American stock car since the '37 Cord and Buick to crack the century mark. He clocked a Lincoln with overdrive at 102.5 and a Cosmopolitan with overdrive at 102.

The 1949 Lincoln and Lincoln Cosmopolitan made their public appearance on April 22, 1948, a week before the Mercury and two months before the revolutionary '49 Ford. While the Lincolns preceded the introduction of the ohv V-8 '49 Cadillac by three months, they did

Styling of the '49-'51 Lincolns has always been controversial. They certainly can't be mistaken for any other make of car offered at the time.

How the 1951 Lincoln Became America's Economy Champ

Bob Estes is the well known Inglewood, California, Lincoln-Mercury dealer who sponsored cars in the Mexican Road Races. (See SIA #105.) Estes had a particular interest in the 1949-51 Lincolns, as opposed to the Lincoln Cosmopolitans, for their economy and performance potential. He entered a 1950 Lincoln in the Mobilgas Economy Run and got a third place in class. A 1950 Mercury won first. "This kind of stirred me up as to what might be done with an an all-out effort, and I gave it a lot of thought," Estes told SIA in that issue. "In 1951 we entered a 1951 Lincoln sport sedan and won the Sweepstakes award with a ton mpg figure of 66.484 and a mpg figure of 25.488. We had a standard-shift transmission and 3.31:1 rear end, with 2.39:1 ratio overdrive." The car was super tuned by Bill Stroppe and Clay Smith in Long Beach and driven by Les Viland, a professional. But it was strictly stock. Chrysler was so unhappy about the Lincoln win that they protested. The car was impounded and torn down after the race, where it was shown to be 100 percent original, unmodified."

For the July issue of *Motor Trend*, Editor Griff Borgeson obtained Estes's practice car for the Grand Canyon run. He wrote, "Frankly, we expected little performance from this car other than good economy at steady speeds. But after almost a thousand miles of driving the machine through traffic, deserts, mountains, at every speed and under almost every road condition, it became apparent that the Lincoln is one of the best cars on the market today, in every way."

Motor Trend's average mileage with stick and overdrive was 25.448. Their fastest run was 100.67 mph, with an average of 97.08 mph for four runs. If the car had been fitted with sea-level carburetor jets instead of high-altitude, they might have gotten another four or five mph. The 3.31:1 "plains" rear end dispelled any rumor that the car was slow.

Their 0-60 time through the gears was 15.58 seconds. A standing quarter mile was covered in 19.90 seconds.

Borgeson's comments on the engine were especially interesting. He wrote, "When Les Viland delivered the Economy Run car to my door I had my pet vintage machine—a 1928 Lincoln touring car—out to meet its newest descendant. The 23-year-old job still goes like a bomb, and Les went over it carefully while I checked myself out on the new car. We talked about the long tradition of Lincoln quality, and about the most significant point of all today, Ford's almost three decades of experience with production of the V-8 engine. The Leland Lincoln became Ford's first V-8, and Ford has been the world's biggest producer of this type of engine, has had years of experience in acquiring and developing know-how—a pleasant position to be in as the automotive world awakens to the superiority of the V layout.

"As far as I know, not even its manufacturer calls attention to the fact that Lincoln's engine is the biggest being fitted to a passenger car today, anywhere in the world—the reason being, I suppose, an understandable desire to avoid creating the impression of a gas-eating gargantuan in the economy-conscious public mind. However, economy-wise, a big engine lightly stressed is equal to or better than a small engine pushed to its limit.

"The Lincoln engine reeks of reliability; its simple, ungadgety design has been refined to the ultimate degree over the years. Outstanding features are its forged crankshaft (not cast, as in the Mercury), excellent crankcase ventilating system, fore and aft vibration dampers (the flexible flywheel doubles in this capacity), and hydraulic valve lifters. There's nothing more annoying than tappets that don't tap, and we've encountered them in more than one hydraulic-tappet engine. We were pleased to find that, in spite of deliberate high over-revving, the Lincoln's tappets did their job properly and in silence. They operate at zero clearance, regardless of valve condition or engine temperature, and require no adjustment. Like the rest of the car, they're made to serve silently and faithfully."

By no means did this fine engine pass from the scene after 1951. Originally designed as a Ford truck engine, it was continued up until the mid fifties as a Ford truck engine, but with the hydraulic lifters exchanged for solid lifters. These engines are not easy to find today because they served out long lives in trucks, many achieving over 200,000 miles, then being rebuilt and going another 150,000 miles or more. In rebuilding a Lincoln of the 1949-51 period, finding another engine could be a problem. Fortunately, most of the Lincolns still have good rebuildable engines, even if the cars have reached the 200,000 mile mark.

specifications

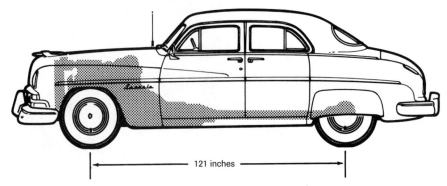

58.5 inches

121 inches

1950 Lincoln Sport Sedan, Model L-74

Price when new	$2,576 f.o.b. Dearborn standard equipment
Options	HydraMatic, radio, vacuum antenna, heater, rear fender skirts, whitewalls

ENGINE

Type	L-head, 90-degree V-8, cast-iron block, water-cooled, 3 mains, full pressure lubrication
Bore x stroke	3.5 inches x 4.375 inches
Displacement	336.7 cubic inches
Horsepower @ rpm	152 @ 3,600
Torque @ rpm	265 ft./lb. @ 2,000
Compression ratio	7:1
Induction system	Single 2-bbl. carb, mechanical fuel pump
Exhaust system	Cast-iron manifolds, crossover pipe, single muffler
Electrical system	6-volt battery/coil

TRANSMISSION

Type	HydraMatic 4-speed with planetary gearsets
Ratios: 1st	3.82:1
2nd	2.63:1
3rd	1.45:1
4th	1.00:1
Reverse	4.30:1

DIFFERENTIAL

Type	Hypoid, spiral-bevel gears
Ratio	3.31:1

Drive axles	Semi-floating

STEERING

Ratio	27.2d:1
Turns lock-to-lock	5.5
Turn circle	42 feet

BRAKES

Type	4-wheel hydraulic, internal expanding drums
Drum diameter	12 inches
Total lining area	196.4 square inches

CHASSIS & BODY

Frame	Box section steel, central X-member, forward K-member reinforcement
Body construction	All steel
Body style	Four-door sedan

SUSPENSION

Front	Independent, unequal A-arms, coil springs, direct-acting tubular shocks, torsional stabilizer bar
Rear	Solid axle, longitudinal semi-elliptic leaf springs, tubular hydraulic shocks
Tires	8.00 x 15 whitewall, 4-ply tube type
Wheels	Pressed steel disc, drop-center rim, lug-bolted to brake drum

WEIGHTS AND MEASURES

Wheelbase	121 inches
Overall length	214 inches
Overall width	76.7 inches
Overall height	63.6 inches
Front track	58.5 inches
Rear track	60.0 inches
Ground clearance	7.4 inches
Curb weight	4,375 pounds

CAPACITIES

Crankcase	6 quarts
Cooling system	35.5 quarts
Fuel tank	19.5 gallons

PERFORMANCE

1951 Lincoln sport sedan with standard transmission and overdrive tested by *Motor Trend*, July 1951.

Standing start 1/4 mile	19.9 seconds
0-60 through gears	15.58 seconds
10-60 in high gear	23.42 seconds
30-60 in high gear	12.83 seconds
Top speed:	
Fastest one-way run	100.67 mph
Average of four runs	97.08 mph

This page: Lincoln hood ornament lacked strong visual identification with the marque. *Facing page, top:* Sad-eyed, sunken headlamp treatment and round tri-lens taillamps are among the Lincoln's recognizable design features. *Bottom left:* Never seen on cars today, rear compartment vent windows. *Right:* Understated wheel covers carry traditional Lincoln crest.

1950 LINCOLN

not win over many GM customers. Total 1949 Lincoln production was 38,384. The factory has never given any breakdown by body styles. The figure compares to 35,123 Lincoln Cosmopolitans and 301,319 Mercurys for the 1949 model year.

Of the three model years, the 1950 is generally considered the best looking. When the Lincoln-Mercury Division was formed in 1945, William F. (Bill) Schmidt was made its first styling director. He did nothing to change Gregorie's original 1949 design, as this was already locked in. The first cars styled under his direction were the 1950 models, which were facelifts. The first thing that went was the eggcrate grille because dealers didn't like it. Schmidt and his crew, which included Tom Hibbard, replaced it with a very clean horizontal chromed grille. But they could do nothing about the sunken headlamps; thus the sad Lincoln look remained throughout the three-year model run. The round parking lamps contained within the '49 grille were replaced with rectangular lamps at the very outer ends. The pull-out 1949 door handles, which were nothing but problems, were replaced with smart pushbutton door handles. The heater and vent systems were completely redesigned, going from one of the worst setups in the industry to one of the best.

Another dealer complaint was the complex five-piece instrument panel with its church organ keys. This was replaced with a clean one-piece unit with all of the instruments housed in a single cluster under clear plastic. The panel flowed gracefully into the doors. In overall concept it was very similar to the 1950 Mercury panel, which is generally regarded as one of the best looking and most functional instrument panels of the period. There were minor improvements in suspension and steering, carburetion, automatic choke and spark control. The engine did not change until late in the 1950 model year.

The Lincoln convertible was dropped because '49 Mercury convertible sales had been so successful. A new model called the Lido was added. This was a coupe with a vinyl top and convertible-like interior. Companions to the Lincoln Lido were the Mercury Monterey coupe and Lincoln Cosmopolitan Capri two-door sedan. All three of these models were introduced mid-year 1950 as Lincoln-Mercury's answer to the new GM hardtops. Ford was caught off guard when GM introduced Cadillac, Buick and Oldsmobile hardtops in mid 1949 and a Chevrolet hardtop for 1950. Ford was so busy implementing its recovery program that it was not able to introduce a Ford hardtop until mid 1951. Lincoln and Mercury hardtops did not appear until 1952.

The most apparent 1951 change was the adaptation of the Mercury's fishtail rear end, which did nothing to improve the styling, and the wider one-piece window, which did much to improve rear visibility. Headlamps were set farther apart with a narrower bezel. The grille

Lincoln in The First Mexican Road Race

Sixteen Lincolns were entered in the first Mexican Road Race held between Ciudad Juarez, Mexico, and El Ocotal, on the Guatemalan border, May 5 through 10, 1950. Twelve of the Lincolns were 1949 Lincolns or Lincoln Cosmopolitans, three were 1950 models and one was a 1947 model. Only four finished, and all were 1949 models. What happened to all the Lincolns is a story in itself.

Enrique Hachmeister, of Guatemala, was killed 19 miles from the start when he lost control on a turn while traveling over 100 mph. He was driving a 1949 Lincoln Cosmopolitan four-door sedan. Harry Sents of Glen Aubry, New York, drove his 1950 Lincoln coupe right through the front door of a house south of Durango. Fortunately, nobody was killed or seriously injured. As pointed out in our driveReport, the road wants to turn, the Lincoln wants to go straight, and that's what happened to most of them. Happier things happened to Marie Brookeson and Ross Barton, two sexy senior citizens who entered a 1949 Lincoln Cosmopolitan two-

door. While they fell out at Mexico City, they continued on for leg prizes and publicity, then returned to Mexico City and were married!

The most memorable Lincoln in the race was #38, a 1949 Lincoln coupe entered by Bob Estes, driven by Johnny Mantz and co-piloted by Bill Stroppe. Mantz might have won were it not for just plain bad luck. He was in the lead down to Mexico City, where he suffered an attack of dysentery. He kept falling behind; then his brakes gave out. But miraculously he remained fourth overall until the ninth and last leg. He finished ninth, coming in on his rubberless wheel rims. He couldn't have gone another mile. Then, neither could the winner, Hershel McGriff, in a 1950 Olds 88. He ruptured his oil pan on a sharp rock just a short distance from the finish line.

This was Bob Estes's first entry into a Mexican Road Race. His support car, which followed the racing team, was a 1950 Lincoln sport sedan, same as our driveReport car. He was ably assisted by

Les Viland. Because of this race, although some time after it, Estes was able to talk Benson Ford into making an all-out Lincoln effort for 1952-54. This was Ford's first return to racing after World War II and the death of Edsel and old Henry. Of course, the rest is history. Estes recalls that right after the race the Mantz car, now in a shambles, was sold to a Mexican. Several years later, while in Mexico City, Estes saw the car, looking rougher than ever, but still running.

The first Mexican Road Race is an exciting story of little guys battling each other in mostly stock cars, of all makes and models, from all over the world. While the later races were spectacular, they were slicker, with international factory support and more professional competition. The first Mexican Road Race remains a monument to the cars of the 1936-50 era, the people who loved them and had the nerve to put them to the test of the world's toughest and most dangerous racing course, 2,135 miles of Mexico, border to border.

Above left to right: "Suicide" rear doors give car an old-fashioned look. Restrained use of chrome out back. Speedo is quite legible. **Below left:** Lots of soft coddling for rear passengers. **Right:** Driver exit and entry is easy.

1950 LINCOLN

The Early '49 Lincoln: Was It A Lemon?

Was the '49 Lincoln really that bad? Yes, the very early models really were that bad! Or, as Bob Hope once quipped, "Here in California we grow oranges. Back in Detroit they've got a whole new crop of lemons." Remember, the '49 Lincoln was introduced on April 22, 1948, the earliest of any '49 model. Henry Ford II was anxious to be the first kid on the block with '49s—and his eagerness for publicity ultimately cost him a lot of customers. The '49 Lincolns got a bad—and justly deserved—reputation very early. Strangely, the '49 Mercurys, introduced just one week later, fared much better. The '49 Fords, introduced in late June, weren't quite as bad as the Lincolns, even though they were quite poorly assembled.

I remember as a kid in Minneapolis seeing a guy driving around in a light metallic brown '49 coupe with signs on both sides and the trunk reading "Lemon." I guess he was trying to shame the dealer into taking it back.

We discussed the engine balancing and oil consumption problems earlier. A variety of other defects soon surfaced. The fuel pump on the Cosmopolitan was too close to the firewall and scraped against it. The floorboard screws were too long and hit the bell housing, making a terrible screeching noise. The hydraulic cylinders in the Cosmo's doors worked loose. They also leaked, causing paint damage. Dust and water entered through the doors and trunk. The handbrake didn't hold. The five-piece instrument panel squeaked. Soft trim and hardware rattled everywhere. There wasn't enough space between the tires and the wheel housing

for mounting tire chains. These problems and many others were addressed at top management meetings as early as July 1948. Finally, at the end of December 1948, it was agreed to redesign the car as much as possible for 1950.

Paul Woudenberg has noted in his book, *Lincoln & Continental, the Postwar Years*, "Dealer frustration rose to a boiling point by mid-1949. Zone by zone, the dealers got together and went to Dearborn to vent their discouragement and anger. Little could be done to help them. The commitment to body dies could not be less than three years, and the only prospect for improvement was the announcement of the 1950 models, made rather late on January 27, 1950, which had meant a single model run of some 21 months." This is not to say that all 1949 Lincolns were bad cars. By the end of calendar year 1948, most of the major bugs were worked out. Those cars built in 1949 were much better, and the closer it got to 1950, the better the 1949 Lincolns became. But a reputation for poor quality dogged all 1949 models, and 1950 and 1951 models as well. Quality control problems of 1949 models should not be a consideration in purchasing one today. If any '49 Lincoln has lasted this long, it was probably one of the better ones. Moreover, it is not difficult to correct the faults in restoration. Plus, there is sort of a reverse snob appeal in owning a dog in its day. Look at what has happened to the Edsel, chrome-dripping GMs and 1958-60 Lincolns. Besides, car collecting for most of us isn't even remotely related to the realities of the times in which these cars lived.

was reworked again. The '49 bumpers gave way to a cleaner design which in the front began to integrate the bumper and grille, a styling theme which would be carried much farther in 1952. Interior changes were minor.

The biggest change was in the engine. This actually occurred late in the 1950 model year. As mentioned earlier, the vibration damper filled with a silicone fluid did not work out very well. This was blamed for a lot of complaints about engine vibration. Another problem was oil consumption. Lincoln had four piston rings in 1949 and early 1950, but this did not stop oil consumption. Going on the theory that the fourth ring dragged, they tried three rings later in 1950. This cured the problem and gave a slight horsepower boost. They further discovered that the vibration complaints stemmed not so much from the vibration damper as from a poorly balanced engine. Later 1950 models and all 1951s have improved engine balancing and improved vibration damping. The cylinder blocks were made with more alloy to increase cylinder bore durability. Minor engine improvements included the addition of distribution tubes in the water passages for better cooling to the exhaust valves.

The three-model lineup was continued: coupe, Lido coupe and sport sedan. Production was 4,482 coupes and Lido coupes and 12,279 sedans or 16,761 Lincolns, along with 15,813 Lincoln Cosmopolitans. Lincoln sales should not be disregarded despite their small numbers. The cars were being sold by established Lincoln-Mercury dealers, and it was much easier for them to sell a Mercury. Consider the prices. A 1950 Lincoln sport sedan like our driveReport car had a base price of $2,576, compared to $2,032 for a Mercury sport sedan. The car was actually priced midway between the Olds 98 deluxe sedan at $2,393 and the Buick Roadmaster sedan at $2,633, both of which had overhead-valve engines. Dynaflow was standard on the Buick Roadmaster. HydraMatic was optional on both the Olds and Lincoln. Ford was entirely correct in offering this junior Lincoln in order to compete as effectively as possible with GM and Chrysler, all of which had overhead-valve engines. But the car should have been priced closer to the Mercury, or there should have been a lower-priced version, say at around $2,250. 👓

Acknowledgments and Bibliography

1951 Lincoln Motor Trial, Motor Trend, *July 1951; Tom McCahill tests the 1949 Mercury, Lincoln & Lincoln Cosmopolitan,* Mechanix Illustrated, *June 1949; 1950 Lincoln Cosmo,* SIA #16; *1950 Mercury,* SIA #12; *The Bob Estes Story,* SIA #105; *1950 Mercury/Olds 88 Comparison,* SIA #124; Encyclopedia of American Cars, 1930-1980, *Auto Editors of Consumer Guide;* Standard Catalog of Ford, 1903-1990, *Krause Publications;* Lincoln & Continental, The Postwar Years, *Paul R. Woudenberg, Motorbooks International;* Mexican Road Race, 1950 Border to Border, *published by Floyd Clymer. Special thanks to Don Williams, MD, San Diego, California, and Bob Estes, Beverly Hills, California.*

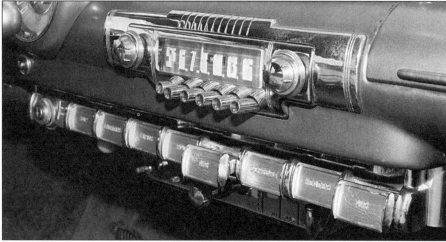

Above: *Despite curvaceous body there's lots of trunk space.* **Left:** *'49 Lincoln dash featured "pipe organ" style controls.* **Below:** *Big flathead V-8 pulled 152 horses from 336.7 cubes.*

Luxury in a Tidy Package

OR A DOZEN years following the demise of the heavy K-series cars early in 1940, the Lincoln was a car in search of its identity. Was it a luxury marque of the Cadillac's caliber, or was it a car for middle America-like the Buick?

It was the Lincoln-Zephyr that had kept the division alive, of course, ever since the smaller car's introduction late in 1935. But the Zephyr. strictly speaking, wasn't a Lincoln at all. In both concept and execution it was a glorified 12-cylinder Ford, even to the extent that a number of parts interchanged with its lesser brother. And of course it was priced to compete with the likes of the Buick Century. It was not, in short, a luxury automobile.

To be sure, there was the classic Continental; and in 1941-42 there was even a huge. sumptuously appointed sedan known as the Lincoln Custom. Neither was inexpensive. But underneath the glamour, both were pure Zephyr. Lincoln had, to all intents and purposes, abandoned the fine-car field.

At least temporarily.

When the assembly lines began to move again after World War II the big Custom series was gone. So was the Zephyr name. But the 12-cylinder Lincoln of 1946-48 was, apart from a minor facelift and a couple of much-needed mechanical modifications, a warmed-over '42 Zephyr (see *SIA* #68). Its performance was no match for most of its competitors; and its ride, thanks to the archaic, transverse leaf-spring suspension, wasn't all that it should have been.

But under the direction of E.T. "Bob" Gregorie, plans for a new Lincoln were long since under way; two new Lincolns, in fact, perhaps reflecting the company's uncertainty as to their place in the scheme of things. The new cars appeared in April 1948, billed as 1949 models. The base Lincoln, like the unlamented Zephyr, was priced in the upper-medium range, about $100 less than the Buick Roadmaster. But unlike the Zephyr, which had featured styling of its own, this one shared the Mercury's new body shell.

It was the larger model, known as the Lincoln Cosmopolitan, that marked the division's return to the high-priced field. $3,238 at the factory may not seem like a luxury-car price today, but in 1949 it was $162 higher than the Cadillac series Sixty-Two.

1952 LINCOLN

by Arch Brown
photos by Bud Juneau

Replacing the hoary V-12 was a new V-8 engine, used by both the new Lincolns. With a displacement of 336.7 cubic inches, it developed 152 horsepower, a generous 22 percent increase over the old V-12. Since the weight of the standard Lincoln was about the same as that of the car it replaced, the difference in performance was spectacular. Even the Cosmopolitan, 250 pounds heavier, was a faster, nimbler car than previous Lincolns had been.

There was really nothing all that different about the new engine. Basically it was an oversized Ford V-8, a heavy, sturdy long-stroker of L-head configuration. Like the earliest Ford V-8s back in 1932, it turned out to have an appetite for oil. More than a year was spent in identifying the problem—which, as it turned out, had to do with the engine's balance, or lack of it. The situation rectified, the engine went on to give excellent service, notably in the F-7 and F-8 series Ford trucks.

Styling of both Lincolns was totally new, and underneath were a number of other improvements: a stout new frame, better brakes, hypoid gearing for a lower

silhouette and—at last—coil springs and independent suspension in front.

Now, Lincoln had a competitive product to sell. Or so it seemed, at least for a time. But within a matter of months Cadillac and Oldsmobile would upstage both new Lincolns with a pair of high-performance, lightweight. short-stroke, overhead-valve V-8s which instantly rendered obsolete every other engine on the market—Lincoln's included. And then a year later GM topped its own act with crisp new bodies that left the Lincolns looking a trifle bulbous by comparison.

Sales began to fall. One problem, of course, was that the Ford Motor Company had no automatic transmission. Their one endeavor in that area, the Liqua-Matic of 1942, had been—as previously noted in these pages (see SIA #68)—a calamity. A proper replacement had yet to be developed. so starting in June 1949—with some swallowing of corporate pride, no doubt—Lincoln offered GM's HydraMatic transmission as an option.

Sales of the nearly identical 1950 models slipped a little, but still held at better-than-prewar levels. One of the problems was that there was no body style comparable to GM's sensational "hardtop convertibles"—sporty, pillarless two-door sedans. Hastily, Lincoln countered with a pair of upscale coupes, the "Lido" on the smaller chassis and the Cosmopolitan "Capri." Both were adorned with vinyl tops, a novelty at that time.

Restyling was again minimal for 1951, but the simple addition of a bold stainless steel belt rib made the Cosmopolitan appear less bulgy than before, and may have helped account for a sales increase in that model. The "Baby Lincoln," meanwhile, though it was setting no sales records, made a phenomenal showing in the Mobilgas Economy Run. Its 25,448-mile-per-gallon average was hard for some people to believe, but it was honestly achieved with a combination of a high-altitude carburetor and very tall gears: 2.39:1 overall, with the overdrive engaged.

But meanwhile, another new Lincoln was under development, one which would return Ford's prestige car strictly to the luxury field. Introduced on February 6, 1952, it was a beautiful automobile, featuring a number of important developments:

• A brand new "over-square" engine,

Originally published in Special Interest Autos #73, Jan.-Feb. 1983

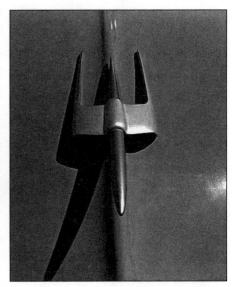

Right: Lincoln's fluted, three-dimensional taillamp lenses still look quite modern today. *Far right:* Hood ornament design was carried over from 1949-'51 Lincolns. *Below:* Leading edge of front fenders is accented by little semi-abstract knights' helmets. Headlamp rims also show nice styling detailing. *Bottom:* '52 Lincoln represented a profound turnaround from previous Lincoln styling and engineering. Finally, Lincoln had a modern luxury car instead of a stopgap.

1952 LINCOLN

the first of Ford Motor Company's coming family of overhead-valve V-8s, furnished the power. Piston travel was reduced 20 percent compared with the old flathead, contributing both to economy and—especially—engine longevity. Smaller than the older engine, it nevertheless generated six more horsepower while providing plenty of potential for further power increases. Since the car had been relieved of some 360 pounds of excess weight, performance was substantially improved.

• A new suspension system designed by Lincoln-Mercury's vice president and chief engineer, Earle S. MacPherson (a recent recruit from Chevrolet), utilized balljoints instead of kingpins—a "first"

Left: *Gone are the toothy grilles and sad eyes of the '49-'51 cars.* **Below:** *Squared-off styling gave more practical trunk space, too.* **Below center:** *Lincoln followed Cadillac's lead with "bullet" bumper guards.*

for an American production automobile. Servicing was made simpler, and steering was easier and more positive than before.

• Styling, developed under the direction of Bill Schmidt, was clean and crisp, featuring an integrated bumper and grille, high-crowned front fenders, and—on the dashboard—aircraft-style controls.

• Brakes were again improved, and the brake pedal—along with the clutch, on those few cars that had one—was suspended, eliminating the drafty hole in the floorboard. This, too, was a "first" for an American car.

• Perhaps most important, the medium-priced "Baby" Lincoln was gone. This time, Lincoln had clearly defined its turf: squarely in the luxury field, The Cosmopolitan, now the "base" model, was priced—in coupe form—just $15 lower than the corresponding Cadillac; while the top-of-the-line Capri series was within $200 of Caddy's Coupe deVille.

It has been said that Earle Macpherson intended the 1952 Lincoln to compete with the Oldsmobile Ninety-Eight,

rather than with the Cadillac. If this is true, the car's price tag must have come as a shock to him. In coupe form the Lincoln was marginally heavier than the Cadillac and only an inch-and-a-half shorter (though the Caddy sedans and Coupe deVilles stretched out another five inches). So, while the new Lincoln was nearly six-and-a-half inches shorter overall (and with three inches less wheelbase) than the '51 Cosmopolitan,

it was still a large automobile. And although its engine, at 317.5 cubic inches, lay mid-way in size between those of Cadillac and Oldsmobile, it proved to be a very creditable performer.

Critics of the '52 Lincoln have pointed out that production was actually below the 1951 figure. While that allegation is true, it overlooks two important points: First, due to the February introduction date, the model year was an abbreviated

A Passion for Precision: Henry M. Leland

It's an interesting historical footnote that America's two remaining luxury marques—Cadillac and Lincoln—trace their origins to the same man: Henry Martyn Leland.

It was Leland, a fanatic when it came to precision work, who had designed the engine for the very first Cadillac back in 1902. Drawing upon his earlier experience in the firearms business, Leland introduced the principle of interchangeable parts. International recognition of this achievement came in 1908 in the form of the coveted Dewar trophy. With Britain's prestigious Royal Automobile Club looking on, three Cadillacs were disassembled, their parts piled together—and then reassembled. The foundation had been laid for mass production.

Henry Leland went on to design, among other things, Cadillac's first V-8, setting the stage for another revolution in the industry. And always, his goal was preci-

sion workmanship. He insisted upon it from his workers, and from his suppliers as well. His impact upon the entire industry is impossible to overstate.

In 1917 Henry Leland and his almost equally talented son Wilfred left Cadillac. The United States had entered World War I and Leland, ever the patriot, wanted to become involved in the war production effort. GM president Billy Durant didn't; he was a pacifist.

And so the Lincoln Motor Company was born, named for the hero of Henry Martyn Leland's youth. (Leland's first vote had been cast for Abraham Lincoln, running for re-election in 1864.)

Again, the goal was precision. But not, this time, in the automobile industry. The Lincoln Motor Company's stock-in-trade was aircraft engines: the fabled Liberty V-12.

For a time, that is. Less than a year after production started, the war was over; and

the Lelands found themselves with a fine factory, a skilled work force (much of it recruited from Cadillac)—and nothing to do. Thus, of necessity, was born the Lincoln automobile. Or perhaps wily old Henry Leland had that in mind in the first place.

One has to wonder what the Lelands, father and son, would think of the Lincoln car of a generation later—our driveReport car. Certainly it came far closer to their ideal than the Lincoln Zephyr had ever done. No doubt they—or at least old Henry—would have pointed out ways in which the product could have been improved, for he was never satisfied, even with his own exacting work.

But in terms of its advanced engineering and its high level of fit and finish, we think Henry Martyn Leland would have been proud to see the Lincoln name on the car that was produced so many years after he had passed from the scene.

His legacy of quality was still evident.

1952 Lincoln Comparison Chart

(The 1952 Lincoln has been compared with both Cadillac and Oldsmobile, and of course it makes an interesting contrast to previous Lincolns.)

	1952 Lincoln Cosmopolitan Coupe	1952 Cadillac "62" Coupe	1951 Lincoln "98" Holiday Coupe	1951 Lincoln Cosmopolitan Coupe
Price*	$3,293	$3,308	$2,750	$2,975
Wheelbase	123 inches	126 inches	124 inches	125 inches
Overall length	214.1 inches	215.5 inches	214 inches	222.5 inches
Weight (lb.)	4,155	4,050	3,755 (est)	4,420
Bore/stroke	3.8″/3.5″	3.8″/3.6″	3.75″/3.4″	3.5″/4.4″
Displacement (cubic inches)	317.5	331.0	303.7	336.7
Bhp @ rpm	160/3,900	190/4,000	160/3,600	154/3,600
Compression ratio	7.5:1	7.5:1	7.5:1	7.0:1

* Prices f.o.b. factory, with standard equipment, plus federal excise tax.

Sources: *Automotive Industries*, March 15, 1951, and March 15, 1952. Thomas E. Bonsall, *The Lincoln Motorcar*.

Right: Lincoln's styling is somewhat illusory; it appears smaller than it actually is. Below and below right: Hardtop's side roof trim is repeated on the inside of the car.

1952 LINCOLN

one. And second, with the coming of the 1952 modeL Lincoln abandoned the medium-priced field where the so-called "Baby Lincoln" had accounted, during 1949-51, for more than half of the division's sales. Comparing 1952 Lincoln production with that of 1951's luxury cars—i.e., the Cosmopolitan series—sales were up by 72.5 percent, the ten-month model year notwithstanding!

The new car represented a bold move for Lincoln, in the sense that only rarely does a manufacturer try out his latest innovations first on his luxury line. Yet here was the over-square, overhead-valve V-8 showing up in the Lincoln two years ahead of its appearance in Mercury and Ford. The same was true of Earle MacPherson's radical ball-joint suspension. In a clean break with the past, Lincoln had become one of the industry's prime innovators.

Nor did the company rest on its laurels. The 1953 Lincoln may be almost impossible to distinguish from the '52 in terms of appearance, but there were a number of exciting additions and improvements. Saginaw power steering was made available, along with four-way power seats. (The latter were particularly novel at the time.)

But the biggest news for 1953 had to do with the Lincoln engine. Redesigned cylinder heads with higher compression ratios and larger valves, larger manifolds, a four-barrel carburetor, dual exhausts and a high-lift camshaft raised the horsepower from 160 to a neck-snapping 205. For the first time since the Duesenberg an American car had topped the 200 mark—and all this without an increase in the engine's comparatively modest displacement.

The difference in performance was startling. Lincoln had cut four seconds off its zero-to-sixty time with a car that could top 115 miles an hour! The stage was set for three years of ding-dong competition in which the Lincoln would be pitted against some of the fastest production sedans in the world—and emerge on top.

After a production increase of nearly 50 percent for the 1953 model year, Lincoln dropped off a little in 1954. It could have been worse: they were fielding a mildly facelifted version of the 1952-53 car against a totally restyled Cadillac that featured the then-popular (though ultimately infamous) "dog-leg" wrap-around windshield. Yet Lincoln's market share, vis-a-vis Cadillac's, held steady.

Incidentally, it is interesting to note that from the start the upscale Capri outsold the base Cosmopolitan series; and its lead increased year-by-year until in 1955 it was outselling the less-expensive series six times over.

There should by rights have been a fully redesigned Lincoln for the 1955 season. From the start the car had been criticized for looking "too much like a Mercury." Now, to make matters worse, it looked like last year's Mercury—or at least that's how it was perceived. For both Mercury and Ford were restyled for 1955, while Lincoln had to make do with another facelift. Or "fanny lift," rather; for the principal modification was an eight-inch extension of the rear quarter panels, giving the illusion of greater length.

Mechanical modifications were another matter. For 1955 Lincoln at last had an automatic transmission of its own: "Turbo-Drive." Smoother than the HydraMatic, it also did away with GM's odd (and potentially dangerous) quadrant, wherein one had to go through the forward gears in order to find reverse. The Turbo-Drive also carried lower numerical gearing in the rear end, enhancing the Lincoln's already admirable fuel economy.

Nor was that all. Factory-installed air-conditioning—a cumbersome, trunk-mounted unit—was available for the first time. And the engine, thanks to an increase in the bore and higher compression, was boosted to 225 horsepower. An inch-and-a-half was added to the rear tread, increasing further the Lincoln's stability in cornering.

Sales, however, were dismal. Not only

Far left: *Interior appointment and fabrics are quite restrained in rear compartment.*
Left: *Dashboard shape is carried through onto front doors.*

was the huge (and in retrospect rather less-than-graceful) Cadillac extremely popular, but Chrysler's Imperial doubled its sales with an attractive new car; and with the help of its new V-8 engine, sales of the senior Packard virtually trebled. All three of Lincoln's luxury-class rivals carried larger engines with higher horsepower ratings than did the pride of Ford Motor Company.

The 1955 Lincoln was, of course, no more than an "interim" car. On September 8, 1955, the dramatic, all-new Lincoln Premiere made its bow to a public reception so enthusiastic that sales nearly doubled. You'll find a driveReport on that one in *SIA* #60.

Lincoln had at last established its identity. Not in the stratospheric range of the gargantuan "K" series; and not in the medium-priced field like the Zephyr and the "Baby" Lincoln that followed it. Squarely in the mainstream of the luxury market now, Lincoln had found its niche.

And it was doing rather well for itself!

Driving Impressions

Our first reaction, when we slipped behind the wheel of Marc Henig's '52 Cosmopolitan, had to do with the seats.

	Body Style	Price*	Shipping Weight	Production
Cosmopolitan	Sport coupe	$3,293	4,155 lb.	4,545
	Sport sedan	$3,198	4,125 lb.	**
Capri	Sport coupe	$3,518	4,235 lb.	5,681
	Sport sedan	$3,381	4,140 lb.	**
	Convertible	$3,665	4,350 lb.	1,191

1952 Lincoln
Model Availability, Price and Production

Total 1952 model year production: 27,271
* Prices shown are f.o.b. factory with standard equipment, exclusive of federal excise tax.
** Combined total, Cosmopolitan and Capri sedans: 15,854

Sources: *Automotive Industries*, March 15, 1952. Thomas E. Bonsall, *The Lincoln Motorcar*.

They're marvelous! Firm, supportive, chair-height; one could sit here in total comfort all day long. Leg room is ample, too.

And there's a full complement of gauges. No "idiot lights" in this dashboard display. Something else to like.

At the touch of a solenoid on the dashboard the overhead-valve V-8 came to life. One lifter stuck momentarily—a characteristic of these cars—then all was quiet. We dropped the dual-range HydraMatic into D-3 position for town driving; then, once on the open road,

into D-4. Top gear in this setup amounts to an overdrive ratio. Nice.

We could feel the shifts as the transmission changed gears; but it's smooth. The only time we experienced any "lurching" effect was when, after cruising down the highway in fourth gear, we slowed abruptly and turned into a steep driveway. At that point there were two downshifts in rapid succession, and the second one made itself felt Really, the only thing we don't like about this gearbox is the way reverse is positioned: right where "low" is found on a standard

A Fine Car Made Even Finer: The 1954 Lincoln Capri

After having driven Marc Henig's fine 1952 Lincoln Cosmopolitan, we were anxious to try out one of the succeeding models to see how much difference the extra 45 horsepower of the 1953-54 cars would make; and of course, to get the feel of the power steering and power brakes that were available on the later cars.

Bob Boruck, of Oakland, California, was kind enough to put his near-mint 1954 Capri sedan at our disposal for this purpose. It's a gorgeous, all-original car. No restoration work of any kind has ever been done to it, nor is any needed. Its original owner, an elderly lady, used it for 20 years to drive back and forth between her two homes in Pomona and Palm Springs. Its odometer registered 50,000 miles when Bob was fortunate enough to become its second owner. Another 12,000 miles have been added with Bob's hands on the wheel.

Certain differences are immediately apparent, as compared with Marc Henig's car. First of all, it's a four-door sedan, a little taller than the coupe and somewhat more formal in appearance. The head

room would do credit to a limousine; even the tallest driver can wear his hat in this automobile. Yet in no sense does it appear "top heavy."

Second, of course, it's the top-of-the-line model; and as nicely as the Cosmopolitan is appointed, this one is even better.

The four-way power seat can be raised and lowered electrically, as well as moved forward and back. Bob keeps it well elevated, affording unusually good visibility.

On the road, the difference in acceleration between the '54 and the '52 is noticeable, but not quite as great as we had expected. If one really wants one of these cars to *move*, the trick is to pop the HydraMatic selector into D-3. At that point the big Lincoln fairly jumps ahead! Bob reports that its best cruising speed is between 70 and 75.

The Saginaw power steering unit preserves a good deal of "road feel." The driver is hardly conscious of it on the open highway. In parking maneuvers it comes into its own, however. For not only does it

make the wheel light and easy to turn, but it cuts a little more than one and a half turns off the lock-to-lock turning.

The power brakes are another delight. Not at all inclined to grab, they nevertheless relieve the driver of the necessity of applying hard pressure to bring the heavy Lincoln to a stop.

We're impressed! Lincoln took an already excellent automobile, their 1952 model, and by 1954 turned it into a superb—and throughly modern—car that's a joy to drive under just about any circumstance!

specifications

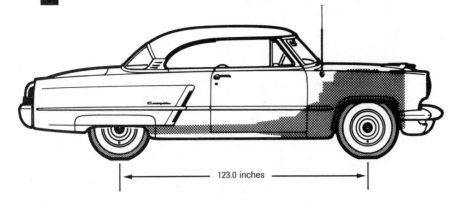

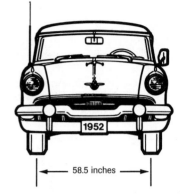

123.0 inches

58.5 inches

1952

1952 Lincoln Cosmopolitan

Price	$3,293 f.o.b. factory with standard equipment, plus federal excise tax
Options on dR car	Hydra-Matic transmission, power windows, radio, windshield washers, backup light, left outside mirror

ENGINE

Type	90-degree overhead-valve V-8, wedge-head
Bore x stroke	3.8 inches x 3.5 inches
Displacement	317.5 cubic inches
Horsepower @ rpm	·160 @ 3,900
Taxable horsepower	46.2
Torque @ rpm	284 @ 1,800
Compression ratio	7.5:1
Main bearings	5
Induction system	Holley dual downdraft carburetor, concentric bowl type
Lubrication system	Pressure
Exhaust system	Oval, 3-passage single muffler
Electrical system	6-volt

TRANSMISSION

Type	Hydra-Matic, automatic planetary gearset
Ratios: 1st	3.8195:1
2nd	2.6341
3rd	1/4500:1
4th	1.00:1
Reverse	4.3045:1

DIFFERENTIAL

Type	Hypoid, Hotchkiss drive
Ratio	3.31:1
Drive axles	Semi-floating

STEERING

Type	Worm and roller, symmetrical linkage
Turns lock-to-lock	4.625
Ratio	26.1:1
Turn circle	45 feet, 3 inches

BRAKES

Type	Duo-Servo internal expanding, hydraulic
Drum diameter	11 inches
Total braking area	190.89 square inches

CHASSIS & BODY

Frame	I-beam, double-braced X-type, 6 crossmembers
Body construction	All steel
Body style	Sport coupe (2-door hardtop)

SUSPENSION

Front	Independent, helical coil springs, ball joints, steel torsion bar stabilizer
Rear	54.75-inch longitudinal leaf springs
Tires	8.00 x 15
Wheels	Disc, drop-center rims

WEIGHTS AND MEASURES

Wheelbase	123 inches
Overall length	214.1 inches
Overall height	62.6 inches (loaded)
Overall width	77.5 inches
Front track	58.5 inches
Rear track	58.5 inches
Ground clearance	7.2 inches
Shipping weight	4,155 pounds
Weight distribution	55.3 percent front, 44.7 percent rear

CAPACITIES

Crankcase	5 quarts (6 with filter)
Cooling system	24.5 quarts
Fuel tank	20 gallons

PERFORMANCE

Top speed	100.5
Acceleration 0-60	13.5 seconds
Fuel consumption	17.2 mpg (497 mile average)
Stopping distance	237 feet (from 60 mph)

From (Speed Age, June 1952)
Note: Test car was equipped with standard transmission and overdrive

PERFORMANCE

Top speed	98.3 mph
Acceleration 0-60	16.6 seconds
Fuel consumption	15.6 mpg (traffic)

From (Motor Trend, June 1952)
Note: Test car was equipped with Hydra-Matic transmission

1952 LINCOLN

three-speed transmission. That struck us as both stupid and dangerous when the HydraMatic first appeared, back in 1940. We still see it that way.

In order to assess the new-for-1952 suspension we took the Lincoln out on the Marsh Creek Road, a winding, back-country stretch just a few miles east of Marc Henig's Concord, California, home. It's a superb road car, solid and heavy, yet not at all cumbersome. Cornering is remarkably flat, even under some pressure. The non-power steering is a little slow, but feather-light at speed. (Parking is another matter, of course. Maneuvering two tons of Lincoln sitting on those fat tires—even though Marc keeps a few extra pounds of air in them—requires a bit of muscle!)

Acceleration, while hardly startling, is more than adequate, Marc reports that the Lincoln "ran like a striped ape when we could get decent gasoline." Today, with the timing backed off just a hair, it performs very nicely on a

50-50 blend of leaded and unleaded premium fuels, a combination which yields an octane rating of about 94.

We didn't try any high-speed runs, but Marc Henig is obviously correct when he observes that the Lincoln is "happier" at 65 to 70 than it is at 55. An all-day cruising speed of 80 could be sustained with ease; and of course this car could be downright embarrassing to the anemic pursuit cars presently employed by the highway patrol.

The brakes do their job well, but a good deal of pedal pressure is required. A power assist would be a big help in this department, And the horn: it could wake the dead!

This is no "show" car. Henig bought it in 1974 as a daily driver, and it alternates even now with a '55 Ford Ranch Wagon as his regular transport. The Lincoln's original owner, who bought it from Van Etta Motors, San Francisco, on May 23, 1952, suffered a stroke only a couple of years after taking delivery. So when Marc purchased it, for an incredible $525, it had been driven only 18,000 miles! Today, with the mileage approaching 100,000, no major mechanical work has been required.

Since this is a Korean War-era car, the chrome plating, which has never been restored, could use some help. The car was repainted a year ago, however, in its original Raven Black over Lakewood Green; and despite the imperfections in the chrome, it's a neat, smart-looking automobile.

And to Marc Henig, whose dad drove a Lincoln like this one years ago, the Cosmopolitan represents the American automobile at its very best! ∂

Acknowledgments and Bibliography

Automotive Industries, *January 15, 1952: March15, 1952:* Motor Age, *June 1952: Floyd Clymer, "Report on the '52 Lincoln,"* Popular Mechanics, *October 1952: Tim Howley, "A Look at the Postwar Lincolns,"* Automobile Quarterly, *Vol. 17, No. 2: Walt Woron, "'52 Lincoln Road Test,"* Motor Trend, *June 1952: Thomas Bonsall,* The Lincoln Motor Car: Sixty Years of Excellence; *Jerry Heasley,* The Production Figure Book for US Cars; *Maurice Hendry,* Lincoln; *Richard M. Langworth,* Encyclopedia of American Cars, 1940-1970: *James H. Maloney and George H. Dammann,* Encyclopedia of American Cars, 1946 to 1959; *Lincoln Owners Manual, 1952. Our thanks to Tom Bonsall, Baltimore, Maryland: John and Claudia Cavagnaro, Stockton, California: Ralph Dunwoodie, Sun Valley, Nevada: Pat Kellner, Hillsborough, California: Bob Rodenberg, Clayton, California: Harry and Sherry Wynn, Concord, California. Special thanks to Marc Henig, Concord, California: Bob Boruck, Oakland, California.*

Above: Lincoln's dashboard styling was very airplane-like in general appearance, as were Mercurys of the time. Full instrumentation was used; controls and switches conveniently grouped near driver. Below: Lincoln styling has been criticized for looking like a "big Mercury." However, no one knocks the Merc for looking like a "small Lincoln."

RACE CAR/LUXURY CAR

by Arch Brown
photos by Roy Query

I T isn't reasonable to expect championship road-racing performance of a luxury automobile. The two concepts simply aren't compatible.

Or so it seems. Yet between 1952 and 1954, Lincoln racked up an incredible record in the bruising, bloody Carrera Panamericana — the legendary Mexican national road race.

The race, plans for which had taken form in 1949, was conceived by the Mexican government as a means of increasing tourism by celebrating the completion of its new highway, which extended border-to-border on the north-south axis, from the United States to Guatemala. the contest was to be conducted under the sanction and rules of the Federation Internationale de L'Automobile (FIA); and the course was to run from Ciudad Juarez, just across from El Paso, to El Ocotal, just north of the Guatemalan border. The total distance came to 2,135 very hard miles, ranging from sea level to elevations as high as 10,486 feet.

Appropriately, the starting gun for the first Carrera Panamericana was fired on a major Mexican holiday, Cinco de Mayo: May 5, 1950. Entrants were limited to five-passenger, closed automobiles — strictly stock, though factory options were permitted. Contestants ranged all the way from Cadillac and Packard to Nash and Studebaker to Alfa Romeo and Jaguar.

And yes, there were Lincolns as well,

in that initial race. One of them, piloted by Enrique Hachmeister, accounted for the contest's first fatality, when it crashed just a few miles from the starting line, killing its driver instantly.

Lincoln had abandoned its silky-smooth but underpowered and trouble-prone V-12 following the 1948 model year. In its place, the completely redesigned 1949 Lincolns — introduced on April 22, 1948 — were powered by a 152-horsepower, 336.7-cubic-inch flat-head V-8. In the face of the over-square, overhead-valve powerplants about to be introduced by Cadillac and Olds, the new Lincoln mill was essentially obsolete the day it first appeared, but it was nevertheless capable of giving a pretty good account of itself. Witness the fine showing made by midget car champion Johnny Mantz in the Mexican Road Race. Driving his own personal 1949 Lincoln, Mantz, together with co-pilot Bill Stroppe, ended up in ninth place with an average speed of 91 miles an hour. It was a highly creditable run, especially given the nature of the competition, and the Lincoln might have done even better had it not been beset, in the final leg of the race, by persistent tire troubles.

After the initial race in 1950, the course was reversed so that the cars ran from south to north, a change which provided much better press coverage (as well as superior hotel accommodations) at the finish line. At the same time the route was shortened to 1,933 miles, through the elimination of the original finish line town of El Ocotal. This time, the race would commence at Tuxtla Gutierrez and end at Ciudad Juarez.

The 1951 contest was a free-for-all, with all contestants competing head-to-head, regardless of class. Modifications to the engine and running gear were permitted that year, in a reversal of the original policy. There was another reversal for 1952, however, requiring all cars to meet factory specifications, and at the same time two classes — Sports Car and Standard Stock — were established.

Conspicuous by its absence, at first, was any participation by the Lincoln factory. But as the time approached for the 1952 race, Bill Stroppe, who together with his partner, Clay Smith, had signed on with the Ford Motor

Company to handle competition projects on the West Coast. They suggested to Benson Ford, head of Lincoln-Mercury, that the contest could become a publicity bonanza for Lincoln. Ford was reluctant at first, fearing the possibility of failure and the ridicule that it would bring to his cars, but Stroppe remained hopeful.

For the second time in less than four years (just three model years, actually), the Lincoln had been completely redesigned for 1952. Styling, developed by chief Lincoln stylist Bill Schmidt working under the general direction of corporate styling director George Walker, was crisp, clean and extremely attractive, representing a radical departure from the bulky designs of 1949-51. Equally new and different was the chassis. A more rigid frame, better brakes and larger shocks were featured.

Even more importantly, Earle S. MacPherson, Lincoln-Mercury's chief engineer, had developed a highly advanced ball joint front suspension, the first to be employed by an American automobile. Far simpler than the system it replaced, the new suspension cut

the number of lubrication fittings from 16 to four. Unsprung weight was reduced, and steering was lighter and more precise than before.

Best of all, there was a new, over-square, 317.5-c.i.d. overhead-valve V-8, as modern as any engine then on the market.

But it wasn't the 1952 Lincoln that Bill Stroppe had in mind for that year's Carrera Panamericana. This time, the contest was scheduled for November, which meant that the 1953 models would be available. And thanks to redesigned heads, larger manifolds and valves, greater valve lift, four-barrel carburetion and a higher compression ratio, for 1953, the bhp of Lincoln's fine new engine had been raised — with no change in displacement — from 160 in its initial form to a rousing 205, marking the first time since the demise of the Duesenberg that an American automobile had offered more than 200 standard horsepower.

Finally, in the spring of 1952, Bill Stroppe received his long-awaited telephone call from Benson Ford, instructing him to put together a team for

1954 LINCOLN CAPRI

1954 LINCOLN CAPRI

Above: *Plane-like hood ornament is a far cry from Lincoln's classic greyhound.* **Below:** *Lincoln "coat of arms" nestles in big chromed V on front of hood.*

the Pan American. Ford told Stroppe that a prototype 1953 Lincoln was ready to go at the company's test facility at Colorado Springs. He asked that Bill, along with Clay Smith, pick up the car and drive it back to Stroppe's shop in Long Beach. The idea was that this extended run would enable the two men to make sure that the '53 Lincoln really was fast enough to compete successfully in the Carrera Panamericana. Benson Ford had to be absolutely certain of his car before giving the project the green light.

The prototype car had already undergone some brutal testing at Pike's Peak before Stroppe and Smith took it over, and Clay — a mechanic's mechanic if ever there was one — detected a noise he didn't like. Valves. So after the car arrived in Long Beach, the engine was torn down and the problem corrected. At that point, Smith and Stroppe turned around and headed back to the Bonneville Salt Flats. There, on the 10-mile oval, the Lincoln ran consistently at 118 mph. Plenty of speed for the Pan American.

Returning to Long Beach, Stroppe called Benson Ford to confirm the results of his test run. An agreement was struck whereby the company would field a team of Lincolns for the 1952 race. Three new cars were stripped to the bare chassis and every component was meticulously checked. The rules that year forbade any modifications from stock factory specifications, apart from safety measures, which included among other items two Houdaille shocks at each front wheel, and air-lifts at the rear along with oversized tubular shocks. The rear ends were raised about four inches, in the interest of better control. Tires were inflated with nitrogen, in order to maintain constant

1954 Luxury Hardtops Compared

	Lincoln Capri	Buick Roadmaster	Cadillac 62	Chrysler New Yorker	Packard Pacific
Price (f.o.b. factory)	$3,869	$3,373	$3,838	$3,672	$3,827
Weight	4,250 lb.	4,215 lb.	4,350 lb.	4,095 lb.	4,040 lb.
Wheelbase	123 inches	127 inches	129 inches	125.5 inches	122 inches
Overall length	214.75 inches	216.75 inches	216.4375 inches	215.5625 inches	215.5 inches
Engine	Ohv V-8	Ohv V-8	Ohv V-8	Ohv V-8	L-head str. 8
C.I.D.	317.5	321.7	331.1	331.1	358.8
Horsepower @ rpm	205/4,200	200/4,100	230/4,400	235/4,400	212/4,000
Torque @ rpm	305/2,650	309/2,400	330/2,700	330/2,600	330/2,200
Compression ratio	8.00:1	8.50:1	8.25:1	7.50:1	8.70:1
Braking area (sq. in.)	220.1	219.1	211.6	201.0	209.3
Transmission	HydraMatic	Dynaflow	HydraMatic	PowerFlite	Ultramatic
Axle ratio	3.31:1	3.40:1	3.36:1*	3.54:1	3.54:1
Horsepower per c.i.d.	.646	.622	.695	.710	.591
Weight (lb.) per horsepower	20.7	21.1	18.9	17.4	19.1
Weight per c.i.d.	13.4	13.1	13.1	12.4	11.3
Weight per sq. in. (brakes)	19.3	19.2	20.6	20.4	19.3

* Or 3.07

pressure despite extreme variations in temperature; and a large fuel tank replaced the rear seat. Fortunately, there was nothing in the rule book to prevent Clay Smith, assisted by Chuck Daigh, from carefully blueprinting and balancing the engines. Intake and exhaust ports could not be polished, but nothing was said about matching the manifolds and ports. Then without breaking the rules — though he may perhaps have bent them just a little — Stroppe installed heater fans in the trunk of each car, with flex hoses leading to the rear brakes. Bill knew from experience that the mountainous roads could all too easily spell brake failure. Smith, meanwhile, secured permission to substitute solid valve lifters for the hydraulics supplied by Lincoln as standard issue.

Transmission wizard Vern Houle was recruited, in order to work his magic on the HydraMatic units with which the Lincolns were equipped. Each transmission was recalibrated to shift into fourth gear at 84 miles an hour, and once again, tolerances were adjusted to precision standards. The transmissions were strictly "according to Hoyle" — make that Houle — but somehow they worked better than the units coming off the assembly line.

Clay Smith, who had been involved in the Indy 500, among other contests, had a number of other tricks up his sleeve. For instance, differentials were lubricated with a mixture of castor-bean oil and powdered lead. Again, no violation of the rules was involved, but it was this attention to detail that gave

1954 Lincoln Table of Prices, Weights and Production

	Price	Weight	Production
Cosmopolitan Series			
Sport Coupe (hardtop)	$3,625	4,155 lb.	2,994
Sedan, 4-door	$3,522	4,135 lb.	4,447
Capri Series			
Sport Coupe (hardtop)	$3,869	4,250 lb.	14,003
Sedan, 4-door	$3,711	4,245 lb.	13,598
Convertible	$4,031	4,310 lb.	1,951
TOTAL MODEL YEAR PRODUCTION			36,993
CALENDAR YEAR PRODUCTION			35,733

Above: Lincoln name and symbol figured prominently on racer's rear quarters. **Below:** Not exactly kitted out to take you to the country club dance, but the car did meet the rules of stock class.

specifications

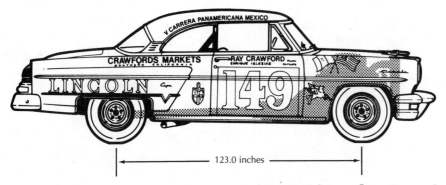

←—— 123.0 inches ——→

←—— 58.5 inches ——→

1954 Lincoln Capri

Original price	$3,869 f.o.b. factory, in stock condition, federal excise tax included

ENGINE

Type	Overhead-valve, 90-degree V-8
Bore x stroke	3.8 inches x 3.5 inches
Displacement	317.5 cubic inches
Compression ratio	8.0:1
Horsepower @ rpm	205 @ 4,200
Torque @ rpm	305 @ 2,650
Taxable horsepower	46.2
Valve lifters	Hydraulic
Main bearings	5
Fuel system	Holley 2140 four-barrel down-draft carburetor, mechanical pump
Lubrication system	Pressure
Cooling system	Centrifugal pump
Exhaust system	Single
Electrical system	6-volt

TRANSMISSION

Type	HydraMatic 4-speed automatic planetary
Ratios: 1st	3.82:1
2nd	2.63:1
3rd	1.45:1
4th	1.00:1
Reverse	4.30:1

DIFFERENTIAL

Type	Hypoid
Ratio	3.31:1
Drive axles	Semi-floating
Torque medium	Rear springs

STEERING

Type	Gemmer worm-and-roller
Ratios	20.4 gear, 26.1 overall
Turns, lock-to-lock	4.25
Turning diameter	45' 9"

BRAKES

Type	4-wheel internal hydraulic, drum type, power assisted
Drum diameter	12 inches
Total swept area	220.1 square inches

CONSTRUCTION

Type	Body-on-frame
Frame	I-section, double braced X-type, 6 cross members
Body construction	All steel
Body style	Hardtop coupe

SUSPENSION

Front	Independent, coil springs, ball joints, torsion bar stabilizer
Rear	Rigid axle, longitudinal semi-elliptic leaf springs
Shock absorbers	Direct acting
Wheels	Pressed steel, drop-center rims
Tires	8.00/15

WEIGHTS AND MEASURES

Wheelbase	123"
Overall length	214.8"
Overall width	77.1"
Overall height	64.2"
Track, front/rear	58.5"/58.5"
Min. road clearance	7.4"
Shipping weight	4,250 pounds

INTERIOR MEASURES

(front seat only)

Head room	35.5"
Shoulder room	57.5"
Hip room	62.3"
Leg room	45.3"

CAPACITIES

Crankcase	6 quarts (with filter)
Automatic transmission	11 quarts
Cooling system	24.5 quarts (w/heater)
Fuel tank	20 gallons
Differential	3.5 pints

CALCULATED DATA

Horsepower per c.i.d.	.646
Weight per hp	20.7 pounds
Weight per c.i.d.	13.4 pounds
Weight per sq. in.	19.3 pounds (brakes)

PERFORMANCE

Top speed (average)	110.7 mph
Acceleration 0-30 mph	4.1 seconds
0-60 mph	12.3 seconds
10-30 mph	3.5 seconds
30-50 mph	5.9 seconds
50-80 mph	15.0 seconds
Standing ¼ mile	18.4 seconds/76 mph
Braking distances:	
from 30 mph	42 feet
from 45 mph	92 feet
from 60 mph	167 feet

(From *Motor Trend,* August 1954)

DriveReport car in action during the Carrera Panamericana.

Price List: Popular 1954 Lincoln Options

Power Steering	$145
Power Brakes	$40
Power Windows	$65
Power Seat (4-way)	$165
Radio	$122
Heater	$113
Air Conditioning	$647
White Sidewall Tires	$37

Note: HydraMatic transmission was standard.

1954 LINCOLN CAPRI

the Lincoln team that all-important competitive edge.

Not to forget the drivers. Stroppe and Smith, well known on the racing circuit, recruited the best in the business, selecting Walt Faulkner, Johnny Mantz and Chuck Stevenson to pilot the three factory-sponsored Lincolns.

As the 1952 race approached, Stroppe, with characteristic precision, had a sign painter prepare roll maps of the entire route, showing every detail of each town along the way and indicating the maximum speed at which each corner could be negotiated.

Tires were a potential problem, especially as the cars came through the mountains, for the roads were narrow and there were no turnouts where tire changes could be effected. In his excellent biography of Bill Stroppe, Tom Madigan describes what Bill did about it: "Late on the afternoon of practice…Stroppe discovered a small turnout where local buses could unload passengers. Half hidden by brush was a small soda-pop stand to serve the bus passengers. Knowing that all public traffic would be halted during the race, Stroppe rented the turnout for those days. He and his crew then embarked upon a masterpiece of one-upmanship. In the brush Stroppe hid six front tires, two for each team car. Then he carefully dug a huge hole and buried a cylinder of compressed air and hoses connected to a small platform. Next he hollowed out two ruts for the front tires. In the center of the two ditches he buried the platform. Two air wrenches were also hidden. When the Lincolns would roll into place, the driver and co-pilot would jump out, connect the air cylinder, and the platform would pop up under the front cross member and raise the car. Using the air-powered wrenches, the men could quickly mount two new tires in a matter of seconds. When quizzed later about his little innovation, Stroppe replied, 'It wasn't cheating. There was nothing in the rules about stopping for tires!'"

In the end, the Lincolns finished one-two-three, with drivers Stevenson, Mantz and Faulkner crossing the finish line in that order. It was a remarkable achievement, and Lincoln's public relations people made the most of it.

For 1953 the rules were changed, to require that cars used in the race must have been in production during the year of the event. No longer would it be possible to employ models yet to be introduced in the showrooms. So once again, 1953 Lincolns were used. This time the team had five official cars, and Stroppe and his crew prepared one additional

Above: *The car as displayed in Reno, today.* **Below left:** *Extra safety catches were installed on hood and trunk.* **Below right:** *Backup lamps were removed for racing.*

machine for Ray Crawford. Known as the "Flying Grocer," Crawford had been a participant in each of the previous contests, though he had not been conspicuously successful. To all intents and purposes his car would be a member of the Lincoln team, although it was funded by Ray personally, rather than by Lincoln-Mercury.

Bill Vukovich, fresh from his victory in the 1953 Indianapolis 500, was added to the roster of Lincoln drivers, along with Jack McGrath, another Indy veteran. Classes were further refined that year, with large and small cars — both stock and sports — being separately categorized.

Three hours were allowed each night for the cars to be checked and repaired, and put in order for the next day's race. So refined had the Lincoln team's procedures become that during that brief period tires and brakes — and even rear ends and transmissions, if necessary — could be replaced with new stock. And as a final precaution Stroppe and Smith brought along a self-contained food

wagon, insisting that each driver and crew member take all his meals and beverages from that source. Johnny Mantz had very nearly been laid low by a digestive upset during the 1950 race. This time the team would take no chances with food poisoning or contaminated water.

Perhaps the results were predictable: Team Lincolns placed First, Second, Third and Fourth, with drivers Chuck Stevenson, Walt Faulkner, Jack McGrath and Johnny Mantz arriving at Juarez in that order. Bill Vukovich, unfortunately, had bombed out on the first leg with a blown transmission.

But tragedy had stalked the 1953 race. Mickey Thompson, swerving to avoid hitting a child, careened over an embankment and killed four spectators. Six more deaths occurred when a Lancia team driver lost control coming through a corner. And driver Antonio Stagnoli lost his life when his Ferrari crashed in flames. Bill Stroppe later recalled the foolhardy chances taken by the crowd: "Going into Mexico City, the

Above: *A Spanish-speaking Dennis the Menace adorned the hood as a good-luck mascot.*
Below: *Driver and navigator were securely belted into Lincoln's slick seats. Huge fuel tank occupies rear seat area.*

1954 LINCOLN CAPRI

people would stand in the roadway, inches from the cars, and try to touch them as they went by at 120 mph." Perhaps the wonder is that the carnage wasn't even worse.

Tragedy struck even closer to home as preparations were being made for the 1954 race. Working an AAA big car race at DuQuoin, Illinois, that year, Clay Smith was killed instantly when a race car spun out of control and careened into the pit. Stroppe was stunned, for Clay, in addition to being his business partner, was Bill's best friend. The question became, could the Lincoln team recover?

It could, and did, although things were never again quite the same. A full team of six Lincolns appeared under the Ford Motor Company banner, along with two Fords. Stroppe, already bowed down by grief over the death of his friend, was worried about the risks posed by the race's ever-increasing speeds. Four drivers and co-pilots were killed in practice. The omens were not good. Several changes characterized the 1954 contest. For one thing, the term "stock" was more closely defined than before, with the result that solid valve lifters could no longer be substituted for the factory-installed hydraulics. As matters developed, however, the change made no appreciable difference in the cars' performance. To make sure that no unauthorized modifications were made, all cars were impounded about three weeks before the race commenced. "I don't think there has ever been a race that was so tightly controlled," Bill Stroppe recalled in a recent conversation with this writer.

Other changes for 1954 included the use of tubeless racing tires, and the addition of a small European stock car class. Meanwhile, at Lincoln an important modification was made in the factory specifications: Ribbed, 12-inch brake drums replaced the previous 11-inch, plain type, and the lining surface was increased from 202.3 to 220.1 square inches, a difference of nearly nine percent.

But the luck of the Lincoln fleet had run out. Four of the six company-sponsored cars fell by the wayside on the very first leg of the race, leaving only Bill Vukovich and Walt Faulkner to represent the factory team. Within the first 72 miles Leeuw Murphy's engine blew, Jack McGrath's car went off the road and Chuck Stevenson burned a piston. Then toward the end of the first leg Johnny Mantz crashed off the road. Nor was that the end of the bad news. On the second day of the race Vukovich spun out and went over a cliff. Of the

1954

Almost any way you look at it, 1954 has to be considered a landmark year.

Well, maybe not in the automobile industry, for with the exception of the senior General Motors cars, the '54's were essentially carry-over models, displaying only minor differences from their predecessors. But consider what was happening elsewhere:

• The United States Supreme Court, in a rare, unanimous decision, declared racial segregation in the public schools to be unconstitutional.

• The Senate, in an almost unprecedented action, censured Senator Joseph McCarthy for the smear tactics he had employed as head of an investigating subcommittee. McCarthy's once-powerful influence faded rapidly thereafter, and by 1957 he was dead.

• The now-familiar controversy over the connection between cigarette-smoking and lung cancer erupted.

• And the United States launched the *Nautilus,* the world's first nuclear-powered submarine.

Still, taken all in all it was a tranquil time. The Korean War was behind us, and hardly any of us could have found Vietnam on the map. The economy was prospering, and Americans were content.

It was a prolific year for writers of fiction. Irving Stone gave us *Love Is Eternal,* a bio-

graphical novel based on the life of Mary Todd Lincoln. From the ever-popular Daphne DuMaurier came the thriller, *Mary Anne.* Mac Hyman amused us with *No Time for Sergeants,* and A.J. Cronin followed his many earlier successes with *Beyond This Place.* William Faulkner's *A Fable* would receive the Pulitzer Prize for fiction in 1955, but it was Lloyd C. Douglas's 1953 novel *The Robe* that continued to head the best-seller list.

Hollywood's top money-maker that year was *White Christmas,* starring Bing Crosby and Danny Kaye. Other notable films included *The Caine Mutiny,* with Humphrey Bogart; *The Glenn Miller Story,* with Jimmy Stewart and June Allyson; *Magnificent Obsession,* with Jane Wyman and Rock Hudson; and a re-make of 1938's *A Star Is Born,* this time featuring Judy Garland and James Mason.

On Broadway, two outstanding musicals came to the end of their long runs: *South Pacific,* after 1,925 performances; and *The King and I,* after having been staged 1,246 times. Other Broadway hits included *Witness for the Prosecution, Caine Mutiny Court Martial, The Saint of Bleecker Street,* and the rollicking musical, *The Pajama Game.*

Meanwhile, popularized by band leader Perez Prado, the Cuban mambo had become the latest dance craze.

six factory-sponsored drivers, only Walt Faulkner remained in the contest.

Fortunately, Ray Crawford and his co-pilot, Enrique "Ricky" Iglesias, were hanging tough. Exactly how the two of them communicated is not entirely clear, for Iglesias's English was extremely limited. But Ricky had other talents, not the least of which was the fact that he was a highly skilled mechanic. Crawford, who was not a mechanic, turned that responsibility over entirely to his co-pilot. According to Bill Stroppe, he was probably the only driver in the race to do so.

Crawford hadn't had any luck to speak of in the four previous races, but this time he was doing everything right. In the end his Lincoln, Car Number 149, took first place among the large stockers, averaging 92.22 miles an hour. Right behind him was the factory-sponsored car driven by Walt Faulkner, with an average speed of 92.09 mph. For the third year in a row, a Lincoln had won its class in the Carrera Panamericana.

Whether Lincoln could have repeated its victorious performance in 1955 will forever be open to question, for the restyled rear end of that year's model tended to form a vacuum, handicapping the new Lincoln's top speed to some extent. The issue became irrelevant, however, when the Mexican government cancelled the event, citing too many casualties (eight deaths, all told, during the 1954 race). Other racing deaths also contributed to public pressure to put an end to the slaughter. Bill Vukovich, a popular favorite wherever he raced, was killed that year at Indianapolis, and at LeMans a crash had taken 80 lives. For a time there were rumors that automobile racing might be banned altogether.

Above: *Crossed Mexican and U.S. flags symbolize international flavor of the challenging race.* **Below:** *Car looks nearly stock up front.*

Driving Impressions

Following its victory in the Carrera Panamericana, Ray Crawford's winning Lincoln, a Capri coupe, was returned to Detroit and its engine removed. It came into the possession of Andy Hotten, a private contractor who did custom work for the Ford Motor Company, and Hotten stored it for many years.

Then in the late 1960s, Car Number 149 was acquired by the Harrah Automobile Collection. Harrah's turned the car over once again to Bill Stroppe, who installed a replacement engine and returned the car to the mechanical condition in which it had been raced, nearly 15 years earlier. Cosmetic work was done in the Harrah shops, so that the Lincoln looked, as well as ran, just as it had at the start of the 1954 race.

Thanks to its donation by Holiday

1954 LINCOLN CAPRI

Above: The grueling route traversed nearly the entire length of Mexico. **Below:** Rugged Lincoln V-8 carried Crawford through the race at better than 92 mph average!

Officially Sponsored by Comité Nacional de la Carrera Panamericana, A.C. Nov. 19-23, 1954

Inns, successor to Harrah's, the winning 1954 road race Lincoln is on display at the National Automobile Museum in Reno. Through the courtesy of Chuck Hilton, the museum's executive director, and with the help of Master Technician Bob MacMillan and automotive technician Rod Lungstrom, *SIA* was able to take this record-breaking automobile out for a drive.

It's a noisy brute, for it has no muffler. It stands higher off the ground than your average, garden-variety Lincoln. It rides firmer, too, thanks to its special shocks and six-ply tires. (To learn how stock Lincolns of this vintage ride and handle, see the 1952 driveReport in *SIA* #73.)

But basically, this is the same Lincoln that Paul Woudenberg has described as the "finest road car of its time." The non-powered steering is precise, but rather heavy when the car is being parked. Still, it is probable that in 1954 very few of these cars were delivered without the optional power-assist.

Acceleration is very good for a heavy car of this vintage. *Motor Trend*, road-testing a stock '54 Lincoln, did the 0-60

number in a highly creditable 12.3 seconds. Brakes are excellent, requiring only light pedal pressure, thanks to the power-assist.

Taken all in all, it's a hell of an automobile. 🔧

Acknowledgments and Bibliography
Automotive Industries, *March 15, 1954; Bonsall, Thomas E.,* The Lincoln Motorcar; *Borgeson, Griff,* "Mexican Road Race," *Motor Life, February 1955; Dammann, George H. and James K. Wagner,* The Cars of Lincoln-Mercury; *Gunnell, John A. (ed.),* Standard Catalog of American Cars, 1946-1975; *Howley, Tim,* "A Look at the Postwar Lincolns," *Automobile Quarterly, Vol. XVII, No. 2; Langworth, Richard M.,* Encyclopedia of American Cars, 1940-1970; *Madigan, Tom,* Boss: The Bill Stroppe Story; *Woron, Walt,* "'54 Lincoln," *Motor Trend, August 1954; Woudenberg, Paul,* Lincoln & Continental: The Postwar Years.

Our Thanks to Ralph Dunwoodie, Sun Valley, Nevada; Bill Stroppe, Long Beach, California. Special thanks to the staff of the National Automobile Museum, Reno, Nevada. Especially: Charles C. "Chuck" Hilton, Executive Director; Bob McMillan, Master Technician; Rod Lungstrom, Automotive Technician; Janet Ross, Librarian.

BLUEPRINTS

1961 Lincoln
by Bob Hovorka

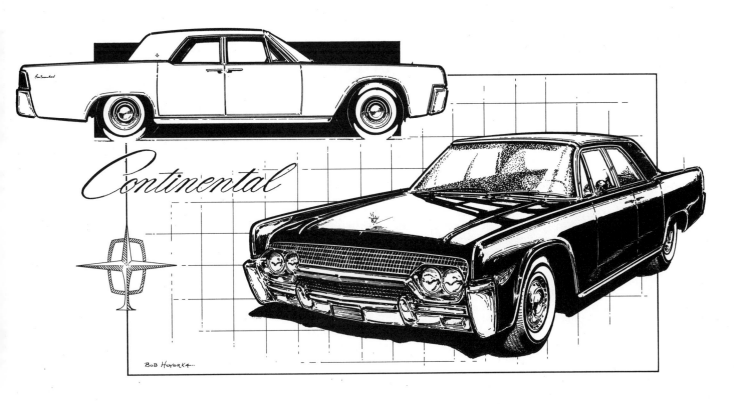

Continental

BoB Hovorka

BOTH Cadillac and Lincoln were new that year. The Buck Rogers style '59 Caddy had its towering tail fins toned down for 1960—for '61, it was completely revised. Lincoln kept its architecturally sculptured sheet metal from 1958 through 1960. For '61, it too was all new.

Shunning popular side chrome and body creases, the new Lincoln was as slab sided as a flat iron. Only a narrow ribbon of bright work topped its smooth fender line. Across the bottom, thin wheel arches connected by a narrow rocker molding were the only concession to glitter. In contrast, a garish grille contained over 500 intricate honeycomb cells. Compounding the contradiction, two elegant taillights that harkened back to the '56 Mark II were bridged by a phony rear grille.

However, there was one thing that wasn't phony: the quality built into every 1961 Lincoln. *Each* engine, for example, was run for three full hours, then partially torn down and inspected. A similar, though shorter, running test was made of each transmission. Every tenth body was pulled from the line and checked for major component fits. Once each day, a body was sent to a master

jig for thorough inspection; once each week, a new body was completely cut apart to check welds and tolerances. In addition, *every* car was actually road tested before it was shipped—not on some factory-controlled test loop, but in the real world, on public streets and highways. After correcting any imperfections turned up by the lengthy check list, the cars were subjected to a high pressure water test, then taken up a ramp where inspectors checked for underside oil leaks. After realigning the front end, the cars were finally deemed ready for delivery.

And just what kind of car did that high-paying customer get for over six thousand 1961 dollars? To start with, he got a car that was shorter and narrower than either Cadillac or Imperial, yet still weighed nearly two and a half tons. Powered by a 430-cubic-inch V-8, it would loaf all day at 80-plus miles per hour. Available as either a four-door pillared sedan or four-door convertible, all versions were branded "Continental." As the open-topped four-door reverted to an earlier era, so did its forward opening rear doors. They were oft labeled "suicide doors," and Lincoln took extra care to insure

they would not live up to their nickname. An automatic warning light notified the driver if any door was ajar. A vacuum system locked all four doors from the driver's seat.

Interiors basked in simple elegance. Dashboards featured a horizontal speedometer framed by two vertical pods that carried all necessary instrumentation. If the optional air conditioning system was ordered, a separate panel dropped down from the dashboard to reveal temperature controls. Seats were bench type and, of course, luxurious, with fold-down center arm rests giving a secure, semi-bucket feeling. A quick twist of the left side-mounted ignition switch started the big V-8. After the initial whirring, everything fell silent. With 465 foot pounds of torque at a mere 2,000 rpm, acceleration was not screeching, but rather like a giant catapult silently pressing you from behind.

Neither sports cars nor factory hot rods, Lincolns never garnered best handling or fastest accelerating awards. But if you wanted quiet luxury and outstanding dependability, they were nearly impossible to beat back then—and just about as hard to beat today! ☜

Lonesome Lincoln

The fascinating, forgotten Ford of 1955

By Tim Howley

Photography by David Gooley

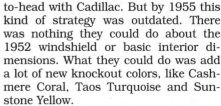

The 1955 Lincoln remains the most obscure and forgotten Lincoln of all time. Having been overshadowed by the Mexican Road Race models of 1952–'54 and the forthcoming 1956 models and Continental Mark II, it's the car that nobody seems to remember in the year that no car lover can forget.

It was the year of the new V-8 Chevrolet and Pontiac, Ford's new Thunderbird and Crown Victoria, and Chrysler's debut of Virgil Exner's exciting "Forward Look." But where was Lincoln? Without a lot of fanfare, Lincoln greatly reworked a then four-year-old body, and production fell from 36,993 to 27,222, as the public yawned. Buyers weren't about to gobble up anything without the wraparound windshield look. Lincoln fans knew that something really new and big was just around the corner; so they stayed out of the showrooms. Even the dean of all new car reporters, Tom McCahill, who swore on a pile of his dog's favorite bones that the 1955 Lincoln was the hottest ever, couldn't pull

his favorite make out of the mud.

As Laurel & Hardy might have said of the 1955 Lincoln, "A fine kettle of fish they've gotten themselves into." Cadillac had an all-new body with wraparound windshield in '54, Chrysler in '55. Packard also had a wraparound windshield and all-new outer skin in '55, yet poor Lincoln still had a 1952 body. The reason was that in those days the Ford Division was top priority; Lincoln really didn't get a lot of consideration until 1952. At that time it was planned there would be an all-new Lincoln body for 1956, in addition to the Continental Mark II. But the competition got the jump, and Lincoln was forced to do the best they could to make the Lincoln look new in '55 when it was still a '52 model at heart.

When the 1952 Lincoln was developed, Ford's corporate head of engineering, Earle S. MacPherson, insisted that its overall dimensions and engine size be essentially the same as the Olds 98. He felt that Lincoln was not in a strong enough marketing position to go head-

to-head with Cadillac. But by 1955 this kind of strategy was outdated. There was nothing they could do about the 1952 windshield or basic interior dimensions. What they could do was add a lot of new knockout colors, like Cashmere Coral, Taos Turquoise and Sunstone Yellow.

During 1955 Lincoln and Mercury were split to become two separate divisions. This was all a part of the attempted remaking of Ford to compete with GM on a division-to-division basis. At this same time the separate Edsel Division was formed. But in 1957, Lincoln and Mercury were folded back into one division.

The changes in Lincoln's looks for '55 were a redesigned grille, headlights, and considerable reworking of the rear fenders and taillights. The rear bumpers were reshaped, and dual exhausts now protruded in the rear. For the first time Lincoln had "frenched" headlights, a theme that would become more pronounced in the next few years. The Lin-

Originally published in Special Interest Autos #177, May-June 2000

coln name was again printed in chromed blocks on the front of the hood, as it had been in 1953. The rear fender shield was changed to be more pronounced, and the Lincoln Knight appeared on the hood and decklid ornaments. The idea of the 1955 styling revisions was to make the car look longer, but in actuality it was only .6 inches longer than the 1954. The body style lineup remained the same as 1952–54, but the standard series was renamed Custom from Cosmopolitan during the '54 model year. The upscale series remained the Capri.

The V-8's engine size was increased in 1955 from 317.5 cubic inches to 341, by enlarging the bores to 3.94 inches from 3.80. The 3.5-inch stroke remained, but the compression ratio was boosted to 8.5 from 8.0. Along with a new high-lift camshaft that had less overlap, a four-barrel carburetor with larger secondary barrels, a new air cleaner for easier breathing, and 10 percent larger intake passages, these changes increased

horsepower to 225 from 205, and torque to 332 lb. ft. at 2,500 rpm from 305. This gave smoother and faster acceleration and a smoother idle, but failed to help at the top-end or at wide-open throttle. To decrease tappet noise, Lincoln redesigned the hydraulic lifters with a higher oil reservoir. Other changes included standard dual exhausts, fan and water pump belts that were widened from 3/8-inch to 1/2-inch for longer wear and less stretch, a larger radiator to cool the bigger engine, and a rocker arm assembly that was now pressure-lubricated continuously rather than intermittently as in the past. Also, the rear axle was increased to 60 inches of tread width for better stability—the front remained at 58.5.

But the big news for 1955 was Lincoln's own new automatic transmission, replacing five years of GM's Hydra-Matic. Tom McCahill called it, "one of the smoothest, non-jerking automatic transmissions ever built," which it was.

The one-shot Multi-Luber lubrication

system was also available for the first time, allowing the driver to lubricate the chassis, suspension, and steering systems from a button located on the instrument panel that lit up green when pressed. It worked from a master cylinder in the engine bay that fed these parts via stainless steel tubing. Available as a factory item or dealer installed, it can easily be made to fit any ball-jointed Lincoln or Mercury from 1952 to 1957. However, two universal joint fittings still had to be lubricated by hand. Engine vacuum forces grease to the fittings for 225 grease jobs before renewal of the lubricant supply which is stored in a seven-ounce can placed upside down in the engine compartment, next to the radiator. Replacement canisters were available from the dealer. It was recommended that the owner operate the Multi-Luber once every 50 miles. There is an instant audible "thud" when it is put into action. The Multi-Luber quickly fell out of fashion because the lines tended to clog up in about three

For maximum public awareness, Lincolns were adorned with lots of badges and emblems.

years, and owners forgot to use them. They were replaced in the early sixties by extended lubrication intervals.

Power steering, power brakes, Multi-Luber, power windows, power seats, tinted glass, heater, air-conditioning, and whitewall tires all remained options, even on the Capri series. The Startmaster option automatically cranked up the engine if it stalled. Some of the rarer and now much sought-after options are three different types of spotlights, safety door locks, automatic starter, rear compartment draft deflectors, rear window wiper, windshield washer, traffic signal viewer, and illuminated auto compass.

Today, 45 years later, 1955 Lincolns are as obscure as collector cars as they were in the days of drive-ins, pink and turquoise bungalows, and Davy Crockett caps. You rarely see them at old car

WHAT TO PAY

Low	Avg.	High
$4,500	$9,000	$16,000

TOM'S TOYS

One of the foremost specialists on 1955 Lincolns is Tom Griffith of Madison, Wisconsin. Since buying his first '55 fifteen years ago, Tom

became so enamoured with this one-year-only beauty that he now owns 10 examples, from show queens to parts cars.

Due to his dedication to '55s, and his ample supply of parts, Tom is viewed by many as the guru of the '55 Lincoln. According to Tom, "When you live and breathe a single year and make of a particular car, people can't help but turn to you for guidance. They figure anyone that in love with a car must have acquired some accurate knowledge over the years, right? And that 341-inch V-8 with Ford's Turbo-Drive transmission will put all the wisecracks to rest pretty quickly. As far as restoring one, parts availability, cost, and patience rank

right up there, along with the difficulty in restoring the beast. Obviously these concerns apply to any classic car, but in the case of the '55 Lincoln, simply multiply by three. Since there are so few left, and the fact that repro parts are at a minimum, parts can be very expensive. Original factory accessories are worth their weight in gold, literally!"

To ensure that the '55 is judged correctly at club meets, Tom applied his knowledge and experience of owning ten of these cars, plus four months of research, and wrote a manual on authenticity. He states, "There are just some things about the production and manufacture of this car that are simply not in any original Lincoln body and chassis manual. Questions like 'What month was it built?' have a lot to do with the difference that can be found between one '55 and another. To own a '55 Lincoln, you must be obsessed, and hunting down parts becomes a life-long obsession. If you're not committed, buy something else...."

For those who are committed to the '55, a copy of Tom's very useful *Authenticity Manual* is a must. Just send $12.00 postpaid to Tom Griffith, 1818 Thackeray Road, Madison, WI 53704.

– *Richard A. Lentinello*

meets, even in the Lincoln & Continental Owner's Club. We had a hard time finding one in California for our driveReport, and in California, theoretically, you can find anything.

The car we eventually located is a mostly restored Palomino Buff and white Capri coupe owned by Frank Casaus of Northridge. He bought the car 12 years ago in North Hollywood. It was a solid, original, rust-free California car of undetermined mileage, and needed just about everything. Being a '55 Lincoln lover from way back, he went through the car thoroughly, but stopped short of a body-off restoration. Frank restored the car to be a driver, not a show car. This meant going through the engine and transmission, bodywork and repainting, rechroming, straightening the stainless trim, and lots of detailing. The seats were redone in vinyl to match the exterior colors. They were not redone in leather, which they were originally. The car looks beautiful and drives wonderfully. It has all of the usual options that came with the Capri—power steering, brakes, seats and windows, and AM radio. It has aftermarket A/C. The only rare option on this stunning car is a Multi-Luber.

Having owned both 1954 and 1955 Lincolns, I personally do not see any improvements in 1955 other than a major styling facelift, and new colors and interiors. The legendary road-race Lincoln handling is just a tad softer in 1955 than '54 or '56. It's obvious that Lincoln in '55 was trying desperately to compete with Cadillac when it wasn't ready to. In so doing, it created a car that competed poorly in the marketplace. On the plus side, the 1955 Lincoln is a fine automobile. Quality of construction and attention to detail is at a peak, and its boulevard ride is superb. And because the '55s are not as popular with collectors as earlier and later years, the prices tend to be lower. In short, you get a lot of car for your money when you buy a 1955 Lincoln.

While I am well aware that early Turbo-Drive transmissions were troublesome, I personally like them. A properly rebuilt 1955 Turbo-Drive is one of the quietest and smoothest transmissions of its time. You hardly notice the upshift, and shifting to low at higher speeds brings no jarring deceleration. Turbo-Drive is not as flexible as Hydra-Matics in the mountains, however. And I really like the kickdown feature. I don't see any improvement in this transmission in my own 1956 Lincoln, but there was plenty of improvement in the 1957 unit.

Here's what *Motor Trend* had to say about the 1955 Lincoln's roadability: "...continues to be a favorite on *MT*'s mountain test course. What you do with it depends on your intelligence and skill.

Rear-end styling was unique to the '55, and previewed the shape of the fins on the '57.

Everything about Lincoln reflects good taste

Wherever it goes, it does it without front-end mushiness, without uncontrolled sliding, without protest. Drifts evenly, gives warning of every movement. Turbo-Drive doesn't give immediate throttle response for power recovery, but the car tracks accurately, breaks traction gradually enough for easy steering control. Even at top speed, moves like it was built as a high-speed machine. No wander, no front-end float." Brakes were described as being nearly identical to the '54 at all speeds tested. Although hardly noted by *MT*, suspension improvements were minor and now included increased rear tread width of 60 inches, formerly the same as 58.5-inch front width.

Tom McCahill did not comment on the handling of the 1955 Lincoln when he road tested a Capri hardtop for *Mechanix Illustrated* for their March 1955 issue. Since he practically single handedly was responsible for keeping Lincoln on the map in those years, his rosy report was to be expected. Unfortunately he made the car appear a lot newer than it really was when he wrote, "How can you improve on a hole-in-one, score better than a knockout without killing, or bowl better than a 300 game? Making better out of best is the problem the Lincoln kids were confronted with in 1955. Since '53 this writer has rated Lincoln America's number one car. I see no reason to change my thinking. I have no doubt that the '56 Lincoln will be radically different in looks but in '55 the big changes are where they count, in the engine room and other functional points." He then went on to rattle off Lincoln's long list of mechanical improvements without commenting on the handling. Here's how he summed up the performance: "Zero to 60 averages 12 seconds on the nose, which is four-tenths of a second faster than '54, but the 0–30 time is two-tenths of a second slower at 4.6. At 70, however, the new

Lincoln is still moving away, taking 16.4 seconds, or eight-tenths of a second faster than last year's 17.2. In top speed this car, with its increased power but less overlapping cam, will not show any improvement over the '54, which isn't in the least bad at 110 plus. It is suspected by the writer, although I couldn't get any proof of this at this writing, that the new transmission sops up just a bit more horsepower at open throttle than the old four-speed Hydra-Matic."

It was high time Lincoln had its own automatic transmission, and unfortunate that Lincoln did not have an all-new body to go along with it. Turbo-Drive lowered the rear axle ratio for better fuel economy but not for better acceleration. The hydraulic part of this system made possible low-gear operation with a selector, while in the drive range, by simply jumping the throttle. Turbo-Drive had a kickdown feature, similar to the kickdown in overdrive. From a standing start, with the transmission in the drive range, you can

---

IN THE MOVIES

Ford put 1955 Lincolns in at least four motion pictures: *There's Always Tomorrow,* with Fred MacMurray and Barbara Stanwyck; *Rebel Without a Cause* and *Giant,* with James Dean; and *Picnic,* with William Holden and Kim Novak, which is the most famous.

William Holden portrays a drifter, who arrives by boxcar in a small Kansas town. Nick Adams is his old college buddy, whose father owns a '55 Lincoln Capri coupe. Adams has a pal, Cliff Robertson, who owns a Cashmere Coral '55 Lincoln convertible, and is engaged to Kim Novak. Novak is dazzled by Holden, and there's an unforgettable scene of them dancing in the moonlight to the movie's theme song, "Picnic." Holden dashes off in the '55 convertible with Novak. The car is not his to take, and he is accused of stealing the car. There are some good chase scenes, but the police never catch him. It's a good movie, one of the best of the period, with an all-star cast. If you're a 1955 Lincoln fan, watch it!

Elegant detail of blending C pillar with badge.

Frank Casaus restored the '55 for go, not show.

jump the throttle and it will wind up in low gear, only jumping to intermediate at around 35 mph. Keep your foot floored and stay in intermediate until you're going a full 75.

Lincolns in '54 won the Mexican Road Race for the third consecutive year, but just barely. There's no doubt that the '53–'54 Lincolns had the fastest straight-line acceleration and top speed in Mexico, the finest roadability of any car made in America, good brakes, controllable balance and an engine that was second to none.

Some years ago I asked the late Bill Stroppe how he thought Lincoln would have faired in the 1955 Mexican Road Race that was canceled by the Mexican government at the last moment. To my surprise I learned that Stroppe's crew would have run Mercurys in 1955, not Lincolns, and here's his reason. The tail

of the '55 was redesigned literally to "outfanny" Cadillac. Lincoln designers gave no thought to aerodynamics and Mexican Road Racing. When Bill Stroppe and his crew took some early production '55 Lincolns to the Bonneville Salt Flats they found that, contrary to what Tom McCahill reported, they were slower than the '54s. The rear body design with the big tail allowed the air to form a vacuum, slowing the car's high-speed acceleration and top speed. Anyway, it's all academic. The Mexican government, reviewing 1955 as a year of racing disasters, and reviewing their own previous problems of crowd control and closing off 2,000 miles of a main highway for five days, decided to call it quits.

There were also some other factors in making the 1955 Lincoln less competitive in racing than the 1954. With the

new Turbo-Drive transmission, the rear axle ratio went down from 3.31 to 3.07, except for cars equipped with A/C. Tom McCahill aside, some will argue that the '55 was slower than the '54. This is probably true and is supported by *Motor Trend* who reported these acceleration figures for 1954 and 1955.

	1955	1954
Standing 1/4 mile:	77 mph, 18.5 sec.	77 mph, 18.4 sec.
0-30	4.2 sec.	4.1
0-60	12.4	12.3
10-30	3.4	3.5
30-50	5.3	5.9
50-80	13.7	15.0
Top speed	104.1 mph	110.7 mph

Except for the '52 models, 1955 Lincolns are the most difficult to find today. The reason isn't simply that there were fewer produced than most other Lincolns in the fifties, but because it wasn't until very recently they were not looked upon as very collectible or worth saving. In retrospect, the car seems to be much more appreciated today than when it was new. These have been unsung cars for much too long, however demand is increasing.

Few body parts are interchangeable with the 1952–'54 cars except the doors, hood, and decklid. The headlight area on the front fenders is quite different from earlier years, and the rear fenders and taillights are completely different. Most exterior trim pieces are not interchangeable with the '54 model, except a few grille/front bumper parts. Wheel covers and hood ornaments are not the same as the '54s.

Oddly enough, the '55 trunk ornament/lock is the same as the '56. Most interior trim is interchangeable with earlier years, but seat and door panel patterns, fabrics and colors are much changed from the three earlier years. Instruments have different faces and backings, and the steering wheels are whiter.

1955 Lincolns have most of the same

AUTHOR'S TALE

In 1972 I owned a Taos Turquoise 1955 Lincoln for about a year. At the same time, I

owned a blue 1956 Lincoln convertible. The stupidest thing I ever did in my life with cars was to sell both of these fine cars. I paid $200 for the 1955, and $500 for the '56, and they

were both pretty nice, original cars. At the time, I lived in San Rafael, California. A man in nearby Corte Madera had the 1955 Lincoln. I approached him in a supermarket parking lot, and asked him if he wanted to sell it. He didn't, but he took my card. A few months later he called informing me he hit a tree, lost his driving privileges, and was ready to sell the Lincoln for $200. And that price included a garage full of parts. I found a right front fender and some trim parts, and had the bodywork done, including straightening the frame, for about $500. For another $200 or so I redid the heads. A year later I had so many cars that the '55 had to go.

This was a nice car, but I was unable to sell it for $800. In those days a '56 was worth about

twice that, but '55s were not very collectible. Eventually I found a buyer. Foolishly, I took a $300 down payment, and she agreed in writing to make monthly payments. Stupidly, again, I did not keep the title in my name. She made one or two payments and that was it. I was never able to collect. A year or so later she sold the car at a tidy profit. The car changed hands several times in California, always at a profit to somebody. The last I heard it went to Europe about 15 years ago. Today, this would be about a $20,000 car in the condition it was in 1973. Two years ago, in Houston, I came across another for $15,000, and that is the lowest price I have heard for a 1955 Lincoln convertible in recent years. Now, even the hardtops will bring that much. What was once a "dog" of a year has now turned into a very desirable year because of its rarity.

specifications

illustrations by Russell von Sauers, The Graphic Automobile Studio

© copyright 2000, Special Interest Autos

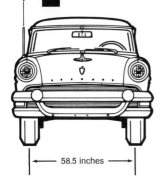
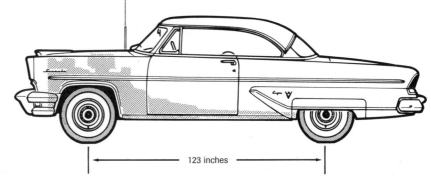

58.5 inches

123 inches

1955 Lincoln Capri Hardtop Coupe

Base price	$3,910
Standard equipment	Turbo-Drive automatic transmission
Options on dR car	Power steering, power brakes, power seats, power windows, vacuum antenna, AM radio, white sidewall tires, aftermarket A/C, Multi-Luber

ENGINE

Type	Overhead valve V-8
Bore x stroke	3.94 x 3.50 inches
Displacement	341 cubic inches
Horsepower @ rpm	160 @ 3,800 rpm
Taxable horsepower	49.68
Torque @ rpm	332 @ 2,500 rpm
Compression ratio	8.5:1
Pistons	Aluminum
Main bearings	5
Valve lifters	Hydraulic
Induction system	4-barrel downdraft carburetor
Lubrication system	Pressure
Electrical system	6-volt
Exhaust system	Dual

TRANSMISSION

Type	Turbo-Drive, 3-element torque converter with 3-speed planetary gear train

DIFFERENTIAL

Type	Hypoid, Hotchkiss drive
Ratio	3.07:1
Drive axles	Semi-floating

STEERING

Type	Worm and roller
Ratio	21.3:1
Turns lock-to-lock	4.25
Turning radius	45 feet, 9 inchies

BRAKES

Type	4-wheel hydraulic drums
Drum diameter	12 inches
Total swept area	207.54 square inches

CHASSIS & BODY

Frame type	Steel X-member
Body construction	Semi-unitized, all steel
Body style	Two-door hardtop

SUSPENSION

Front	Independent ball-joint with coil springs and hydraulic shock absorbers
Rear	Semi-elliptic leaf springs with hydraulic shock absorbers
Tires	8.00 x 15 4-ply whitewalls
Wheels	Pressed steel, drop center safety rims

WEIGHTS AND MEASURES

Wheelbase	123 inches
Overall length	215.6 inches
Overall width	77.6 inches
Overall height	62.7 inches
Front track	58.5 inches
Rear track	60 inches
Ground clearance	7.4 inches
Shipping weight	4,305 pounds

CAPACITIES

Crankcase	5 quarts, plus one quart when replacing filter cartridge
Cooling system	25.2 quarts
Fuel tank	20 gallons
Turbo-Drive	11 quarts
Differential	4 lb.

PERFORMANCE

Standing 1/4 mile	77 mph & 18.5 seconds
0-30	4.2 seconds
0-60	12.4 seconds
10-30	3.4 seconds
30-50	5.3 seconds
50-80	13.7 seconds
Top speed	104.1 mph

good and bad qualities as the 1952–'54 models. When in good operating condition they are reasonably economical, handle well, and are not difficult to repair; and nearly all mechanical components are easy to find through standard parts sources. These cars make really nice drivers, and are very adaptable to modern roads and driving conditions. In their day they were considered low and sleek. Now, they look so tall among all of today's jellybean cars that they are easy to find in shopping mall parking lots.

As far as problem areas go, look for worn-out suspensions, trouble with the Turbo-Drive transmission, and ruined exhaust systems. From 1955 until 1980 Lincoln used dual exhaust systems that were designed in such a way that mois-

Apart from an inherent valve lifter problem, the 160-hp 341-cu.in. V-8 is extremely smooth.

Options include power seats, windows, brakes and steering, vacuum antenna, and Multi-Luber.

Couch-like rear seat fits three adults.

Optimistic speedometer reads 130 mph.

ture collected in the pipes, mufflers, and resonators, thus rusting them out quickly, especially on seldom-used cars. The solution is a stainless steel exhaust system which, although expensive, is what many Fifties Lincoln collectors chose.

Especially troublesome with all '52–'57 Lincoln ohv V-8s are the hydraulic valve lifters, which are prone to collapsing or sticking. This is a problem inherent to the design of these engines. Even the best of additives do not seem to provide an effective solution. Disassemble the hydraulic lifter arms to be sure that all the tiny oil passages are clean; then clean out the oil return passages in the heads. Remove the oil pan and check

the oil pump screen to make sure that it's not clogged, and install a higher capacity oil pump. For whatever reason, Lincolns in this era tend to build up sludge faster than Cadillacs, Chryslers, and Packards. If you're buying a Fifties Lincoln of undetermined mileage, it's a good idea to remove the oil pan and clean out the sludge.

A real annoyance is using a 6-volt electrical system to turn over the 341-cu.in. engine. The battery is located in a box at the bottom of the firewall, passenger's side, and can only be accessed through the interior floor. Lincoln did it this way from 1952–'57; and lots of collectors today would like to get their hands on the engineer who dreamed

PRODUCTION

Body/Style Number	Factory Price	Shipping Weight	Production
Custom			
60C Sport coupe	$3,666	4,185	1,362
73A Sedan	$3,563	4,235	2,187
Capri			
60A Sport coupe	$3,910	4,305	11,462
73B Sedan	$3,752	4,245	10,724
76A Convertible	$4,072	4,415	1,487
Total Production			27,222

that up. Therefore you have to go into the interior, using a flashlight, to charge the battery, and probably bang your head against the firewall or instrument panel in order to check the battery water level. It also means spilling battery acid on the carpet when removing the battery. Those battery boxes down below the floorboards rusted out easily, and more than one Lincoln of this era dropped its battery on the driveway or, worse yet, on the highway. There's no solution to the battery location problem if you want to stay authentic. Going to an 8-volt battery or the heaviest duty 6-volt will help. Interstate Batteries are probably your best bet.

The rear spark plugs are nearly impossible to reach, but if you look under the fenders in back of the front wheels you will find a hole that will provide easy access to those two rear plugs. However, you must first remove the tire. Other items worth noting: In 1955 Lincoln changed the power steering box and its line connections; added a large fiberglass air deflector in front of the radiator; and, for whatever reason, midway through the year took the word "Lincoln" off the rear bumper, where it was stamped on.

At one time rebuilt and new parts were nearly impossible to get for fifties-era Lincolns. That has changed dramatically in recent years, to the point where almost everything is now being made for these cars, especially mechanical parts. Trim parts unique to '55 are the most difficult to find, and are expensive. The unique upholstery patterns are no longer being made, although old fabric may exist for the patient searcher. Joining both the Lincoln & Continental Owners Club and the Mexican Road Race Register is a must for the 1955 Lincoln restorer. ✆

1955 LINCOLN PREMIERE

Collectors associate the name Premiere with the 1956 Lincoln. The original Lincoln Premiere was a 1954 show car. It was such a dead ringer for the 1955 Lincoln that one wonders why it was put on the show circuit before the '55 model's introduction. This one-off car was a black hardtop with a mostly white and black interior. The rear section of the hardtop was covered with white vinyl, and the front section of the top was transparent tinted plastic, à la 1954 Ford Skyliner and Mercury Sun Valley. According to an article in the May-June 1954 issue of *Lincoln-Mercury Times*, "The Lincoln Premiere is a car for first-nighters and party-goers. The front half of the top is a solar panel of plastic material through which the occupant can see the bright lights of theater row. Inside, the occupants sit between a ceiling of white and a floor of black. Seat cushions are worsted broadcloth in gray, black and white stripes. Moldings are black leather and chrome. There's something new in lighting, too, with an arch of lights extending over the rear window." Who knows what happened to the Premiere? Most likely the factory destroyed it years ago. Although many of Ford's famous show cars from the fifties have turned up in recent years, this one has not.

For a fairly large car, its well-proportioned design makes it appear moderately compact.

MARILYN'S '55

It has been 39 years since the untimely and mysterious death of Marilyn Monroe. Yet the fragile image she created on the silver screen haunts us to this day. Like James Dean, Buddy Holly, and Elvis Presley, Marilyn remains one of the great icons of the fifties. Along with icons go cars. With James Dean it's the 1949 Mercury, with Elvis, pink Cadillacs, and with Marilyn it's a 1955 Lincoln Capri convertible in Cashmere Coral, a standard 1955 Lincoln color.

Marilyn's 1955 Lincoln is on display today in the Imperial Palace Collection in Las Vegas. While there seems to be no photographic record of her with the car when it was new, there is no doubt that it was her car. There is a tag on the firewall stating that it was built for Marilyn Monroe. The Imperial Palace has the original title in her name. George Barris clearly remembers customizing it for Marilyn by adding a few inches and a Continental kit to the already long tail.

We do not know how much she drove the car, or if she drove it at all. George Barris distinctly remembers that later he customized a circa 1959 Chrysler 300 convertible, which she kept until her death in 1962. Extended tails and Continental kits seem to have been a Marilyn Monroe trademark. It is believed that she did the same thing with an early fifties Cadillac convertible, leading collectors to think in later years that she owned a 1953 Cadillac Eldorado convertible. The color pink or a coral color may also have been Marilyn Monroe trademarks in her cars. Why Marilyn picked a 1955 Lincoln we do not know, but we suspect that it was given to her by Ford in order to gain publicity in a year of sagging Lincoln sales. This may have been the same convertible that William Holden drove in the motion picture *Picnic*, but we have no proof. Ford did that kind of thing with a few celebrities in those years. Or maybe it was a gift from an unknown admirer. Of all the unknown sides of Marilyn Monroe, her 1955 Lincoln is one of the most mysterious.

THE 1957 LINCOLN

AND THE LINCOLN FUTURA

by Tim Howley
photos by David Gooley

EVER since the first fin-tailed 1957 Lincoln hit dealer showrooms, arguments have raged on about 1957 versus 1956 Lincolns. Buyers contended then and collectors contend today that "They ruined it with the fins." William M. "Bill" Schmidt, the 1956 Lincoln stylist, told me time and time again, "I had nothing to do with the '57." Recent evidence suggests that Schmidt had a lot more to do with the '57 than he ever admitted. Collectors who shy away from '57s really don't understand. Underneath, the '56 and '57 are both pretty much the same car, although the '57 has significant mechanical and production improvements.

The 1956-57 Lincoln project began in 1952, about the same time that Ford decided to create the Continental Mark II and set up a separate division to produce it. During the 1952-55 period, Lincoln was not going directly up against Cadillac. The target market was the

Olds 98 and Buick Roadmaster. Ford Corporate's chief engineer at the time, Earl S. MacPherson, was convinced that Lincoln had no business going head-to-head against Cadillac. Sales for models of these years convinced top level Ford executives that MacPherson was going down the wrong road. Consequently Bill Schmidt's 1956 Lincoln styling exercise was selected for a $100 million attack on Cadillac and the entire 200,000-plus luxury car market.

Bill Schmidt told the story time and time again, and it's still worth repeating. "We felt that MacPherson's direction was all wrong. So we went behind the blackboards in the studio and started modeling a full-sized car of our own. It was a

much longer car. One day we had a management meeting. During the lunch hour Ernest R. "Ernie" Breech [Henry Ford II's number two man] came into the studio and started poking around. He discovered the car and asked me what it was. I told him it was our thinking for a '56 Lincoln. He thought it was great. He went back into the meeting of 14 vice presidents, had me wheel in the car, and told them that was the way to go. MacPherson was against it. He gave all of the standard engineering reasons. It would require more horsepower, bigger brakes; it would be more expensive. But Mr. Breech said, 'No, this is the way we ought to go,' and Benson Ford said so, too, and so did everybody else in the room, and that was the way they went."

It was a very correct decision. The larger '56 actually handled and performed better than the '52-55 models. Production broke 50,000, which was about a 33 percent increase over the

Originally published in Special Interest Autos #136, Jul.-Aug. 1993

average of the previous four years. Buyers loved the understated '56 Lincoln design in a package that actually outsized Cadillac.

The design of the '56 Lincoln was tied very tightly with the Futura show car. Schmidt, an avid skin diver, tells the story best. "The original idea for these cars grew out of my observations made while skin-diving in the clear waters off the Florida Keys and the Bahamas. I was impressed by the graceful movements of the fish and their wonderful streamlining. One of the first designs I did was the Manta, inspired by the manta ray, and that one led directly to the '56 Lincoln. A close study of the mako shark, actually too close for comfort, resulted in the forward-thrusting headlamps. The Futura came out of this same underwater study. Before we did any of them I spent three weeks under water."

It was a single school of thought, literally. It resulted in the X-100 show car done by Elwood Engel and Joe Oros and the XL-500 done by Schmidt, the Mystere done by Bill Boyer and the Futura, again done by Schmidt. If you look at any Ford product which appeared in '55-56 you will see the fish influence, and this even includes the Thunderbird done by Frank Hershey, assisted by Bill Boyer, Damon Woods and several others.

In addition to the 1956 Lincoln, which got produced, and all the others which were shown, Schmidt worked on a very skilled blending of the Futura and the 1956 Lincoln. This appeared in the form of a quarter-size clay of a Town Car with an open chauffeur's compartment and sketches of a four-door landau. Both of these models carried the Futura fins. The Town Car carried the Futura's front end. These cars are quite obviously the inspiration for the '57 Lincoln (see *SIA* #60). The photos were provided to *SIA* from Schmidt's personal collection. When that issue of *SIA* came out, I called Bill Schmidt and asked him if he still denied having anything to do with the '57 Lincoln. His answer was, "Yep." When asked why these cars looked so much like the '57 Lincoln his answer was, "Tim, you're entitled to your own opinion; I prefer to disown the '57 Lincoln."

When Schmidt left for Studebaker-Packard in 1955, Johnny Najjar inherited the '57 facelift project. It was his very first assignment upon succeeding Schmidt as head of Lincoln-Mercury styling. Said Najjar, "Schmidt may have been forced to design the 1957 Lincoln under the influence of management, probably influenced by Elwood Engel who was sort of a roving stylist for all divisions. Schmidt left me with fins that were much higher than on the final product. [The factory called them 'cant-

Above: *Long, low '56 Lincoln profile looks even longer with '57's fins.* ***Below:*** *Lincoln's tall taillamps were certainly inspired by the Futura's treatment of these items.*

ed blades.'] I tried getting them down as far as I could. Well, I got them down as far as management would let me. If they had allowed it, I would have taken them down even more to be closer to the '56. Schmidt's rear bumpers wrapped all the way around to the wheel cutout which made the car appear shorter. I moved these bumpers back further for a longer appearance. Another problem was the headlights. The front of that car was lit up like a Christmas tree, and it was very difficult to work with as a stylist."

After conversations with Schmidt and later Najjar, here is what this author thinks happened. Schmidt wanted to do something along the lines of the cars shown in *SIA* #126 ("GM's Far-Out '59s"). Management forced him to design "canted blades" that stuck way up in the air. Schmidt got mad and resigned. It remained a very sensitive subject with him for the remainder of his career. Najjar took over. With their chief stylist walking out over the fins, Ford management decided maybe they should subdue them a bit, but not quite to the

extent of Schmidt's original proposal.

It was really a goofy time at Ford's top level. There was an endless series of meetings over the '57 Lincoln in which Ernie Breech browbeat Louis D. Crusoe, head of finance and organizational planning. Move a piece of trim up here; no, move it down there. The two men were like little kids, literally down on their hands and knees going over drawings. What emerged was a 1956 Lincoln with Quadra-Lites and fins, improved mechanically, but looking as though everybody including the cleaning lady had a hand in the styling. Supposedly, Crusoe walked out of the meeting shaking his head and muttering, "I don't have to take this #*%!." Not long after, he had a heart attack, and later was given early retirement. The public's reaction to the fins and Quadra-Lites: Production dropped from 50,288 in 1956 to 41,123 for 1957, and for 1958 Lincoln was to build a completely redone unitized car which performed even worse in the marketplace.

Horsepower for 1957 was up to 300 from 285, achieved mainly from an increase in the compression ratio from 9:1 to 10:1 and an improved Carter four-barrel carburetor. Another improvement, not adding directly to performance, was a filament air cleaner replacing the oil bath setup. Lincoln's Turbo-Drive transmission, introduced in 1955, was greatly improved with a 12-inch steel torque converter replacing the rather delicate aluminum unit. Stronger gears were used throughout. The radiator was larger than in 1956 to improve transmission cooling. A popular option was the Power-Directed limited-slip differential which prevents the car from being immobilized when one wheel is stuck in the snow. There were a number of subtle suspension improvements, and the frame was beefed up considerably in the Landau to increase body rigidity.

One of the most unusual features of the '57 Lincoln is its Quadra-Lite headlamps. A true dual headlamp setup was not legal in many states until 1958. With Quadra-Lites the top lamp is a true seven-inch unit with high and low

Above left: *Wheel covers are same as '56.* ***Above right:*** *Rear fender "airscoops" also came from Futura design.* ***Below:*** *Lincoln's semi-abstract starburst design appears on trunk lid.*

beams. The lower lamp is an auxiliary road lamp operated independently from a toggle switch only when the headlamps or parking lights are turned on. Essentially, the motorist has four lighting options: 1) low beams; 2) high beams; 3) high or low beams with or without the auxiliary lights; 4) auxiliary lights and parking lights only.

Perhaps the most exciting change was in the four-door models. The traditional four-door sedan with its tiny rear quar-

ter windows was replaced with a four-door without rear quarters. Although it had pillars, it looked like a hardtop. This car is a fairly faithful execution of what Bill Schmidt had done before he left Ford. In addition, there was a new "Landau," model, a four-door pillarless model, a truly beautiful automobile and a tough one for Schmidt to disown.

1957 Lincoln interiors were fabulous and came in an even wider choice of colors and patterns than the 1956 models. In the convertible, two leather seat choices were offered: button and biscuit like our driveReport car, or pleated. Seat surfaces were all leather, in two tones with buttons and biscuits, three tones with pleats. Bolsters, backs and door panels were high-grade vinyl. In the Premiere hardtops and sedans, button and biscuit seats were nylon inserts in leather. As an option you could have button and biscuit seats in leather or pleats in leather. Capri interiors were all fabric, but offered in twice as many fabrics and colors as in 1956.

Lincoln added quite a number of options for 1957 including power vent windows, electric door locks, improved Multi-Luber with an automatic cycling device, and the Power-Directed differential mentioned earlier. Factory advertising billed the '57 as the "most automatic car in the world."

At 224.6 inches overall, more than two inches longer than the '56, the '57 Lincoln was longer than anything in the industry including the Imperial. Whether you like the fins or not, you'll have to

The Original Lincoln Futura

In 1952 when he dreamed about it and in 1954 when he created it, the Futura was Bill Schmidt's ultimate work of "automotive fish art." It rode on a special chassis with a highly modified '55 Lincoln engine. The Futura was first done in clay and then plaster body casts were sent to Ghia in Turin, Italy, so that a car could be executed in steel. Along with the clay went the blueprints, detailed specifications, and Bill Schmidt. What came back to the states was mind boggling.

Benson Ford, who then headed the Lincoln-Mercury Division, called it "a $250,000 laboratory on wheels." He stated at the time, "We speak of the Futura as the 'car of tomorrow' because it embodies many advanced styling mechanical designs which we feel will be found in future production cars. We expect to gather a great deal of important engineering data from it and also test public reaction to its very advanced styling." Bill Schmidt recalled not long before he died, "We first had it on the Ed Sullivan Show, then on the Dave Garroway Show. Then Bill Ford and I drove it down Park Avenue and up to the Tavern on the Green. This was all just before the '56 Lincoln was announced. The '56 Lincoln and the Futura were both done about the same time and they did not want to show the Futura to the public too soon

because it was so similar to the '56 Lincoln. I think that the Futura trip to New York was one of the most exciting events in my styling career with Ford. I left right after that to go to Studebaker-Packard."

The Futura was almost 19 feet long but only 52.8 inches high. The wheelbase, at 126 inches, was the same as the '56 Lincoln. Its body was painted a dazzling white pearlescent, bordering on frost blue. The paint was made from the distillation of fish scales which gave it an iridescent quality. This was a fairly common color for Ford show cars at the time. But it was prohibitively expensive to put into production. The interior was done in matching pearlescent white leather and black.

The special 1955 Lincoln engine delivered 330 horsepower as opposed to 225 for a stock '55 Lincoln engine. The Lincoln Turbo-Drive transmission had push-button controls on the center pedestal armrest. Indicator lights, on the cowl in front of the driver, showed the gear being used. All gauges were contained within the center of the steering wheel. It was sort of a binnacle arrangement with the wheel revolving around the binnacle. A compass was mounted in front of the driver and a clock was mounted in front of the passenger.

A circular radio antenna combined with

an approach microphone mounted on the rear package tray picked up and amplified the sounds of cars approaching from behind. The windows did not roll down. To enter and exit the car you had to lift the canopy. Outside door handles were flush with the top of the doors. It was all operated electronically/hydraulically once you touched the door handles from outside or in. The top flipped up and the doors popped open. Hood and trunk also operated electronically/hydraulically.

Air scoops at the leading edge of the canted blades directed air into the air-conditioning system and also air-cooled the rear brakes. (In the 1957 Lincoln the air scoops are strictly ornamental.) An air intake in the top combined with an air intake and exhaust louvers behind the seats, provided fresh air for the driving compartment.

It was a fantastic creation, and the very epitome of Ford's advanced designs. The Futura was a sensation wherever it was shown. Unfortunately, it was Ford's policy to destroy all of them after a few years. As much as collectors bemoan the Batmobile, at least Barris saved the original from the crusher. Without the Batmobile for molds, Butts could never have built the Futura replica.

admit that they were far more subdued than the Chrysler offerings, and were tame compared to what Cadillac had in the wings for 1959. Any way you look at it, any where you drive it, the '57 Lincoln was a fabulous automobile. With it, Lincoln achieved an all-time high in quality control to date. This kind of quality would not be seen in Lincoln again until the sixties. In a separate body and frame car, it would not return to Lincoln until the 1969 Mark III.

The '57 Lincoln was best summed up by Tom McCahill who wrote in *Mechanix Illustrated*, "The car now boasts four headlights which give it the appearance from head-on of Paul Bunyan and his brother challenging you with over-and-under shotguns. The rear fins have been flared out and the taillights now remind you of a fire in a Gothic chapel. The long, uninterrupted hood line could easily serve as a picnic table for the Notre Dame football squad. Any way you slice it, this car is not quite as conservative in appearance as it was in '56, but the added garnishes do not detract from the overall dignity any more than a good custom-made striped shirt detracts from an expensive blue suit.

Driving Impressions

Our driveReport car is owned by Bob Knapp's Deer Park Winery and car collection near Escondido, California. The Winery and collection are open seven days a week and the grounds are a pop-

Busier headlamp cove treatment and a bit more chrome trim also differentiate '57 Lincolns from their immediate predecessors.

ular site for San Diego area car shows. The '59 Buick Electra 225 convertible in *SIA* #126 came from this collection.

This Lincoln Premiere convertible has quite a history. It comes from "Lincoln Acres," a collection of about 80 Lincolns which sat out in the San Diego sun for 20-plus years. The county finally went in and crushed most of them about a year ago, although they gave the owner quite some time to get rid of them beforehand. Many of these cars were '57s because that was one of the owner's favorite years. The owner, Bob Moeller, can only be described as a likable good old boy and ex-Navy man who just loved

old Lincolns but never had the financial resources to restore them or keep them out of sight of nosy neighbors and the long and nasty arm of the law. Bob Knapp got this convertible before Moeller's ruckus with the law began or the car might have been lost completely. It was a very rough car. Most collectors would have not attempted restoring it. It was one of those cars that needs another car to bring it back to life. Over a period of two years Bob's crew did a beautiful job, but were still not quite finished when we arrived to photograph and drive the car. This required a second trip back for the test drive.

William M. Schmidt, Fifties Lincoln-Mercury Stylist

William M. "Bill" Schmidt, who styled the 1956 Lincoln and the Lincoln Futura, but denied the 1957, joined Ford in 1940. He worked in early Ford styling under Edsel Ford and survived the 1943-45 shakeup to be appointed Lincoln-Mercury's first Chief Stylist in 1946. Since the 1949 Lincolns done by E.T. "Bob" Gregorie had already been completed, his first contributions were the 1950 and 1951 facelifts. The first Lincoln credited to him from scratch was the 1952 model, dictated by some very strict dimensions set down by Corporate Chief Engineer Earl S. MacPherson, to compete with the Olds 98. In 1952-53, Schmidt's styling talents came into full bloom with the Lincoln XL-500 show car and an assortment of "fish-inspired" creations including the 1956 Lincoln and the Lincoln Futura. All of these were done about the same time.

Schmidt never let his top design talents and position go to his head. He shunned Detroit style politics and was always quite modest about his achievements. He avoided conflicts with George Walker, Ernie Breech and Henry Ford II, which polished off quite a few others. But he contended that by the time they got into styling the 1957 Lincoln he was ready to move on. He moved on to Studebaker-Packard, where he and Dick Teague did the 1956 Packard

Predictor. In a last-ditch effort to save the Packard, James Nance seriously considered buying the 1956 Lincoln dies from Ford. Schmidt did some sketches; essentially it was 1956 Packard-style trim on a 1956 Lincoln with the Lincoln instrument panel and a new interior. That's as far as it ever got. Schmidt contended it was not his idea. After Studebaker-Packard he went over to Chrysler from 1957 to 1959, where he played a key role in designing many of

the Chrysler products of the early to mid-sixties. In 1959 he started his own design consulting firm, William M. Schmidt Design Associates, Harper Woods, Michigan. Bill Schmidt died quite suddenly of a heart attack at his winter home in Florida in February 1990. He was 68 years old. The design firm he founded is now headed by his son John.

Of Lincoln-Mercury styling in the fifties, Schmidt once said, "It was a very exciting time. Originally it was a fairly small group. Unrestricted by layers upon layers of management, it was able to carry out some pretty radical styling and advanced engineering plans. We started out with a real challenge and then let our imaginations soar. Unfortunately, by the mid-fifties things were starting to change, so I decided it was time to move on."

A fellow Ford stylist of the period, Bob Thomas, describes Schmidt thus: "Bill was quite a guy, and everybody at Ford liked him. He was one of those people who told it like it was, and he was just an incredibly outstanding stylist."

This author had first-hand knowledge of Schmidt's modesty. Not long before his death he told me, "I just don't understand why anybody can be so hooked on 1956 Lincolns!"

Any fine original or well restored 1957 Lincoln is a pleasure to drive. There is really no noticeable improvement in performance over the '56 despite the added horsepower, but there is improvement in handling over the '56, and the ride is just a bit softer. Lincoln engineers carefully tuned the '57 with slight changes in the spring rate and steering geometry, then tied it down with adjustable shock absorbers. The variable control (hard or soft) was on the shocks and had to be adjusted by the owner or dealer by getting under the car. Of course, today you can buy automatic, variable-control shocks, which will accomplish the same thing without all the under-car hassles of 1957.

Motor Trend's best times (with or without manual downshift) were 0-30 in 4.3 seconds (about 0.2 less than the '56), and 0-60 in 11.5 seconds (about the same as the '56). Their cruising speeds were again quite comparable to the '56, going from 30 to 50 in four seconds and 50 to 80 in 12.2 seconds. Commenting on roadability, *MT* wrote: "The ride remains soft but not mushy, and oscillation is conspicuous by its absence even over coordinated bumps that normally make a car act more like a bronco. We whipped this new Lincoln into really tight turns at spine-tingling speeds, and the only protest to be heard came from a set of screeching tires. Definite understeer was noted along with minimum body lean; the car goes into a four-wheel drift rather than just breaking loose at the rear end. When we purposely ran afoul of the basic laws of physics, the resultant skid was easily checked and directional control regained by a quick twist of the power-operated wheel. There appears to be a deliberate attempt to compromise between oversteer and understeer."

Braking is no better or worse than Cadillac's. At 4,676 pounds, a '57 Lin-

specifications

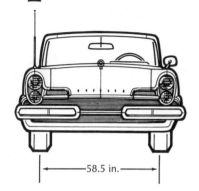

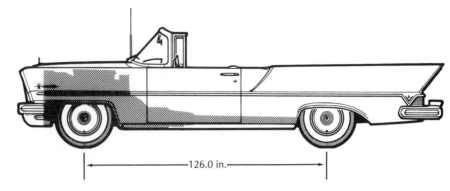

58.5 in.

126.0 in.

1957 Lincoln Premiere Convertible

Price when new	$5,381
Standard equipment	Power steering, power brakes, power windows, power seat, Turbo-Drive transmission, heater, radio

ENGINE

Type	Overhead-valve V-8
Bore x stroke	4.00 inches x 3.66 inches
Displacement	368 cubic inches
Compression ratio	10.0:1
Max. bhp @ rpm	300 @ 4,800
Max. torque @ rpm	415 @ 3,000
Induction system	Single 4-bbl carburetor with vacuum-operated secondary barrels
Exhaust system	Dual, with reverse-flow muffler and resonator
Electrical system	12-volt battery/coil

TRANSMISSION

Type	Fluid torque converter with 3-speed planetary gear train
Ratios: 1st	2.40:1
2nd	1.47:1
3rd	1.00:1
Reverse	2.00:1

DIFFERENTIAL

Type	Hotchkiss drive
Ratio	3.07:1 standard, 3.31:1 optional
Drive axles	Semi-floating

STEERING

Type	Saginaw recirculating ball, power assisted
Turns, lock to lock	3.3
Ratio	20.9:1
Turning circle	45 feet, 54 inches

BRAKES

Type	Hydraulic drum with power assist
Drum diameter	12 inches
Total swept area	207.54 inches

CHASSIS & BODY

Frame	Full-length boxed siderail with submerged X-member
Body construction	All-steel, welded
Body style	Two-door, 6-passenger convertible

SUSPENSION

Front	Independent coil, ball joint with telescopic, adjustable shock absorbers
Rear	8-leaf springs with telescopic, adjustable shock absorbers
Wheels	Five-lug steel disc
Tires	8.20 x 15

WEIGHTS AND MEASURES

Wheelbase	126 inches
Overall length	224.6 inches
Overall width	80 inches
Overall height	61 inches
Front track	58.5 inches
Rear track	60 inches
Ground clearance	6.8 inches
Shipping weight	4,676 pounds

CAPACITIES

Crankcase	5 quarts
Cooling system	25.25 quarts
Fuel tank	20 gallons

Opposite page top left: Starburst also replaced Lincoln's traditional knight on the hood. **Opposite page top right:** Rear seat cushion is almost vertical to clear the top. **Opposite page below:** Door panels were given colorful, contemporary design treatment. **Opposite page bottom:** For its size and weight, Lincoln's acceleration is very respectable. **This page:** "Quad" headlamps on '57s are foolers. Lower pair are auxiliary driving lamps.

THE LINCOLN FUTURA REPLICA

Above left: Original Futura became TV Batmobile, so Bob Butts built this replica.
Above right: Twin cockpit canopies were obviously inspired by jet fighters.

Above left: Clever combo of tach and speedo. Above right: Dash would cause horrid reflections both day and night. Below left: Where the '57's fender scoop began. Right: Now there are some proper fins!

We had a very unusual opportunity for photography with this 1957 Lincoln convertible. Only 40 miles away in El Cajon, California, is the only existing replica of the 1955 Lincoln Futura, whose fins inspired those on the '57 Lincoln. So SIA decided to bring the two cars together for some very unique photographs.

The original Futura was Ford's most widely publicized show car ever; its fate is a bitter pill for most collectors to swallow. After a fantastic reception on the show circuit, the beautiful pearlescent white Futura went to California to appear in the Glenn Ford and Debbie Reynolds movie, *It Started With a Kiss.* Normal Ford policy is to destroy these show cars after the party is over; somehow this time it didn't happen. The car just sat at MGM and finally went to George Barris for storage. It wasn't too long before Barris sued Ford for storage fees. Ford counter-sued Barris. Barris went to Dearborn and came back with legal possession of the Futura, another advanced design called the Beldone, a small Ford wagon, and a Mercury wagon. We do not know what happened to the wagons, but the Futura and the Beldone survive! Barris totally destroyed the originality of the Futura, turning it into the *Batmobile* for the popular sixties TV series, *Batman.* He built four more Batmobiles from it and sold them all, but to this day retains the original Futura/Batmobile.

Bob Butts owns a company called Fantasy Cars in El Cajon. For years he has been building cars for the movies, and consequently has a large number of Hollywood connections, including George Barris. In 1984 he bought the Beldone from Barris, and later Barris allowed him to take molds from the original Batmobile so that he could build Batmobile replicas in fiberglass. He built one and sold it, and plans to build more. Interestingly, Butts is a Futura enthusiast. He has researched the car for years and finally decided to use the Batmobile molds to build a Futura. The color is red with the red and black interior. He plans to market Futura body kits so that others can build Futuras with more modern Ford running gear. He admits it's a pretty specialized market because very few people understand what the Futura was all about; even knowledgeable Lincoln collectors have a limited awareness of it.

The Butts re-creation is very faithful in body specifications. The interior is about as close as he could come within a budget. It could very easily cost over a million dollars to re-create the Futura in steel today. The Butts Futura was done for under six figures. The first Butts Batmobile utilized a 1957 Lincoln frame and engine. This did not work out too well because the engine protrudes too high into the hood. This Futura was done with the lower profile 1962 Ford frame and engine, and this worked out quite well. The chassis was stretched five and a half inches at the outer ends, and the engine is a Ford 390. A second Butts Batmobile is being built on a 1971 Ford chassis with a Ford 351 Cleveland engine. Butts believes this is the best frame and engine combination for any future Futuras/ Batmobiles he may build. This Futura has its hood hinged at the cowl. The original factory Futura had its hood hinged at the front, and any future Butts Futuras will have cowl-hinged hoods. The instruments, mounted in the steering column, are motorcycle instruments. The doors are released from the underside of the car. The clear top is plexiglass. Butts has not been satisfied with the tops he has had molded to date and is having another one made. Because the top/windshield is plexiglass, the car cannot have windshield wipers. For this and other reasons the car cannot be made street legal in California, but it can be street legalized in several other states.

coln convertible is a lot of car to bring to a halt, even at 30 mph. Tom McCahill concluded otherwise when General Tire hired him to see if he could rip their new General Dual 90 tires off the wheels of a new '57 Lincoln Landau on the Ford Proving grounds. He could not, and the Lincoln brakes grooved a straight line down the roadway coming down from in excess of 100 mph.

The GM Saginaw power steering retains just enough road feel, and remains quite effortless when parking. The whole car seems really tied together. It's not any one thing but everything that makes the '57 Lincoln a pleasure to drive. The car has excellent stability in high cross winds and at high speeds. Shifting is quite smooth for a car of this era. A lot of its overall excellence had to be derived from the Continental Mark II, offered in 1956 and '57, but it would be hard to say exactly where or how this was being accomplished. Drive either a Mark II or a '57 Lincoln and you really experience state-of-the-art engineering at the time.

What we like most about the '57 Lincoln is the availability of good, solid cars at reasonable prices, now 36 years after they left the factory. It's partly a tribute to the overall quality and partly due to the fact that they do not command nearly the prices of the '56s. In September 1992, in Minneapolis, I could have bought a beautiful, 64,000-original-mile 1957 Lincoln convertible for $9,000 or best offer. While we were photographing this convertible, I learned of another one near by, 40,000 original miles, and the asking price was $15,000. Try to find a nice original '56 Lincoln convertible for sale today at any price. ᏚᎦ

Acknowledgements and Bibliography

1957 Lincoln drive reports, Car Life *and* Motor Trend, *November 1956; "McCahill Tests the '57 Lincoln,"* Mechanix Illustrated, *February 1957;* The Fords, An American Epic, *by Peter Collier and David Horowitz. Special thanks to Johnny Najjar, Sarasota, Florida, and the family of the late William M. Schmidt, Harper Woods, Michigan. Thanks also to Bob Thomas, San Diego, California; Bob Knapp and the staff at Deer Park; Bob Butts and the staff at Fantasy Cars, and the Lincoln & Continental Owners Club, PO Box 68308, Portland, Oregon 97268.*

Above: Lincoln V-8 added 15 bhp for '57. Left: Top quality materials are used throughout the interior. Below left: Window controls are on dashboard extension. Below right: Dash design is very close to '56 cars. Bottom left: Even with the canted fenders, Lincoln's lines remain understated compared to its contemporary competition. Bottom right: From this aspect rear fender treatment is very graceful.

1958 LINCOLN CONTINENTAL

BIGGER AND BETTER?

by Tim Howley
photos by David Gooley

THE late fifties is a fascinating era in automobile styling. It produced the ultimate in baroque automobile architecture, especially in the biggest American cars. We think of the 1959 Cadillac and 1957-59 Imperial as being the most bizarre examples.

But when you set them alongside the 1958 Lincoln Continental, and to a degree the 1959 and 1960 versions, they don't even begin to compare in terms of uniqueness of design. The 1958 Lincoln has been called the "Pink Pagoda Lincoln," a "Brontosaurus," by the late Alex Tremulis, "Cleopatra's barge," and even worse. What makes this car so unique and collectible today is that it is the largest unitized car ever built and it is totally novel in almost every other respect.

Coming right after the beautiful 1956 Lincoln Premiere and the classic 1956-57 Continental, the 1958 Lincoln is a "puzzlement," as Yul Brynner used to say. To understand this docile dragon you have to understand how the Ford Motor Company was thinking in its highest ivory towers at that time.

In 1955 there was a popular belief in Detroit that unitized was the wave of the future. Now unitized construction was nothing new in America. The Chrysler-Airflow and the Lincoln-Zephyr in the thirties were in a sense unitized. Actually, they were of a cage or "monocoque" construction with body frames welded to the chassis. The forties Nash and 1948 Hudson were built along the same engineering principles. When Lincoln broke ground for its new Wixom plant 15 miles northwest of Dearborn in 1955, they decided it was time to build Lincolns a new way, completely unitized. It was also decided the new four-passenger Thunderbirds, also to be unitized, would be built in the same plant. Nobody had ever built a car as large as a Lincoln with unitized construction before. Even the Thunderbird would be something of an experiment.

At the time Ben Mills was the head of the Lincoln Division and Earl S. MacPherson was corporate head of Ford engineering. They both had unitized construction foremost in their minds. Harley Copp was the chief engineer of the Continental Division which had developed the highly advanced perimeter frame for the 1956 Continental Mark II. He understood the potential problems with unitized construction in very large cars. First, he had concerns about the problems of noise vibrations. Copp knew that with a separate frame and body it was not too difficult to isolate the road shock and sounds from the passenger compartment. He also knew that while unitized construction was being done effectively with a number of small European makes, there might be serious structural problems building very large unitized cars.

Anyway, Copp and all wise engineers in his department were overridden by Henry Ford II, Ernie Breech, Ben Mills, Robert McNamara and Earl MacPherson. Their decision, however opposed by the engineers, did have an element of

Originally published in Special Interest Autos #157, Jan.-Feb. 1997

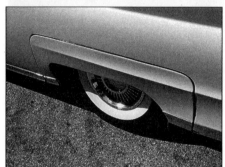

Top left: Deeply coved front fenders were part of Lincoln's new style for '58. Above left: Long, low skirts nearly covered the rear wheels. Above right: Massive shapes and strong horizontal lines made a huge car look even larger. Below: For '58, Continental went from being a separate nameplate to a model designation.

logic. It permitted overall height well below the five-foot mark, and this was accomplished without materially affecting interior room. The tradeoff was weight which came close to 5,000 pounds and over 5,000 pounds in the convertible. The weight was the result of extra body stiffening and extra sound deadening materials required in such a large unitized automobile. The new Lincoln turned out to be the heaviest and the longest built to date since World War II: 4,927 pounds in the convertible, 131-inch wheelbase and 229 inches overall for all models. But it was not the largest car ever built, or even the largest Lincoln. Many of the great Classics of the thirties, including Lincoln, were much larger. In fact, many of the Lincolns, Cadillacs, Oldsmobiles, Buicks and Imperials of the early seventies were longer.

The stylist in charge of the project was John Najjar who had been in Ford styling since 1936. (See sidebar, page 103.) Najjar was told explicitly by Ben Mills that the objective was to beat Cadillac. The new unitized type of construc-

tion dictated a new direction in big car styling. The interior dimensions had to exceed those of Cadillac. Later, so did the exterior dimensions. The new Lincoln could in no way look like a concession to the finny Cadillac with round surfaces and chrome laid on with a trowel. Nor could it follow the Chrysler wedge shape. Management said that the new Lincoln had to exude "fresh individuality," whatever that meant. The car was essentially a cube, and Najjar filled out the cube so completely that the driver could easily see all four corners of the car.

The original inspiration for the 1958 Lincoln was a quarter-size, remote controlled model called "La Tosca," created by Alex Tremulis, head of Ford Advanced Design. Its canted blades forming a fender peak running the entire length of the car and wild rear end theme were the beginnings of the 1958 Lincoln. (It is kind of amusing that Tremulis considered the 1958 Lincoln "just about the ugliest car ever built.") The scalloped front fender of a show car seen in London and Paris inspired the

unusual front fender well treatment. The reverse backlight from the Mercury Turnpike Cruiser was adopted for the Continental Mark III version. Three full-size clay models were created with a different design proposal on each side of the models.

The Continental Mark III was to have been a separate program. In fact, John Reinhart designed a separate Mark Berline. In the end the Continental Division was disbanded and the Continental became a full dress version of the Lincoln body. Reinhart tried to put a Continental kit on the rear, but it never worked. The proportions were all wrong.

At first the wheelbase was set at 126-128 inches, close to that of 1956. But soon it grew to 131 inches, to outdistance Cadillac. The main challenge was how to make an all-new Lincoln in an all-new plant with all new people on a record wheelbase for a unitized car... and in record time.

The roof added much needed stiffness and support. The convertible without a roof was a monumental problem. Obviously, the strength had to come from

1958 Lincoln

underneath. This created near insurmountable engineering problems, as Harley Copp had earlier feared. The more reinforcements they put under the car the more the weight shot up.

While prototypes of the Thunderbird, developed at the same time, were quite satisfactory, the Lincolns were buckling. "Weld effectiveness was only 60 to 70 percent. It was John Dykstra, vice president in charge of quality control for all Ford products, who was able to bring weld effectiveness up to 90 percent, making the 1958 Lincoln a production reality. This 90-percent figure meant that if the car required 100 spot welds, then 10 percent more had to be added. A lot of reinforcement was added to the early engineering versions, and the total weight of the cars soon got up close to 5,000 pounds, as Harley Copp had predicted.

While Earl MacPherson was one of the major proponents for unitized construction in the 1958 Lincoln, he was not in favor of employing the current version of his own MacPherson strut front suspension on these very large cars. Instead they went to the more conventional short and long arm suspension and four coil springs all around. The reason for the rear coils was to accommodate air-suspension, which never did make it into production on the Lincoln or Thunderbird. Two hundred Fords were equipped with air-bags, and a few Mercury prototypes had them. Even though Ford had an air-suspension system superior to GM's, they were afraid to lay it on the public because there were just too many problems that seemed insurmountable.

Up until the nineties, this was the most completely new Lincoln ever built; body, suspension, and engine were completely changed from 1957.

The engine was the famous 430 V-8 which was used by Lincoln through 1965. (See sidebar, below.) In 1958, this was the largest displacement of any American production car engine. This engine had a 10.5:1 compression ratio and a Holley 4150 four-barrel carburetor. It developed 375 horsepower at 4,800 rpm. (Little known is the Mercury Marauder three two-barrel carburetor dealer option which raised the horsepower from 375 to 400.) The horsepower rating was lowered to 350 in 1959 and 315 in 1960.

The front suspension was much like what Lincoln had been using since it introduced ball-joint front suspension to American cars in 1952, but unitized con-

The Lincoln 430 Engine

The 430 was the only engine that Lincoln offered from 1958 through 1965. This engine had a number of advantages over 1952-57 engines. These included placing the combustion chambers in the block instead of the heads, self adjusting valves for the first time in any Ford product, three-stage cooling system for faster warmup, and fully water-jacketed intake manifolds which kept the fuel mixture more stable and uniform than previously. Other advances in this engine were greatly improved intake and exhaust valving. This in conjunction with redesigned intake and exhaust manifolding resulted in significantly better engine breathing.

Concerning the combustion chambers, the top surface of the block on each bank of cylinders is cut at a 10-degree angle, not perpendicular to the bore as was standard practice. Heads were machined flat across, instead of having cast-in chambers. The result was a fully machined, wedge-type combustion chamber — achieved much more economically than was possible with chambers cast in the heads and then sent through a separate, expensive machining process. The primary advantage of all this, in addition to production cost savings, was improved combustion.

Despite its increased displacement, this new engine is actually 17 pounds lighter than the 368-cubic-inch V-8 used in 1956 and 1957. It is also one inch lower in height. Anybody who ever tried getting at the spark plugs of the 1952–57 Lincoln engine had to be pleased with the new plug locations on top of the exhaust manifolds instead of under them. This was not, however, the ideal V-8 by late fifties standards. The fuel pump was in a bizarre location, on top of the engine at the forward end, and the water pump, while in the traditional location, was extremely difficult to replace.

Mercury offered the 430 engine as standard equipment on the Park Lane in 1958 and 1959 and on the Parklane, Montclair and Colony Park in 1960. A shorter stroked, 383-c.i.d. version was offered on other Mercurys during these same years. The Edsel 410 and 361 also utilized the Lincoln 430 block with less cubic inch displacements.

The 410 was the standard engine for the Edsel Corsair and Citation in 1958 and was optional for all Edsel engines in 1959. The 361, which was the smallest version of the 430 ever developed, was the standard engine on the Edsel Ranger and Pacer in 1958 only. The 1958 Ford 352 and 332, while not the same block, were quite similar to the Lincoln 430. It could justly be argued that the Lincoln 430 provided the basis of the fine Total Performance Ford engines of the sixties.

*Facing page, left: Canted bumpers follow angle of headlamps. **Right:** Quad lamps first appeared on Lincolns in '58. **This page, top left:** Hood ornament was update on Continental Mark II's design. **Above left:** Reverse slant rear window was exclusive to Mark IIIs among Lincolns. **Center:** Rear fenders were capped by chromed accents. **Right:** Lincoln shield gave finishing touch to rear fenders.*

struction dictated many design changes. The coil springs now sat in underbody pockets and there was complete redesigning of transverse arms and stabilizer bar. The rear suspension was now coil type, not parallel leaf springs. The rear suspension system now consisted of two trailing arms, two coil springs and shock absorbers and two compression bumpers. The trailing arms were tied to one of the underbody crossmembers at the front and to the rear axle housing at the rear. They curved outward and

extended underneath the axle where they were attached to the axle housing through rubber insulators.

The 1958 Lincoln stands as the most unique car that Lincoln ever built. Its 1959 and 1960 versions, which carry the same dimensions and same general styling theme, are quite subdued. Some people contend incorrectly that these are Continentals. They are not. The true Continental was built for 1956 and 1957 only by the separate Continental Division. The only place the name Lin-

coln appears on these cars is on the windshield wiper bottle! The 1958-60 Continentals are in truth Lincoln Continentals because they were built by the Lincoln Division. The separate Continental Division was disbanded in 1958.

However, these 1958-60 Lincoln Continentals are correctly named the Marks III, IV and V, not to be confused with the same Mark nomenclature of the late sixties and early seventies. In addition to the Marks, there was the lower-priced Premiere series and the very low-end

1959 and 1960 Models

After 1958, the primary stylist, John Najjar, had nothing more to do with the series. The job of the 1959 faceleft went to Don DeLaRossa. His task was to make a very unconventional car look as conventional as possible. Unfortunately, a lot of the car's originality was lost in the process. The most noticeable change was toning down the car's extreme concave scallops around the front wheel wells. They were reduced to a crease that ran into the front doors. The Lincoln grille now had its narrow horizontal bars accented with strong verticals. The Lincoln Continental grille retained its distinctive mesh design. Both grilles were integrated into the slanting quad headlights. Front bumper ends were completely changed, but were no less pronounced. Back bumpers remained the same with the large oval chromed area that framed the taillights. On the Lincoln Continental, the six round taillights were exchanged for rectangular "pods." The two Lincoln taillights were also changed. A very subtle but interesting design change on all models was the addition of a stainless steel strip to the very end of the rear fenders, just a hint of fins. The rear coil springs were retained. The horse-

power went down from 375 to 350 at 4,400 via a compression ratio drop to 10:l and a Carter AFB-2853S four-barrel carburetor. There were a great number of body improvements, most of them in the way of more structural reinforcement, better noise insulation from the interior and better engine mounting and balancing.

The 1958 model lineup was continued for 1959 and 1960 with one important addition. Hess and Eisenhart turned out in very limited numbers a Formal Sedan or Town Car and Executive Limousine built out of four-door sedans. These cars had padded tops, unique rear window design and highly luxurious limousine interiors. One hundred twenty-seven of these unique Lincolns were turned out for 1959, 49 Limousines and 78 Formal Sedans and 170 for 1960, 34 Limousines and 136 Formal Sedans.

For 1960 there were even more changes, so many that no two body panels, not even the hoods, doors and trunk lids, are interchangeable between 1959 and 1960. Front bumpers were changed again. The front bumper lost its wings and the rear bumper was changed just enough that it is not interchangeable with earlier years. The oval

treatment above the rear bumper was changed to a rectangular design. The grilles and all trim pieces changed again. The biggest change was the instrument panel. Najjar's "television screen" instrument panel was sacrificed for four pods containing the main instruments and the heater/air-conditioner controls.

For 1960 the Lincoln finally returned to parallel-leaf rear suspension. This was accompanied by significant improvements in braking. Horsepower went down to 315 at 4,100 with a Carter ABD-2965S two-barrel carburetor and no further compression ratio reduction. There were more improvements in unitized construction and there was a totally redesigned rear engine mount. The Twin-Range Turbo-Drive transmission had several improvements. The unitized Lincoln, which earlier had developed a reputation as a real dog, was now a very fine automobile. It made no difference. Before the 1960 model ever hit the showrooms, Lincoln management was firmly convinced that they had made a terrible mistake. The 1961 Lincoln was very much Thunderbird inspired, and was a much smaller automobile.

specifications

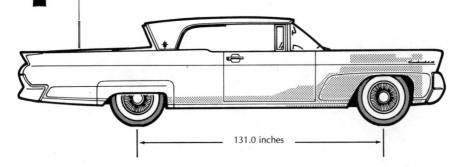

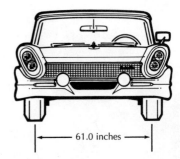

131.0 inches

61.0 inches

1958 Lincoln Continental Mark III two-door hardtop

Base price	$5,765
Price as equipped	$7,000, approximately
Options on this car	Power windows, power vent windows, 6-way seat, whitewall tires, air-conditioner, leather seats, automatic headlamp dimmer, tinted glass, power trunk release

ENGINE

Bore x stroke	4.3 inches x 3.7 inches
Displacement	430 cubic inches
Compression ratio	10.5:1
Horsepower @ rpm	375 @ 4,800 rpm
Torque @ rpm	490 @ 3,100
Electrical system	12-volt battery/coil
Carburetion	Holley 4150 4-barrel
Exhaust system	Dual

TRANSMISSION

Type	Lincoln Turbo-Drive automatic transmission; single stage torque converter with 3-speed fully automatic planetary gear train
Gear ratios: 1st	2.37:1
2nd	1.48:1
3rd	1.00:1

DIFFERENTIAL

Type	Hotchkiss
Final drive ratio	2.87:1 standard; 3.07 with air conditioning
Drive axles	Semi-floating

STEERING

Type	Recirculating ball, power assisted
Turns lock-to-lock	3.44
Steering ratio	19.73:1
Turning diameter	43 feet, 6 inches

BRAKES

Type	4-wheel internal hydraulic drums, power assisted
Drum diameter	11 inches
Brake lining area	297.6 square inches

CHASSIS & BODY

Construction	Unitized
Body style	2-door hardtop

SUSPENSION

Front	Independent, A-arms, coil springs, ball joints, link stabilizer bar, tubular hydraulic shock absorbers
Rear	coil springs with trailing arms, tubular hydraulic shock absorbers
Tires	9.00/14, 9.50/14 with air conditioning
Wheels	5-lug steel disc

WEIGHTS AND MEASURES

Wheelbase	131 inches
Overall length	229 inches
Overall width	80.1 inches
Overall height	57.5 inches
Front track	61 inches
Rear track	61 inches
Shipping weight	4,802 pounds

CAPACITIES

Crankcase	5 quarts
Cooling system	26 quarts
Fuel tank	23 gallons

FUEL CONSUMPTION

Best	13 mpg
Average	10.5 mpg

PERFORMANCE

Acceleration: 0-30 mph	3.8
0-45 mph	5.4 seconds
0-60 mph	9.0 seconds

Source: *Motor Life*, March 1958

Right: Rear deck looks longer than the hood on Mark III. ***Facing page, left:*** *Interior is also huge, with good visibility.* ***Right:*** *Like little brother Mercury, Conti's rear window opens for ventilation and to amaze friends and neighbors.*

1958 Lincoln

Capri series. All three series shared the same unitized body, suspension and engine. Standard on all three models was automatic transmission, power steering, power brakes, windshield washers and padded instrument panel. The Marks did not have any features other than these as standard equipment. Popular extras on all models were radio, air-conditioning, power windows, six-way power seat, whitewall tires, tinted glass, automatic headlight dimmer and power lubricator.

The difference was that only the Marks had the reverse slant rear window plus a distinctive mesh-type grille and trim and a much more luxurious interior. At the rear, the '58 Marks have three round lights set in each side of the grille-like insert above the rear bumper. Capris and Premieres have all rear lights mounted in a single wedge-shaped housing and have a different grillework insert. The rear bumper and massive frame over the bumper are the same for all models.

Initial reception to the 1958 Lincoln Continental and Lincoln was extremely promising. Luxury car buyers liked to see a Continental at half the list price of the 1956-57 models, and with a choice of four body styles. The Premieres listed for about $500 less than the Continentals, and the Capris for $1,000 less. These models did not sell nearly as well during the first few months. At first Continentals accounted for something like 75 percent of all 1958 sales. But things soon began to change. The 1958 Lincolns were introduced at the beginning of the Eisenhower recession which got a lot worse in the last months of 1957 and for nearly all of 1958. Spring 1958 was a disastrous time for all American makes. After 41,123 Lincolns had been produced for the 1957 model year, only 29,684 Lincolns and Lincoln Continentals were produced for 1958, that broke down to 17,134 Premieres and Capris and 12,550 Mark IIIs.

Driving Impressions

Our driveReport car is a pink (Autumn Rose) 1958 Lincoln Continental Mark III hardtop coupe. It is one of two 1958 Lincolns owned by Chris Trexler, of Los Angeles, California, who is stuck on 1958 cars. He also owns a 1958 Buick Limited, a 1958 Pontiac Bonneville and a 1958 Oldsmobile. His other 1958 Lincoln is a convertible.

Trexler is the second owner of the 1958 Lincoln hardtop. The first owners simply gave up on it and parked it after it broke down in 1969 returning from a trip to the Grand Canyon. They simply had it towed back home to San Bernardino, California, and parked it in a carport, but unfortunately they used it as a storage shed, which was the final fate of many 1958-60 Lincolns. For years they were cheaper than storage sheds—and they also have more room!

When Trexler bought the car he found that the only problem was the fuel pump. The car ran fine, although he had the automatic transmission rebuilt. With a little mechanical work, lots and lots of cleaning, new paint only on some panels and a rechromed front bumper, this fat Cinderella emerged beautifully from her cocoon of more than 20 years. At present the car has only 55,000 miles, which is believed to be original.

This car is an early production 1958, meaning that it does not have a low gear on the transmission detent, some trim around the windows on later models is missing, and there is no Continental script on the ash tray.

Trexler says it is the best, most reliable old car he has ever owned. It performs flawlessly, and the air-conditioner will freeze you out of the car. This one debunks everything you have ever heard about 1958 Lincolns being lemons. He claims he would not be afraid to hop in the car and drive it to New York. His only real complaint is the poor gas mileage.

Standing alongside one of these giants, one will instantly conclude that it must ride and handle like a Sherman tank. Driving a properly restored car like Trexler's will come as quite a shock. Lincolns of this period are a pleasure to drive; they handle every bit as well as

1958 Lincoln Production Figures

	Weight	Price	Production
Capri			
53A Four-door sedan	4,799	$4,951	1,184
57A Hardtop sedan, Landau	4,810	$4,951	3,084
63A Hardtop coupe	4,735	$4,803	2,591
Premiere			
53B Four-door sedan	4,802	$5,505	1,660
67B Hardtop sedan, Landau	4,798	$5,505	5,572
63B Hardtop coupe	4,734	$5,259	3,043
Continental Mark III			
54A Four-door sedan	4,888	$6,012	1,283
65A Hardtop coupe	4,802	$5,765	2,328
68A Convertible coupe	4,927	$6,223	3,048
75A Hardtop sedan, Landau	4,884	$6,012	5,891

1959 production was 15,780 Lincolns and 11,126 Lincoln Continentals. 1960 production was 13,734 Lincolns and 11,086 Lincoln Continentals.

1958 Lincoln

conventionally sized and constructed cars of the period and their performance is simply astonishing, as *Motor Life*, *Motor Trend* and *Road & Track* found in 1958.

Motor Life found it to be the first car weighing more than 5,000 pounds that was able to crack nine seconds in 0-60 mph tests! Several of these runs were clocked at 8.9 seconds, and the overall average was a flat nine. That was with a two-door hardtop like Trexler's car. In drive alone, *Motor Trend* attained a 0-60 time of 9.9 seconds, reducing it to 9.5 seconds using low and drive. *Road & Track* beat both these times with a convertible. Their 0-60 time was 8.7 seconds, and they attained a top speed of 116 mph.

One might think that they had the three two-barrel option, but a photo of the engine compartment would indicate that they did not.

Despite the unitized body, the interior of the car is extremely quiet at all speeds, a tribute to the work of Lincoln engineers in solving a very difficult problem with what is essentially a sounding box. Rubber insulators were used at all suspension attachment points. Various insulation materials were used extensively at critical areas.

But just being in these unusual cars takes some getting used to. You step down into the car, à la 1948-54 Hudson. The seats are enormously wide and the dash panel is moved way forward of the passengers. The broad, flat hood gives the impression of extreme width; this is somewhat of an illusion, but not entirely. The interior dimensions of a '58-60 Lincoln are considerably greater than 1956-57, although the 1958 is only 4.4 inches longer and virtually no wider than a '57.

The ride is very comfortable, soft and smooth over practically all surfaces. Because of the weird rear coil spring setup on the 1958 and '59 models, the cars are on the wallowy side and the rear ends will tend to break loose in hard turns. Ride was improved somewhat in 1959 and even more in 1960 when they went to parallel-leaf rear springs.

The Saginaw recirculating-ball power steering is very good, and surprisingly fast. The overall steering gear ratio is nearly 20:1, and less than 3.5 turns of the wheel are required to go from lock to lock. Curb-to-curb turning circle diameter was actually reduced from 1957. The turning circle for the test car was 43.6 feet, compared with 45.5 feet for 1957 Lincolns. Braking is not so good. Because of the change from 15-inch to 14-

1958 Lincoln Memories

I have written on the year 1958 before. That was a very special year year for me. It was the year I graduated from the University of Minnesota to the rude awakening that the world was not exactly waiting for me. It was a combination of a recession year and the fact that inexperienced journalists were about as popular as — well, 1958 Lincolns. One of the first 1958 cars I remember seeing in a showroom was a 1958 Lincoln Premiere hardtop coupe. I have always liked the hardtop coupes the best of any of them. In 1966, while living in Park Ridge, Illinois, I purchased a 1960 Lincoln Premiere coupe for $75. It was a very nice 50,000-mile car. But my wife hated it so much she made me get rid of it.

Very recently, now living in Escondido,

California, I had the opportunity to buy a 1958 Lincoln coupe for about $700. This was a very good running car, low mileage, mostly rust free, but needing paint, chrome and a completely new interior. The unique thing about this car is that 1958 was the only year that Lincoln built three different series, and this was the bottom end series with crank-up windows and manual seat adjustment. (Power windows and power seat were optional on all Lincolns in those years, but you rarely if ever saw a Premiere or Mark without them.) The interior of this model is about as Spartan as a 1958 Ford Custom. But again my wife reminded me that if I bought another 1958-60 vintage Lincoln I could move into it. At last report the car was still for sale.

inch wheels, brake drum diameter was reduced from 12 to 11 inches. To compensate, much wider drums and linings are being used. Both front and rear shoes are 3.5 inches wide. Width in 1957 was 2.5 inches at front, 2 inches rear. This increased effective lining area from 207.5 to 298 square inches, a 43 percent boost. With a car this large it just wasn't enough.

For those who like unique features and gadgets, this car is loaded with them. One feature we particularly like is the power-operated rear window. This window can be lowered as little or as much as you like for ventilation. It's great for clearing window fog in the cold or rain without turning on the heater or defroster. ᧡

Facing page, left: 430 V-8 was also used in top-line Edsels and later Continentals. **Top right:** Electric windows, including vents, were extra-cost option. **Right:** Even interior roof panels were lavishly detailed. **This page, left:** Dash was all new and ultra modern. **Right:** Rear is nearly as flashy as the front end.

Bibliography & Acknowledgments:

Road reports in Motor Trend, *October 1957;* Road & Track, *August 1958;* Motor Life, *March 1958;* Lincoln & Continental, The Postwar Years, *Paul R. Woudenberg;* "The 1958 Lincoln Story," Continental Comments, *national publication of the Lincoln & Continental Owners Club, Third Quarter, 1993;* Standard Catalog of Ford, 1903–1990, Krause Publications. Also see 1958 Lincoln driveReport in SIA #21, March–April, 1974.

Special thanks to Chris Trexler, Los Angeles, California, and retired Lincoln-Mercury stylist John Najjar, Sarasota, Florida.

Chief Stylist John Najjar tells the 1958 Lincoln Design Story

John Najjar had a long and distinguished career with Ford. He was one of Ford's first stylists, having come to Ford by way of the old trade school in 1936, and had worked under E.T. "Bob" Gregorie on the original 1939 Lincoln Continental. Some of his other credits included working with Elwood Engel on the 1952 Lincoln X-100 and working with Bill Schmidt on the 1955 Lincoln Futura. He had also worked with Elwood Engel on the Mercury XM-800 and the 1957 Mercury Turnpike Cruiser production car and show car. So he had a lot of exexprience working on "futuristic" cars when he was assigned the 1958 Lincoln project.

Najjar, now retired and living in Florida, tells his own story of the car:

"I was appointed chief stylist, Lincoln studio, in May 1955, reporting to Mr. G.W. Walker, V.P., and Elwood Engel of Styling, and Mr. Ben D. Mills, V.P. of the Lincoln Division. My charge as chief stylist of Lincoln was this: The facelift of the 1957 Lincoln was to be completed and an all-new 1958 Lincoln series was to be designed. A few months into the 1958 program the 1958 Lincoln Continental was added to my responsibilities.

"We created three full-size clay models for the 1958 Lincoln with a different design proposal on each side of the models. This gave us the opportunity to explore a variety of designs, giving vent to as many proposals. We, of course, soon narrowed the alternatives down while simultaneously creating the interior's instrumentation and seating. My Exterior Design Executive was L. D. Ash, the Interior and Advanced Executive was I. "Bud" Kaufman, and Arthur Miller was in charge of Color and Trim.

"Elwood Engel and I reviewed the small scale models in the Advanced Design Studio headed by Alex Tremulis. A model called 'LaTosca' appealed to us. It had canted blades forming the body sides, and a huge oval chrome ring housed the taillamps forming the rear end. We moved the model into the Lincoln studio and proceeded to use its salient features.

"In the fall of 1955 Mr. George Walker [corporate head of Ford styling] suggested that Elwood Engel and I accompany him on a tour of the Automobile Shows in England and France. While on tour, among other design features, we were impressed with the workout of a scalloped front fender on a show model. This led to the development of the front fender on the 1958 Lincoln.

"We purposely made the Lincoln look wide at the beltline. It formed the peak of the fenderline profile that ran the full length of the car. We nestled the greenhouse area [roof, windshield and backlite] between the two surfaces. This gave the driver the feeling that he was cradled between two pontoons. We had earlier created the reverse-tilt backlight [rear window] on the Mercury Turnpike Cruiser, both the production and show version, so it was carried to the Continental Mark III version of the Lincoln.

"With the advent of having to incorporate the Continental into the Lincoln series with the least number of new, unique body panels, it became mandatory to achieve maximum interchangeability. Hence the roof panel served both the Lincoln and the Lincoln Continental. The basic roof had a normal backlight, aft flowing profile, and was used on the Lincoln, while the Continental used the reverse slant backlite. The reverse backlight was emphasized by a chrome band along the trailing edge of the roof, tapering off onto the deck panel.

"On the convertibles, the reverse backlite was also used to provide deck space for the convertible top in 'down' position. The convertible top in 'down' position required that the deck panel covered it, but it couldn't be designed to collapse to a low 'stack'; so I designed two 'longitudinal nacelles' to hide the inverted roof rails. This permitted the height of the deck lid to be lowered to the same height as that of the sedan. It gave the car a very sleek, finished look when the top was down.

"I designed the instrument panel with a separate housing for the cluster. It looked like a television screen. It was supposed to be removable for repairs, but it never ended up that way. It was designed to be a separate housing with the belt rail sweeping in from the door panels, behind the instrument cluster housing, across the full width of the car at the base of the windshield.

"The most troublesome design area of the Lincoln appeared at the front fenders which canted inboard with the headlamps and the need to protect the sheet metal with the bumper. It ended up looking much like its nickname, 'dog bone,' but it met the need for the proper package protection.

"Considering the styling climate at the time, the 1958 Lincoln and Continental met the objectives of being a large, stately, luxurious vehicle with unique design and engineering features."

Looking back at the 1958 Lincoln in retrospect, Johnny Najjar says, "I see a model about once a year and I am shocked at the height of it and the length of it compared with the cars of today. It looks big. But taking that car and scaling about 1/10th off of it, making it 9/10ths of what it was, I think it would be a good car except for the scallops ahead of the front doors and the way the front bumper terminates at the wheel wells. I would also change the extreme slant of the headlights, I might verticalize them. But for being able to see the four points of the car from the driver's seat, which was one of the objectives of the product planner, it still achieved that, and was pretty good.

"I sure would like to do that car over again. I would get more of the '56 Lincoln theme, the straight line element, but we were too embued with fins, character and sculpture." When asked if, given the management atmosphere in 1955, he would have been allowed to retain more to the 1956 Lincoln theme, Najjar answered, "Oh, no, no, not really. It wasn't until '61 that we began to wake up and realize that we needed smooth-sided, simple cars."

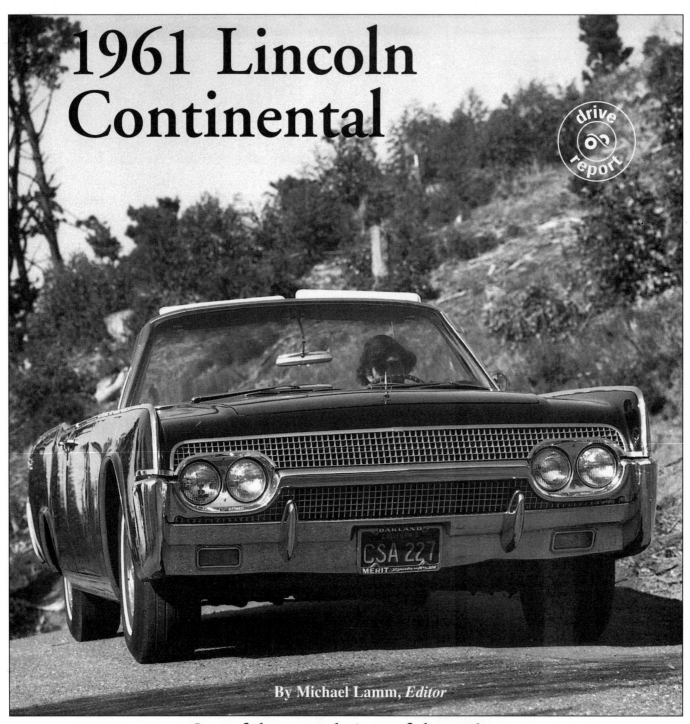

1961 Lincoln Continental

drive report

By Michael Lamm, *Editor*

One of the great designs of the 1960s,
it's more a car of this era—compact, elegant, sporting, finely wrought.

Originally published in Special Interest Autos #34, May-June 1976

The 1961 Lincoln Continental grew out of a Thunderbird design exercise—actually started life *as* a Thunderbird proposal—in Elwood P. Engel's "stiletto studio" down in the basement of Ford's design building. This was in August 1958.

They called it the stiletto studio because the room was long and narrow and so tight that it needed a big mirror along one wall to let visitors see the far sides of full-sized clay models.

What happened is recalled by Mr. Engel. "First of all, my boss was George Walker, and I had my own special projects studio. At the time, I was designing a Thunderbird. They wanted a T-Bird with a Continental flavor. This Thunderbird was pretty close to what the 1961 Continental eventually looked like, but in the Thunderbird proportions.

"Bob McNamara came down there one day, and Walker was with me, and McNamara—he always remained pretty style-conscious—he looked at it [the Thunderbird clay], and he said, 'I wonder what this would look like if it was a Continental.' He turned to me and said, 'How long would it take you to redo this [clay model] to the specifications of the lincoln?'

"'Well,' I said, 'just give me a couple of weeks,' and in those couple of weeks, the two-door Thunderbird was converted to the Lincoln package. And that's how it was bought [by management], hook, line, and sinker, with hardly any changes."

Ironically, Engel's studio, which had been established only 6-8 weeks earlier, had already "sold" management a completely different, much larger Lincoln just before McNamara decided to stretch the T-Bird proposal. Says Colin Neale, Engel's senior stylist at the time and now an executive interior designer at Chrysler, "So here we unsold a car we'd previously sold. It was at this point that we took on a panic timing."

As so often happens, the real work got done after regular working hours. Colin Neale gives a vivid account: "We were working eight hours a day, five hours a night, Saturdays, Sundays, everything. It was an explosive, wild time. The most productive periods were evenings. We'd attend to routine during the day, and everyone would work in a steady, slug-it-out way. Then we'd pop out for dinner, and we'd go back and really burn it up in the evening. It was a very exciting time, but very hard on family life."

The upstairs team, headed by Gene Bordinat and assisted by Don DeLaRossa, was going

nowhere fast. Part of the problem turned out to be the "package"—the specs and dimensions laid down by Management and Engineering for the 1961 Lincoln-to-be. That package called for roughly the same size and shape as the huge 1958-60 Lincolns. In retrospect, it appears that Ford Motor Co. didn't really know *what* it wanted the 1961 Lincoln to become.

Harold C. MacDonald, who acted as the '61 Continental's chief engineer, explains it this way. "You'll recall that the Lincoln had always been fairly large. The 1958-60 was one of the largest cars of all time. There was really the feeling around the company that this car was much too large. We felt, 'Can't we start over on a smaller, more compact sort of car?' Ford felt out of tune with the times."

So, with Bordinat's group going nowhere and with Management apparently not totally happy with Engel's "sold" proposal, McNamara went hot and heavy for the Thunderbird clay. Says Don DeLaRossa: "We were not making any headway upstairs…were just not hacking it, really. Elwood's design was done in a rather free atmosphere—free of all those factors that perhaps were thought by some to be very relevant. But once they had a chance to see this vehicle downstairs—such a complete turn-on—they bought it."

Management, then, suddenly abandoned the 1958-60 package dimensions and adopted a new set to accommodate the stiletto studio's converted Thunderbird. At first, no one really knew what the revised dimensions were. When I asked design analyst Robert M. (Bob) Thomas if there had been any particular problems in converting the T-Bird clay to Lincoln dimensions, he chuckled. "Yes," he told me, "one big one. When I phoned Engineering and asked them about package information [on the Thunderbird package], the only specifications they were concerned with was the structural area around the cowl—the width at the cowl and the front doors.

"You'll remember that back in the late '50s, we were designing cars that were wedge-shaped in plan view. So I remember talking to Elwood about the package and telling him we could really make a nice wedge design out of this…push it out at the back to make the rear extremely wide. The reason we wanted to do that was because the design of this Lincoln was going to follow the 1956 Mark II in respect to the greenhouse [roof section] perched on top of the body shape, with fenders cradling the greenhouse; that feeling.

"So that's the way we designed it, and we had

a real nice flat in there between the fender and greenhouse at the C-pillar—about 4-5 inches wide. It really looked super on the clay model.

"I can remember George Walker coming down into the studio. He used to call me Tommy, and he'd say, 'Tommy-boy, this looks pretty wide in the back. Are you on package?' And I said, 'Yeah, Mr. Walker, we're right on package.' But that was the only package point I had—just at the cowl; no overall width dimension. So we did it that way.

"And then the day before we were to show this model, Engineering came in and told us the overall width figure. We were five inches over package in the back! So we worked all night and pulled in the body sides—pulled them back into package—and I can remember Elwood saying to me around 3:30 in the morning, 'Why you son of a – – – – –, you're lucky you don't have to pay for all this overtime!' It's funny now, but it wasn't then."

There was no mad secrecy between the upstairs and downstairs studios. Each knew what the other was doing—it wasn't a locked-door situation. Nor was it a very fierce competition. As John Najjar comments, "It was a double-pronged effort to use the best talent available. Elwood knew what he wanted in both exterior and interior design. He kept insisting that he wanted a clean, pure car, and he directed us toward that objective." Colin Neale notes that discussions were so open between the studios that he specifically remembers comparisons of sketch styles being made.

Neale had responsibility for the rear aspect of the design. "I had some feeling for what I wanted the rear end to develop toward. It was one of those fixed ideas with me. An awful lot of designers have fixed ideas that they push in many varying forms. And I was very interested in the idea of the back of a car not looking like a solid trunk but looking extremely light and absolutely like a squashed tube! In other words, this was to be a non-solid rear end.

"This whole car's trying to look very light seemed to make it an appropriate vehicle. I just put together sketches with my normal distorted perspective, but I showed that these ideas were achievable by the proper sectioning of the bumper and the handling of these sections. I was then encouraged to put this on the clay. I did so, and it looked pretty neat.

"The original form was not quite the final form. In the original form, the side blades of the body also ended in very, very slimline vertical tubes that were the bumper guards. They even

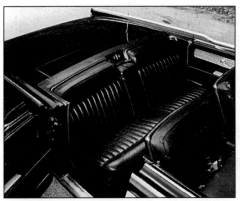

Continental's rear doors open from the front because of body's short coupling.

Big two-barrel 430 V-8 puts out plenty of torque, doesn't crowd engine room.

Hinges for convertible's front-opening decklid are concealed in rear grille.

had tiny round taillight reveals in the sides of these slimline chrome cuffs. So it started *from* that. But as we went along, after McNamara decided to make this the lincoln, we had to go directly to feasibility studies that took innovation and put it under the spotlight, which tended to cool some details. So the theme that started on the blade-mounted taillamps ultimately evolved into the classic old Mark II form."

The grille on the 1961 Continental was something that had "lain around on the shelf" for a long time. Neale worked on the front end, too, and notes, "I don't know that anyone would claim credit in any strong way for the theme, because that front end—the Eversharp razor design—had been around on many, many models. It was like pulling Design #47 off the shelf and saying, 'We'll put that on here.' The grille idea had been on T-Bird proposals and others, and it was just a matter of executing it with squares to make it look like a Continental."

The sheer, very clean sides and profile stretched beautifully into 4-door proportions. And the new 1961 Continental marked the first time anyone had topped off a car's entire beltline and fenders with bold chrome outlines. That simple touch heightened the striking effect of the unadorned, gently puffed sides.

The four doors had to open clamshell style because of the chassis' short coupling. Rear-hinged doors give better entry room. Originally, Engel's studio had hoped to eliminate the B-pillar altogether—go Lancia all the way and have the doors lock into floor rails and the roof. But that couldn't be worked out upstairs.

It was at this point that the design moved upstairs, and "upstairs" meant into Gene Bordinat's lincoln-Mercury studio. Here Bordinat, DeLaRossa, Najjar, and others worked to refine the car and get it ready for production. The body engineers came in, details of the 4-door convertible evolved, and everyone joined in a big, rushed push toward Wixom.

L. David Ash, who at that time was executive stylist of Lincoln-Mercury interiors (he's now director of Ford Motor Co.'s interior design office), talks about his role in the 1961 Lincoln's development: "....we were doing a top-of-the-line car, and the interior had to be appropriate and contemporary. The object was to give it an extreme distinction, an expensive look. The steering wheel got a lot of care and wasn't shared with any other car. Inlays on the door

trim panels and instrument cluster were genuine wood, laminated onto an aluminum carrier. The instruments themselves repeated the shape of the Lincoln compass—the Mark symbol, a truncated diamond. And the entire interior, especially with the clamshell doors, recalls maybe a smidgen of a classic look.

"I sometimes see those cars now, and it's one of the few that I really feel was done in a manner that gives it status. I've been in car design a long time, and I've had to do, one way or another, with a lot of cars, both interiors and exteriors. Some are okay, some were all right for the time but look kind of funny now. That one doesn't. It's becoming a classic, I believe."

The package was controversial then, and it probably always will be. Coming off the huge 1958-60 Lincoln, the 1961 Continental seems more a car of this generation—a compact luxury vehicle.

The '61 Conti's 123-inch wheelbase marked a radical break in Lincoln's growth pattern. The big 1958-60's had spanned a 131-inch wheelbase, and that car stood 14.6 inches longer overall than the '61. That's a tremendous difference, and Ford officials recognized the gamble. Was the change in size a step forward or backward?

More than that, they realized they'd be married to the new Lincoln package for quite some time because, having a unitized body, the basic shape wouldn't be cheap nor easy to change in a hurry. Unit structures cost a lot more money to tool than cars made up of separate bodies and frames. Once you tool for unitized construction, the cost is so fantastic that the company simply has to turn out a lot of cars to get back its investment. In the Lincoln's case, being a relatively low-volume seller, lots of cars meant many years with the same basic body. It's much harder and more expensive to restyle a unit-bodied car than one with a separate body and frame.

So the question arises, Why did Ford decide to go unitized with the 1961 Lincoln anyway?

Many reasons. First, there was Ford's Wixom, Michigan, plant. Wixom had been built specifically to accommodate the unitized 1958 Thunderbirds and Lincolns. Assembly lines for unibodied cars have to be totally different from those that handle body/frame architecture. Wixom, too, had a big overhead in automated welding equipment, again to handle large unit-bodied automobiles.

Without Lincolns to build, Wixom couldn't

stay busy. Thunderbirds alone weren't enough to make the plant pay. So the facility itself demanded another unitized car in addition to the T-Bird, and one with not a terribly high volume. The Lincoln qualified. All 1958-60 Lincolns were put together at Wixom, as were the rest through 1969.

Second, as engineer Harold MacDonald points out, "We wanted to keep the car as compact and low as possible. A separate frame would compromise some of the new Lincoln's foot room and trunk. We were trying to get the maximum space out of this already small package. And we believed we could do an appropriate job NVH-wise [noise, vibration, harshness] in a unitized car."

The last requirement put some strain on the NVH engineers, as did keeping the car really low (the '61 was 3.2 inches lower than the '60). We rarely think of a driveshaft as being anything but a hefty piece of pipe, but in the 1961 Continental, the driveshaft became the eye of Engineering's hurricane. Just as the 1928 Model A Ford had been engineered around its gas tank, the 1961 Lincoln got engineered around its driveshaft. This "piece of pipe" held the key to the car's lowness.

Engineer Daniel Richard (Dick) Veazey, now a supervisor at Ford's Romeo, Michigan, proving grounds, was instrumental in developing the 1961 Lincoln's driveshaft. He reminisces: "The whole design concept revolved [no pun] around the driveline, if we were to get a low silhouette and room for six people. In order to reduce the driveshaft tunnel as much as we did, the shaft itself had to become the most different that we'd ever had in a production automobile."

And different it became. I'll let Mr. Veazey explain in a moment, but first I want to interrupt to mention that L-M Engineering briefly considered and then discarded two far-out ideas: 1) front-wheel drive, and 2) a flexible "rope" driveshaft on the order of the 1961 Tempest's. Fwd would have been very expensive, and the Tempest shaft was neatly sewn up inside GM patents.

But to let Dick Veazey continue: "Lowness became the first demand, and I recall that there was a strong difference of opinion as to whether the lincoln's driveshaft tunnel could be gotten low enough. Ford Division's independent engineering activity said it couldn't be done. We took that as a challenge.

"Before I came to Ford, I worked at GM

Engel's T-Bird proposal evolved into Lincoln (bottom). At one point, Continental sedan was to be pillarless (right).

FORD MOTOR CO.

Upstairs, Bordinat and the advanced Lincoln studio were working on evolutionary mockups on big 1958-60 theme.

FORD MOTOR CO.

Rounded shapes point toward this smaller Lincoln concept clay being executed in the Mercury studio around 1957.

FORD MOTOR CO.

Bordinat's upstairs studio soon expanded Engel's T-Bird to four doors. From this point on, changes were minor.

The Lincoln Players

Ford's basement "stiletto studio" contained four designers: Elwood P. Engel headed it and carried the title chief advanced studio stylist. Engel graduated from Pratt in 1938, then attended GM's design school, joining GM Styling in 1940. He spent the war in the Army Corps of Engineers, and in 1945 he went to work for George W. Walker's independent industrial design firm. Mr. Engel joined Ford's styling staff in 1955, along with Mr. Walker. In 1961, Engel left Ford to become design vice president of Chrysler Corp., a job he got largely on the strength of his 1951 Lincoln. Mr. Engel retired from Chrysler in 1972 and now lives in Michigan and Florida.

Under Engel in the basement studio were: John Najjar, executive stylist then and previously chief stylist of the Lincoln-Mercury production studio, the man charged with the designing the 1958-60 Lincolns. Mr. Najjar participated in the 1956 Mark II competition and is currently assistant director of Ford truck, tractor, and industrial design. Robert M. Thomas, a major contributor to the 1956 Continental Mark II design, was Engel's design analyst. Thomas is described as a classic blackboard designer. He retired recently as design executive of Ford's truck. tractor, and RV design office and now lives in San

Designers involved in '61 Continental (l-r): Thomas, Najjar, Engel, Bordinat, Walker, and DeLaRossa.

Diego. British-born Colin G. Neale joined Engel's Studio as a senior designer after leaving his post as chief stylist for Ford of England. Neale later headed his own interior and exterior studios at Ford. In 1962 he accepted Engel's invitation to take over Chrysler's interior design, color, and material studios. Mr. Neale is currently chief interior design executive at Chrysler.

Upstairs in the Lincoln-Mercury production studio, the principals were: Eugene Bordinat Jr., then director of L-M Styling. a graduate of Cranbrook Academy, who initially joined GM Styling in 1939. He became a supervisor in Fisher Body's tank plant during the war, then went back to GM Styling until 1947, when he switched to Ford. Bordinat moved through various advanced and exterior styling assignments with Mercury and Lincoln, then headed the L-M Studio from 1958 through 1961. When George Walker retired in 1961, Bordinat became Ford's design vice president, a position he holds today. Under Bordinat as executive stylist in the L-M Studio was Don DeLaRossa, who had facelifted the 1959-60 Lincolns and would later become instrumental in the first Mustang's design. His current title is Ford's executive director of exterior and international design.

Both Engel's and Bordinat's Studios answered directly to George W. Walker, who at that time was Ford Motor Co.'s vice president of Styling. Walker had come to Ford as a consultant in 1946, replacing Bob Gregorie. Walker's earlier design career included work for Baker-Raulang, Peerless, Graham-Paige. Willys, Packard, and Nash. Walker came into Ford largely via the 1949 model, a design by Holden M. (Bob) Koto. At that time, Walker ran his own good-sized Detroit industrial design consulting group. He remained an independent consultant to Ford until May 1955, when became aboard as a company vice president. In doing so, he brought along two of his star designers, Elwood Engel and Joe Oros.

Robert S. McNamara was the FoMoCo executive most directly responsible for the 1961 Lincoln's nascence. A graduate of Berkeley and Harvard, McNamara came to Ford after the war as one of the Whiz Kids. He moved quickly through positions as controller. Ford Div. general manager, and he was group v.p. of car divisions when he transformed Engel's T-Bird clay into the '61 Lincoln. In 1960, Mr. McNamara became company president, and from 1961 to 1968 he served as this nation's secretary of defense. He's presently president of the World Bank and makes his home in Washington, D.C.

The man who oversaw the engineering of the '61 Continental was Harold C. MacDonald, who at that time was assistant chief engineer of Ford's car and truck group. MacDonald graduated from Michigan State University in 1940 and went to work as an engine engineer at Packard. After the war he moved to Chevrolet and worked on Earle MacPherson's Cadet light-car project. In 1948, MacDonald followed MacPherson to Ford, where he held high posts at L-M and in the advanced vehicles department. In 1965, MacDonald became chief engineer of Ford Div.. then vice president of car engineering in 1967. His current title is Ford vice president of engineering and research.

To avoid binding, convertible's rear panes roll down automatically when the doors open.

Instruments repeat Continental compasses. Air conditioner controls (not shown) stand inside pod that opens out from center of dashboard.

Extremely rigid unit body allows stubby pillars to function as door locks only.

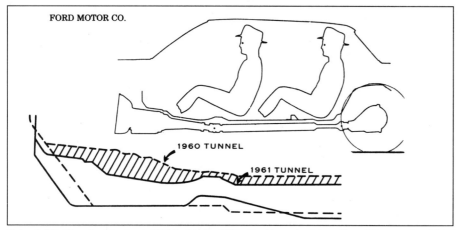

Driveshaft held engineering key to 1961 body's feasibility. Double cardan joints allowed low tunnel and floor for full 6-passenger capacity.

Truck, where I'd been involved in a six-wheel-drive military vehicle. We'd used double-cardan Dana joints at the wheel driveshafts. When I got into the Lincoln Continental program and we were looking for various types of constant velocity joints, the double-cardan seemed to have promise. As it turned out, we ended up using a double-cardan on the front of the 1961 Lincoln driveshaft, and it was that joint that let us beat Ford Division's prediction that we couldn't lower the floor. Without that joint, they would have been right."

Also to drop tunnel height, the engine was moved forward and tipped downward at the rear—a 7-degree angle. The nose of the rear-axle pinion similarly pointed downward, and it was the extreme fore kink that demanded and got the double-cardan.

Lincoln and Dana did a tremendous amount of development work on this joint. Its centering device took a lot of perspiration, but it finally became reliable and quiet. In a military vehicle, noise and minor vibrations weren't really problems, but in a car like the Lincoln they simply couldn't be.

Noise control gave headaches aplenty. Veazey comments: "Unitized vehicles, particularly in the luxury class, are extremely nasty to deal with. When you build a composite test vehicle initially, it exhibits certain characteristics. Then it seems that every stage you go through—from the composite to a cobbled mechanical prototype to a full engineering prototype to a production vehicle—there are continual variations that take place. You'll have a vehicle tuned; then

when the next phase comes along, you have to tweak it again."

Tweaking the final car took many different forms. The transmission support, for example, was finally made from tuned spring steel to compensate for harmonics. The driveshaft itself became one steel tube within another, the two separated but held together by a rubber sleeve in compression. Veazey and the driveline engineers developed a transmission slip joint consisting of twin races of recirculating roller bearings inside splines.

The idea here was to let the driveshaft actually stretch and contract. Without this roller-splined slip yoke, the pinion nose and engine would try to lift on hard acceleration, causing noise and harshness.

Heavy rubber bushings isolated the entire drivetrain and suspension system. To help silence the ride, some 200 pounds of sound deadener insulated the passenger compartment.

Because of the lincoln's relatively low production volume and its expensive-to-tool unit body, Ford Motor Co. decided to offer only two body types in the 1961 Continental: the 4-door sedan and a 4-door convertible.

This rather unusual lineup did make sense, because: 1) interiors, doors, and all sheet metal below the beltline interchanged between the two body styles; 2) the very rigid body structure allowed no torquing—or very little—in the convertible; 3) the convertible added spark and glamour in a youthful, yet classic manner.

The convertible's automatic top mechanism

borrowed heavily from the retractable hardtop program (see *SIA* #3, "All About Fliptops") and the 1958 Thunderbird convertible (*SIA* #11). Details of the self-clamping lock mechanisms, the 11 sequential relays and solenoids, the raising and lowering of the decklid, the "flipper" top boot were all the handiwork of Robert E. (Bob) Hennessey, working under Clair Kramer.

The '61 convertible needed no additional chassis reinforcement over the sedan and thus weighed only about 300 pounds more. Of that, 100 pounds were in tuning weights at the car's four corners (cast-iron weights suspended on leaf springs; these cancelled out harmonic vibrations between 51 and 62 mph), and 200 pounds came from the top mechanism.

All 1961 Continentals harbored a raft of unusual engineering nuances, among them hydraulic windshield wipers that worked off the power steering system. The power-steering pump, by the way, mounted in front of the engine and drove directly off the crankshaft. Air conditioning controls popped out of a pod in the center of the dash, and this same pod contained the duct outlets. The parking brake cable had a nylon inner liner to fight corrosion and binding. All Lincoln bodies used galvanized steel for rockers and other parts exposed to winter salt spray. Electric window lift motors were sealed in liquid rubber and had stainless-steel shafts to assure longevity. The engine timing gear had nylon teeth to silence it.

On the convertible, the curved rear side windows automatically lowered some 4.5 inches whenever the rear doors were opened. This happened to allow clearance between the front and rear glass, which overlapped with the doors closed.

And stepping back a moment, there was more to dropping floor height than just developing a new driveshaft. The engine oil pan became shallower for 1961, as did the pan for the automatic transmission (by 1.42 inches). Engineers reduced the bell housing height 1.2 inches by shrinking the starter ring gear. To get more underhood clearance, they flattened the air cleaner and put in a drop-center intake manifold for the new two-barrel carburetor. These were the major changes to the Lincoln V-8 for 1961. The rest of the drivetrain, including the rear axle and basic engine, were held over from 1960.

Lincoln stayed with the 1961 body shell through 1969, but with continual change. "This was actually Bob McNamara's pet car—his

specifications

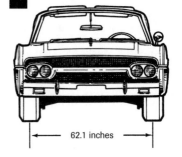

62.1 inches

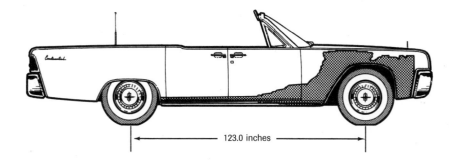

123.0 inches

1961 Lincoln Continental 4-door convertible

Price when new	$6,715 f.o.b. Dearborn (1961)
Standard equipment	Automatic transmission, power seats/steering/brakes, radio, heater, white walls, and tinted glass

ENGINE

Type	Ohv V-8, water-cooled, cast iron block, 5 mains, full pressure lubrication
Bore x stroke	4.297 inches x 3.703 inches
Displacement	430.0 cubic inches
Horsepower @ rpm	300 @ 4,100
Torque @ rpm	465 @ 2,000
Compression ratio	10.0:1
Induction system	2-barrel carb, mechanical fuel pump
Exhaust system	Cast-iron manifolds, twin mufflers and resonators
Electrical system	12-volt battery/coil

TRANSMISSION

Type	Turbo-Drive 3-speed automatic, 3-element torque converter with gears
Ratios: 1st	2.37 x 2.10 stall
2nd	1.48 x 2.10 stall
3rd	1.00 x 2.10 stall
Reverse	1.84:1

CLUTCH

Type	None

DIFFERENTIAL

Type	Hypoid
Ratio	2.89:1
Drive axles	Semi-floating

STEERING

Type	Power-assisted recirculating ball
Ratio	20.5:1
Turns lock-to-lock	3.8
Turn circle	46.7 feet

BRAKES

Type	4-wheel hydraulic drums, internal expanding shoes, power assist
Drum diameter	11.06 inches
Total swept area	416 square inches

CHASSIS & BODY

Frame	Unitized body/frame
Body construction	All steel
Body style	4-door, 6-passenger convertible sedan

SUSPENSION

Front	Unequal A-arms, balljoints, anti-roll and track bars, coil springs, tubular hydraulic shock absorbers
Rear	Solid axle, longitudinal leaf springs, tubular hydraulic shock absorbers

Tires	9.50 x 14 4-ply tubeless whitewalls
Wheels	Pressed steel discs, drop-center rims, lug-bolted to brake drums

WEIGHTS AND MEASURES

Wheelbase	123 inches
Overall length	214.4 inches
Overall height	55.1 inches
Overall width	78.6 inches
Front track	62.1 inches
Rear track	61.0 inches
Ground clearance	5.5 inches
Curb weight	5,220 pounds

CAPACITIES

Crankcase	5.0 quarts
Cooling system	25.0 quarts
Fuel tank	21.0 gallons

FUEL CONSUMPTION

Best	13-15 mpg
Average	10-12 mpg

PERFORMANCE (from **Car Life**, Feb. 1961)

0-30 mph	4.1 seconds
0-40 mph	5.6 seconds
0-50 mph	8.0 seconds
0-60 mph	11.2 seconds
0-70 mph	16.1 seconds
0-80 mph	22.5 seconds
Standard 1/4 mile	18.2 sec. and 74.0 mph
Top speed (av.)	117 mph (est.)

baby. He wanted reliability built into it. It was a real push at the time to pass Cadillac." Those are the words of engineer Harold MacDonald.

J.W. Silviera, the Oakland, California, car collector and realtor, bought this 1961 black four-door convertible in 1965. The odometer showed 40,000 miles at that time. Mr. Silviera drove the Continental as his family car until 1969, when he put it into storage. The odometer now registers 80,000 miles.

I found the big convertible's ride silky smooth, and it glides over even rough roads in supreme silence—no rattles, no whumps, nary a sound from the engine. The 430-c.i.d. V-8 gives amazingly crisp performance to so heavy a car (5,053 pounds at the curb).

Instruments struck me as easy to read, and there's a warning light for DOOR AJAR. This is important with the suicide rear doors, and I understand from Harold MacDonald that Lincoln originally considered putting an ignition

interlock on the rear clamshells. Cost overruled that, though.

Leather seats feel very comfy, with six-way power for the front bench and moderate knee room in back. The inside mirror hangs a little lower than I like, and the glovebox makes for a long reach, but I could find nothing else to complain about with the interior.

The one thing that surprised me—dismayed me—was general handling. Perhaps it's just this one car, but steering response lags. I found myself turning the wheel and then waiting a split second for the car to react. Hard cornering, of course, brought out tire scrub, squealing, and generous understeer. I understand from Al Baumgartner that 15-inch radials and heavy-duty shocks help a bit.

Brakes feel very fine, and they're big, but I hear that they fade badly under sustained use. Front drums of this '61 convertible use flared aluminum shells with cast-iron inserts, like

Buick's Al-Fins, and all Lincolns got these for 1963; then discs in 1965. The powered pedal feels neither too touchy nor too hard.

This car will live, I feel, as one of the great designs of the 1960s. Its simple, clean side treatment and the crisp fender line influenced Olds for 1963; also the mid-1960s Imperial and Chryslers (not surprising, considering where Mr. Engel ended up). The decklid grille idea spread to Studebaker Hawks and a number of other makes. But in my opinion, none of its imitators quite matched the purity and integrated detailing of that original, rather controversial car.

The IDI (Industrial Design Institute), awarded the 1961 Continental's design team a bronze medal that year—an honor accorded relatively few in the auto world. The car's sales figures never did satisfy Ford officials, so from that standpoint the Lincoln might have been something of a disappointment. But in no other way. 🔊

A Mark of Distinction

by Tim Howley
photos by the author

drive report

1969 Lincoln Continental Mark III

RECENTLY considerable contemporary-collector-car attention has been focused on the Lincoln Continental Mark III. Maligned by the press at the time of its introduction (see sidebar, p. 116), it is just as misunderstood by collectors today. If a cachet for a collector car is "failure" (it was too good for the marketplace in its time), then the Mark III fell flat on its Continental rear end. This was the automobile that after nearly 50 years finally put the Lincoln-Mercury Division on the map. It outsold the Cadillac Eldorado in its second model year and was the prime factor in Lincoln's seriously cutting into Cadillac's market. It put Lincoln in the enviable position it enjoys today.

The original 1939-1948 Continental, for all its beauty, was a disappointment in the marketplace, at only 5,324 units produced during five model years. The Continental Mark II, 1956-1957, was no better, with only 3,012 units produced in 20 months. It was both overbuilt at 5,190 pounds (with air conditioning) and overpriced in the mid-fifties at $10,000. The Mark III was a sales success from the day the first models hit the showrooms. Its successors, the Marks IV and V, have been even more successful. And even at this early date, Lincoln-Mercury is highly optimistic about the prospects for the down-sized Mark VI.

The press has judged the Marks by classic standards. Collectors presume they are or soon will be, and many wonder why the Mark III stands today at such bargain prices. Both groups would do well to consider the car from its marketing position.

When the Lincoln-Mercury Division discontinued its Mark II in 1957, there was a gap for a personal luxury car in its lineup. Ford's four-passenger Thunderbird, introduced with the 1958 model, became so successful that by the mid-sixties it was actually taking away Lincoln-Mercury Division buyers. In 1963 Buick came out with the Riviera, in 1966 Olds introduced its Toronado, and finally came the 1967 front-wheel-drive Cadillac Eldorado. By this time there was a $2.5 billion luxury-car market. It included Cadillac and the Eldorado, Lincoln Continental, Imperial, Thunderbird, Corvette, Riviera and Toronado. Production was around 440,000 units. This market continued to grow through the 1979 gas crisis, and even today automobile marketing people contend that the growth may not be over. During the 1974-1975 period it

Originally published in Special Interest Autos #58, Jul.-Aug. 1980

Left: Mark III's forte is ultra-comfortable high-speed cruising. It's a bit slow off the line, but mid-range acceleration is impressive. **Below left:** Headlamp doors are vacuum-operated and have been known to hang up in this position. **Below right:** Hood release is tucked away under front bumper.

actually appeared to be somewhat "recession-proof."

What is the market? It is largely the personal luxury car market previously owned by Cadillac. The Mark III is the first Lincoln ever to seriously threaten Cadillac as "King of the Hill." Year after year, Marks outsell Eldorados. The modern Mark is also the first car in history to be successfully marketed as fashion merchandise, according to Lincoln-Mercury officials.

Contrary to popular belief, the Mark III was not Lincoln-Mercury's answer to the Cadillac Eldorado. The Division wanted its own version of the highly successful Ford Thunderbird. In the beginning it was Lee A. Iacocca's idea. "Iacocca saw that there was a market for a highly styled two-door in the luxury class," recalls Bill Peacock, director of Ford Public Relations. "He moved in to exploit this market and at the same time take advantage of the fact that we had some unused assembly capacity in our Wixom (Michigan) plant. It was a perfect fit from both a marketing and a manufacturing standpoint." Under specific assignment from Iacocca, planning for the car began in September and October 1965. Iacocca worked directly with Ford Design Center, whose director was L. David Ash. Interior styling was done under the direction of the late Damon Woods. Later, Hermann C. Brunn was brought in to coordinate and assemble trim

material and colors for the Mark III. He is the son of Hermann Brunn of classic era body-building fame. Bertil T. Andren was the engineer in charge of the project, and Ralph Peters was the director of product planning. Eugene Bordinat, then and now Ford's vice president of design, oversaw every step in the car's design, and Henry Ford II gave the car an enthusiastic final blessing.

Recalls Andren, now retired and living in Stuart, Florida, "It was finally elected that it would be a reincarnation of the Mark, and the thought was that it shouldn't break our budget. At that time Thunderbird was developing a four-door, and its longer wheelbase became the real clue to the whole project. We knew that if we could use the four-door chassis we could just shove the front seat back, raise the floor a little bit so that we would have a flat floor instead of the deep pocket footwells, and then rearrange the front end a little." The new model would share many of the Thunderbird's inner panels; even the instrumentation could be kept practically identical except for the outer panel and pronounced trim differences. The Division's intent in using so much Thunderbird substructure was twofold—first to hold down costs and second to make assembly easier. The car would be assembled at Wixom, which was already assembling the Thunderbird and the Lincoln Continental.

At first the Thunderbird people resisted the idea. When Iacocca declared that they would simply go ahead with it on their own, Ford division finally gave it their support. This meant that both cars could now share floors and underbody at a considerable savings to both divisions.

From the very inception of the new car, which Ash named "Launcelot," stylists were working within some very rigid dimensional specifications.

At one point Ash and Arthur Querfeld, his assistant on the project, decided to go over to Greenfield Village looking for classic car styling cues. The only two they found which wouldn't make the car appear overdone were the classic-car radiator shell and the octagonal wheel "nuts." Querfeld feels that there was an overall intent to give the car a classic era feeling. This is most evident in the high, short rear deck and the over-six-foot-long hood, the longest hood of any American automobile made at that time.

Work proceeded full speed, and by October 13, 1965, the first clay model proposal had been developed. Lee Iacocca had a far greater hand in styling than is generally known. "Originally we did it with the T-Bird door. We were going to put an applique on it," states Querfeld. "But it didn't work out and Iacocca said 'let's do a new door'." Ash recalls Iacocca's further involvement: "After we had spent some time designing the car

111

and had come up with something rather good looking, Iacocca expressed some pretty strong views," says Ash. "He thought it was rather devoid of character. It was Iacocca who suggested the classic radiator shell and the tire hump on the rear deck. He thought that was what the car needed to give it a distinctive look. As usual, he was right."

Once the final design was approved (March 23-24, 1966), the project became primarily a matter for body engineering. By this time "Launcelot" had been renamed Continental Mark III. While most of the inner panels were shared with the Thunderbird, all of the outer panels, save the roof, were unique to the new Mark. The upper back panel, the piece below the back light, was approximately two inches higher than the 'Bird's. Inner trunk panels were

Above: Handling of the Mark III is good for a large car. Engineers effected a nice compromise between soft ride and moderate body roll. *Right:* Automatic headlamp dimmer is mounted between hood and windshield.

Early and Late Mark III Lincoln Continentals

The first Mark III rolled off the line in March 1968, the last on June 12, 1971. There are subtle but distinct differences between the early models and the later models. The 1970 Lincoln Continental was greatly influenced by the 1968 Mark III. The most important contributions from the Mark were the return to separate body/frame construction and coil-link rear suspension. In return, the 1970 Continental contributed numerous trim and accessory modifications to the 1970 and 1971 Mark IIIs.

Exterior changes were limited to minor modifications in taillamps and parking lamps, new concealed windshield wipers and wheel covers. To accommodate the new recessed wipers, the cowl panel now curved smoothly upward to the hood line, creating a cavity for the wipers. "Bunky" Knudsen, then FoMoCo's president, insisted that Mark III wheel covers be unique to the car. The standard covers now featured a wide center hub with its distinctive Mark III emblem in the center. Surrounding the hub were short radial lines. The vinyl roof was now standard equipment, and buyers could select dark brown or dark blue in addition to black, ivory and green, carried over from previous models. For the first time a sunroof was offered. It was optional on both the 1970 Mark III and Thunderbird.

Some exterior paints were added, others were deleted. Also, four new custom "stardust" paints were offered as options. These new finishes featured a bronze-flake metallic pigmentation covered by a clear high-gloss sealer coat, producing a deep, rich custom finish. The new paint options were available in bronze, green, red and olive tones.

The interior was given the most notice-able change. Both seat and door panel patterns were altered. A change in armrest design put power controls for seats in the arm rests instead of on the seat sides. The former simulated wood inserts were now offered in genuine walnut veneer. The steering wheel now took the Continental's new three-spoke design for better instrument visibility and increased clearance between the wheel and seat. A Cartier electric chronometer was now standard equipment.

A new, automatic, electric seat back latch became standard. Front seat backs now automatically released when the driver's or passenger's door opened, making rear seat entry and exit easier. The arm-rest-mounted ash trays, outside rear-view-mirror control and recessed door handles all contributed to cleaner-looking doors and somewhat greater control convenience. A vanity mirror was now offered in the passenger's visor.

One neat new touch was an automatic time-delay map-light switch. When the driver's door opened, the map light provided illumination for eight to ten seconds, then automatically shut off. Anti-theft protection was increased with a locking steering column. Windshield wipers now offered a choice of two-speed operation or the optionally available intermittent cycle, which provided a delay of one to ten seconds between cycles. This was to prevent "dry-wiping" in light rain or mist conditions.

Mechanically, the 1970 models had Lincoln's new Sure-Track Brake System as standard equipment. Sure-Track is an anti-skid control system that works on the rear wheels only, preventing their locking up during maximum-effort stops by automatically releasing and reapplying shoe pressure three to four times a second. The cycle is

continued until the car slows to about four mph or when the driver releases the brake. Very slight suspension refinements were made to give peak performance with the new standard-equipment Michelin 225R-15s (steel-belted radials) replacing the former belted tires. They offered improved handling and Michelin's 40,000-mile guarantee.

Californians got a new evaporative emission-control system, consisting of elements to collect, filter and store vapors while the car is standing. Vapors are purged through the carburetor when the car is running. The system included a non-vented gas tank and an inner tank to compensate for fuel heat expansion.

The collector buying a 1970 or later model today takes less of a chance with getting a turned-back speedometer than with 1968-69 models. For 1970 a new "tamper-resistant" odometer has a one-way clutch, making it impossible to turn back the mileage indicator by turning the speedometer driveshaft in reverse. Some collectors will argue that the later models benefit from better assembly and quality control. It's a pretty nebulous argument, as quality control was rigid from the very beginning. However, 1970 and later models were given a simulated rather than actual road test of 12miles. Engineers claimed this computer-programmed test was more comprehensive and gave them better control.

Exterior changes from 1970 to 1971 are virtually nil. But if you look closely you will spot a slight difference in the texture of the grille on the 1971 model. The year 1971 also saw the adoption of automatic air conditioning as standard equipment. With it, tinted glass became standard.

raised, as were the rear quarters. This had the visual effect of making the Mark III roof look lower and wider, though actually it was not. Engineers wanted to lop four inches off the front overhang of the approved model, but styling prevailed.

The radiator shell was never intended to be a frank copy of the Rolls-Royce. Stylists were attempting to recreate a classic-era radiator shell that was reminiscent of such makes as Packard, Duesenberg and even Lincoln. Careful study will note that is not on a flat plane like the Rolls, but is a die-cast assembly set at angles. With the exception of the grilles on the Rolls-Royce and Bentley, the Mark III grille was the most costly used to that time on a modern production car. The complex zinc die-casting was given extra care in buffing (and washing) in all stages: bare metal, copper plate, zinc plate and finally chrome. Whereas most grilles at that time may have cost a factory $15 or $20, this one came closer to $200.

The grille spoke of the past. The chassis frame foretold the future. It was the same advanced perimeter-type frame that Thunderbird had gone to in 1967. Unitized construction, introduced on both the Thunderbird and Lincoln Continental for 1958, had proved far less satisfactory than anticipated. Even though the Wixom plant had been built specifically for unit-body construction, there were just enormous quality control problems. They were especially evident with the Lincoln Continental fourdoor convertible sedans. Engineers were deeply relieved to go back to separate body and frame construction for the new Mark. Since 1961 the regular Continental had been getting heavier every year. By 1967 It weighed some 300 pounds more than the original. With the success of the Mark III, engineers were now able to persuade top management to return to a separate body and frame for all Continentals for 1970. Andren states that the Mark III had a tremendous influence on the all-new 1970 Continental, which he feels was a far superior automobile to the Continentals of the previous decade.

The Mark III was produced at Wixom, right in the mix with the 1968 Continental and Thunderbird. It conveniently took up unused production capacity created by the T-Bird's return to body/ frame construction for 1967.

Frame assembly was ingenious. The T-Bird frame was mounted upside-down to facilitate the assembly of front and rear suspension components and the rear axle. The chassis was then lifted off the conveyor, turned over and mounted on a suspended conveyor for additional operations. For 1968 models the frame and chassis assembly lines included both the Mark III and the T-Birds in the mix. T-Bird and Mark III bodies were

also lowered in the same body drop operations. Such major operations as welding of sub assemblies and complete bodies were integrated on the same assembly line for all three cars. However, special arrangements had to be made to accommodate certain components of the Mark. For one thing, it was necessary to provide special facilities for producing the Mark's quarter panel assemblies since the quarter panel has a distinctive wheelhouse as well as different major stampings.

Both the T-Bird and the Mark incorporated the same uniflow ventilation system, but the one for the Mark differed sufficiently to require a separate setup. Body side panels for all three cars were integrated on the same merry-go-round conveyors, but each one required a different welding fixture. As previously discussed, the instrumentation setup was nearly identical for the T-Bird and the Mark. Only the instrument faces, outer instrument panel and trim embellishments differed. But it would not be accurate to brand the Mark's body as merely reworked T-Bird. L-M engineers went to great lengths to offset frame flexibility and reduce body shake. The body structure of the Mark was

much stiffer than that of its brother, the 'Bird. Engineers used stiffening members extensively inside lower body sills, instrument panel cowl structure and rear parcel shelf area. So well was this body constructed that in spite of the over six-foot hood, it is hard to find visible hood shake in Mark IIIs now ten years old with well over 100,000 miles on their odometers. The same degree of structural integrity was to be found in front fenders, cowl, steering column and doors. To say a Mark III Continental is built like a pre-WWII Packard would not be an overstatement.

All three bodies assembled at Wixom were painted in the same shop. All received Ford's electro-coat paint process of first a primer coat, then a sprayed-on second primer, followed by three color coats. At the end process, however, the Mark III bodies were given a special polishing treatment for a brighter surface finish. The final polishing was handled by a special crew of 15 operators, adding about 2½ men for each Mark III body, compared with the T-Bird.

The Mark did get more attention than the others. David Ash recalls taking many trips down to the Wixom plant to

Above: Warning lights for seat belts, open headlamp door, unlatched door and open truck are imbedded overhead between visors. *Left:* Entry and exit from the back seat can be a struggle. *Below:* Classic era feeling is reflected in wheel-cover design, with its suggestion of a wire wheel and big octagonal hubcap.

specifications

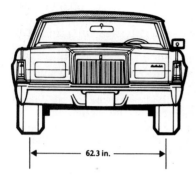

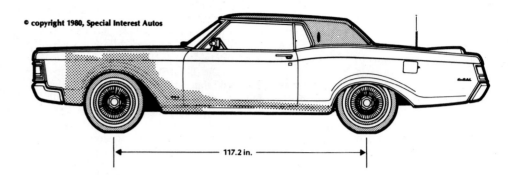

© copyright 1980, Special Interest Autos

62.3 in.

117.2 in.

1969 Lincoln Continental Mark III

Price when new	$9,457 (as equipped)
Standard equipment	Power steering, power windows, power brakes, automatic transmission, electric clock, windshield washers, vanity mirror, automatic parking brake release, rear lamp monitoring system, delayed map light, header warning console, flow-through ventilation system, seat belts, center folding armrests, power seats
Optional equipment	Air conditioning, automatic temperature control, rear window defroster, remote control trunk release, power door locks, cruise control, heavy duty suspension package, tinted glass, automatic headlamp dimmer, AM and AM/FM radios, six-way power seat, 3.00:1 axle ratio, traction-lok differential, tilt steering wheel

ENGINE

Type	Cast-iron ohv V-8
Bore x stroke	4.36 inches x 3.85 inches
Displacement	460 cubic inches
Horsepower @ rpm	365 @ 4,600
Torque @ rpm	500 @ 2,800
Compression ratio	10.5:1
Induction system	One 4-bbl carburetor, cast-iron manifold
Exhaust system	Dual pipes, two mufflers, two resonators
Electrical system	12-volt battery/coil

TRANSMISSION

Type	Select-shift, fully automatic

DIFFERENTIAL

Type	Banjo-housing, hypoid type
Ratio	2.80:1 (3.00:1 optional)
Drive axles	Semi-floating

BRAKES

Type	Front disc/rear drum, power assisted

CHASSIS & BODY

Frame	Perimeter-type, box section side rails
Body construction	All steel

Body style	Two-door hardtop

SUSPENSION

Front	Independent, four-link, coil springs with stabilizer bar
Rear	Coil link with transverse track bar
Tires	9.15 x 15 belted
Wheels	Pressed steel, drop center rims

WEIGHTS AND MEASURES

Wheelbase	117.2 inches
Overall length	216.1 inches
Overall width	79.4 inches
Overall height	53.0 inches
Front track	62.3 inches
Rear track	62.3 inches
Curb weight	4,866 pounds

Marque Club Address
Lincoln Continental Owners Club
PO Box 549
Nogales, AZ 85621

1969 Continental MK III

make sure that the tiniest exterior and interior trim details were installed perfectly. If any piece of door upholstery or trim or an exterior piece of stainless was mounted carelessly, the car simply went back on the line and the work was done over again. After assembly, both the Continental Mark III and the standard Continental received a 12-mile road test. With the introduction of the 1970 models, this test was given on a simulator for better control. All were very high quality cars with infinitely better care in assembly than the more mass-produced models. But the Mark, in particular, came about as close to a hand-assembled car as you could possibly expect to find in today's world of nearly fully auto-

mated automobile production.

Although the Mark III frame and chassis were similar to those used on the four-passenger T-Bird, all the components were tailored to the car. For instance, the frame members running along the outer edges of the body shell between the wheel openings had their own longitudinals designed to control low frequency "shake" disturbances to the chassis, and not the body. The chassis had some distinctive advantages in a car the size of the Mark III. At a 117.2-inch wheelbase (same as the four-passenger 'Bird), it was the shortest-wheelbase Continental ever built. Overall length was nine inches longer than the Thunderbird four-door and eight inches shorter than the 1968 Continental. Overall width was identical to the four-door Continental and two inches greater than the 'Bird. The Mark and the 'Bird were about the same height.

Such relatively compact size for a car that looked as big as the Mark did, provided some distinct handling advantages. Moreover, the car also benefited from a refined version of the T-Bird's suspension, a system which was more advanced than that of the standard Continental with its unitized body/frame. Coil springs were used all around, but they did not result in a "mushy" ride. A substantial link-type stabilizer bar was used on the front suspension to give the car a "glued-to-the-road" feel, even when cornering in tight turns. The rear suspension was a coil-link type, essentially the same as that of the T-Bird, but refined and stiffened.

A nine-inch-shorter wheelbase and eight inches knocked off the bow and stern gave the car noticeably better handling qualities than the regular Continental of the same year. Steering was remarkably quick and positive for such

Lincoln Continental Mark III, IV, V Production Figures		
Source: Lincoln-Mercury Division		
Mark III		
1968	. . . .	7,770
1969	. . . .	23,088
1970	. . . .	21,432
Mark IV		
1971	. . . .	27,091
1972	. . . .	48,591
1973	. . . .	69,437
1974	. . . .	57,316
1975	. . . .	47,145
Mark V		
1976	. . . .	52,269
1977	. . . .	75,628
1978	. . . .	74,996
1979	. . . . . . Not available at press time.	

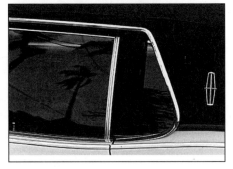

Above: Huge 460 V-8 pumps out 500 foot-pounds of torque at 2,800 rpm, develops 365 hp at 4,600 rpm. It's fairly accessible compared to today's engines that are covered with smog plumbing. *Far left:* Cat's eyes console on rear shelf monitors tail-lamp/stoplamp function. *Left:* Back-seat passengers have limited visibility through small quarter windows. *Below:* Mark's dash boasts full instrumentation. Cartier chronometer was an option in 1969.

a large car, with 3.68 turns lock-to-lock and a radius of 42 feet from curb to curb. With front disc brakes and power assist, braking was excellent. A dual master cylinder served both front and rear. The Lincoln Continental had gone to front disc brakes for 1965, and their braking has left little to criticize since.

The engine was Ford's new 460-c.i.d. Continental V-8, rated at 365 hp at 4,600 rpm. It put out 500 ft. pounds torque at 2,800 rpm. The engine was developed primarily to cope with increasing pollution restrictions, particularly in California, and Ford's improved-combustion emission-control system was an integral part of it. Better breathing and a new four-barrel carburetor were designed for emission control up to legal standards without the use of auxiliary air pumps. This spared the owner the complexity and bother of maintaining air-pump circuitry, and overall operation was superior to previous emission-controlled power plants. Performance and gas mileage were also improved.

Another feature of the new engine was its remarkable smoothness and quietness. You simply could not hear it run once you were inside the car. However, not all of the credit should be given to engine design, balance and engine mounting. Body engineers used a variety of sound-deadening materials throughout, not only to hush the engine

but to literally shut out the entire outside world. Insulation in this car is much more extensive than in the Thunderbird, which is also a remarkably quiet automobile.

The engine was coupled with only one transmission, Lincoln's Select-Shift Turbo-Drive, but shift points were tailored specifically to the car. No running gear drive noise was likely to reach the passenger compartment, either. Wheels, axles, suspension arms, springs and shocks were rubber isolated. No continuous path through steel was left open from the frame to the passenger compartment. The interior was insulated against noise, with 150 pounds of sound-deadening material, including a special aluminum-covered fiberglass blanket.

The interior of the car was never intended to look brilliantly innovative or jet-slick like the Thunderbird's. The whole idea was to make it look like a 1968 version of what might have been a custom Duesenberg. Full instrumentation was placed in rectangular pods. There were five pods in all, with the two directly in front of the driver containing the speedometer and clock. The glove box concealed a remote-control deck lid. Headlamp doors were not remote-controlled, but acted automatically. A header console (a la T-Bird) told you if the headlamp doors were open.

This console also warned of door ajar, seats unbelted and trunk open. Another T-Bird-type console on the rear shelf monitor was visible through the rear-view mirror.

Part of Hermann Brunn's job was to make sure the leather had wrinkles to enhance the classic-car feeling. Manufacturing and quality control didn't like the wrinkles at first, but Brunn's group eventually won their cause. Interestingly enough, leather interior trim was optional though installed in high numbers. Standard interior trim was tricot cloth and vinyl. Tricot is a flat knit material first used on the 1965 Ford LTD. It drapes beautifully and has a slick feel to the hand. It was nicknamed "panty cloth." Originally, there were six color choices in nylon-trim interiors and nine with optional leather. There were two different simulated wood grains for accents—East Indian Rosewood and

Bad Marks for The Mark

"The latest pretender to the Continental throne of plus automobilia is, in essence, a senior Thunderbird. It is a conventionally engineered styling exercise, embodying neo-classic cliches, highlighted by a six-foot-long hood, fronted with a massive plated casting which mimics traditional Rolls-Royce and Mercedes radiator housings.

"Our overall impression of the Continental Mark III can best be summed up by a single word—disappointment. The car is far short on functionality, particularly in space utilization. Styling is difficult to criticize quantitatively, but the Mark III definitely is not in the trendsetting, exciting, early Continental tradition.

"The Mark III is not, however, a bad automobile. On the contrary, the chassis and structure of the Mark III are fine examples of sound automotive engineering applied to a very luxurious vehicle. General performance is certain to be acceptable, even to critical owners. In all, the Mark III represents a polished execution of a lackluster concept."

Car Life, March 1968

"Lincoln has built a luxury car without the luxuries.

"Continental Mark III is a comfortable, quiet, big car with many commendable features. And, it will probably have a successful sales record. But, something seems to be missing; in short, it just doesn't quite turn you on.

Motor Trend, April 1968

"What FoMoCo did, essentially, was take what I think of as being an already overdone car—the Thunderbird—and overdo it some more. The Mark III boils down to a fatter, heavier, even more plush T-Bird.

"Interior styling features a theme perhaps best described as being a cross between a jet cockpit, a stately home of England and Las Vegas moderne. There's something for everybody, particularly the button-happy. Power this and power that abound throughout.

"Available only as a two-door coupe, the Mark III will sell loaded for just a trifle under $10,000. That's a lot for a super T-Bird."

Bill Kilpatrick, Auto Editor
Popular Mechanics, March 1968

Few cars have been more severely criticized at their time of introduction than the Continental Mark III. It has always been very fashionable for the contemporary press to pick on big, fat Lincolns. Yet the collector-car press has always praised the Lincoln, and all of the Mark Continentals in particular, very highly.

Despite the press's brickbats, no luxury car in history has enjoyed more instant success or more enduring success than late-model Continental Marks. The car has become so successful because it is the ultimate American-made status symbol and because it makes such an obvious appeal to the fashion-conscious luxury-car buyer.

What may be overlooked is the automobile's superb engineering and production. From a quality standpoint the Mark III very possibly equals the Mercedes-Benz. For this reason alone it should seriously be considered by collectors, especially at today's bargain prices.

English Oak. Beginning with the 1970 models, authentic walnut veneer was used, but only this one grain was offered.

The optional vinyl-covered roof looked like high-grade cavalry twill. The carpeting was all-nylon cut pile for a shaggy luxury look. One distinctive feature was a split bench seat with two-way power adjustment on each side.

Overall, the press was critical of the car in concept, though not in execution. "From a sales standpoint they were wrong, says Art Querfeld. "When we originally did the clay we had to bring in some people from Wixom, where the car was to be built. Right then and there, laymen from the plants fell in love with the car and we knew we had a winner. The ordinary man liked the car. You don't ordinarily find that, but on this one it was man to man. That was the feeling."

For 1968, 7,770 Marks were produced, nearly the total number of Mark I and Mark IIs combined. In 1969 the number rose to the then-phenomenal figure of 23,088. The 1970 and 1971 models with minor changes were equally successful. Mark IV and V models continued to follow the successful sales pattern of the Mark III. The 1974 recession-year production of 57,316 indicated to its builders that both the car—and the market—were indeed somewhat recession-proof.

The history of great luxury automo-

Facing page: The Mark III has remarkably quick steering for a large car with just 3.68 power-assisted turns from lock to lock. **This page, far left:** *Tremendously long, wide-opening doors make front seat entry as easy as walking into your home.* **Left:** *As you might expect, luxury abounds in the interior. Leather was optional but ordered on most Mark IIIs.* **Below:** *It wouldn't be a Continental without at least the vestige of a Continental spare, would it?*

biles is filled with failures. Duesenberg, Packard, Lincoln V-12, Cadillac V-16 and so many others all ultimately headed into bad times or dying markets. While the Mark III could hardly be compared with the pre-WW II classics, it has been the most successful post-WW II personal luxury car, production-built in the classic tradition of size, look and quality. And it was advertised in the classic car tradition.

According to Bill Peacock, director of Ford Public Relations, "The company looked at the ads of the twenties and thirties to see how they were done. They were essentially an emotional photograph, very little copy.

"They tested a lot of advertising and found this was exactly how to sell this car. The first ad was a spread. It showed a very confident guy leaning against his Mark. He had shooting glasses and he was in the middle of a grain field, and it had a very low amber glow over the whole photo, just as though the sun was setting and he was in a South Dakota grain field after shooting pheasant all day. The ad kind of said, 'I've got the world in my hand, and one of the reasons is that I own a Mark III.' Very little copy. Nothing at all about features.

"The car was a maroon with a black roof, and I think about 75 percent of our initial orders were for that color combination. The car was perceived right from day one as the epitome of what the luxury two-door car should be."

When the last Mark III rolled off the line on June 12, 1971, it had outsold the original Continental and the Continental Mark II tenfold. The Mark IV appeared with much more rounded lines and was built on a 120.4-inch wheelbase. The classic radiator shell, the Continental hump and the octagonal hubs were all retained, but now another classic-era styling cue, the rear-quarter opera windows, were added. Again, it was an immediate success, outselling its only direct domestic rival, the Eldorado, by nearly 20 percent. It retained its leadership and, during its five years of production, 274,758 units were built; an unbelievable figure for a Lincoln Continental run.

Gene Bordinat pretty well summed up the car when he told *Motor Trend,* "We tried to be a little controversial. We did not design to offend anybody... but when they see it, people will be divided into two camps. Some will respond to this sort of thing and will decide they have to have it. Others wouldn't touch it with a ten-foot pole. The buffs may not like it, but people with money will. When you're dealing in 15,000 units a year, you can afford to be controversial. This is far different from designing a Ford, where you have to play the middle ground.

Driving Impressions

Our driveReport car is a Continental Mark III, delivered to its original owner on December 23, 1968. It is registered as a 1969 model. The original owner, Harold Hoersch, is still driving the car, and after 11 years it has logged only 65,000 miles. It's still virtually as tight and quiet as the day it left the showroom floor—a tribute to Mark III body engineering.

Considering its size, it's a very agile automobile. The acceleration was not particularly earth-shattering at lower speeds, perhaps due to California smog devices. And we experienced noticeable lean in low-speed turns. But high-speed stability was excellent, and acceleration was greatly improved over 40 mph. The Mark III is unquestionably a long-distance road car, at its best loafing along the Interstate at 70 mph and covering 700 miles of desert in a day. How much the world has changed since the Mark III was built! It's now illegal to drive it at cruising speed, and at ten mpg you can fly just about anywhere cheaper.

We can well understand why the car now has such burgeoning collector appeal. There is something about it that gives you the feeling of the old classics, particularly the first Continentals. Perhaps it's a combination of things. We said to ourselves, "Had Duesenberg built a car In 1969, this might have been it." That's the total impression we get of the Mark III. We do not agree with the critics who dubbed it a Super Thunderbird. The Thunderbird of this same period was an outstanding automobile, but the Mark is better executed and has its own distinct personality.

What impressed us most about the car is how well it's held up. Every single power contrivance still works perfectly, except the Cartier chronometer. We were a little surprised to see a Cartier in such an early production model, but this one was originally so equipped.

The owner reports that even the automatic temperature control still functions perfectly even though (or perhaps because) the car has been driven daily since new. The low mileage can be accounted for by the owner's short commute to work. He owns San Diego's well known Hob-Nob Hill Restaurant, less than a mile from his home. The car has been repainted, but has never required more than routine maintenance.

The car was purchased new in San Diego, "As I recall, the list price, with all the options, was something like $9,500," says Hoersch. "In those days that was a lot of money, even for a Lincoln. But I had the money and I liked the car. Today, most any new car will cost you that much."

Presently, Lincoln Continental Mark IIIs are going for all-time bargain prices. This is due to two factors: the cost of gasoline and the relatively high number of good Mark IIIs being offered for sale. From a collector standpoint, they could be one of today's best bargains. You can bet there certainly won't be anything like them around in the future. ᐯ

Acknowledgments

Our special thanks to L. David Ash, West Bloomfield, Michigan, and Bert Andren, Stuart, Florida; also to Arthur Querfeld, Ford Design Center; Bill Peacock and Michael W.R. Davis, Ford Public Relations; and Ed Gohrman, Lincoln-Mercury Public Relations.

Lincoln Model Year Production, 1921-1980

Year	Production	Year	Production
1921	2,957	1953	40,762
1922	5,662	1954	36,993
1923	7,875	1955	27,222
1924	7,053	1956	52,878
1925	8,451	1957	41,567
1926	8,787	1958	29,684
1927	7,149	1959	20,906
1928	6,362	1960	24,820
1929	7,641	1961	25,164
1930	3,212	1962	31,061
1931	3,535	1963	31,233
1932	3,644	1964	36,297
1933	1,707	1965	40,180
1934	2,418	1966	54,755
1935	1,411	1967	45,667
1936	16,509	1968	46,904
1937	30,974	1969	61,378
1938	19,527	1970	59,127
1939	21,133	1971	62,642
1940	22,046	1972	94,560
1941	21,994	1973	128,073
1942	6,547	1974	93,985
1946	16,645	1975	101,843
1947	21,460	1976	124,756
1948	7,769	**1977**	**191,355***
1949	73,507	1978	169,620
1950	28,190	1979	189,546
1951	32,574	1980	69,537
1952	27,271		

* Lincoln's biggest production year